GERMAN NATIONAL CINEMA

German National Cinema is the first comprehensive account in English of German cinema from its origins to the present. From *The Cabinet of Dr Caligari* to *Run Lola Run*, Sabine Hake examines a range of films in relation to the social, political, economic and technological events surrounding them.

Hake assesses the work of directors such as Fritz Lang and Rainer Werner Fassbinder, and stars like Marlene Dietrich and Louise Brooks. From the Wilhelmine Empire to post-reunification, she traces the artistic currents, technological innovations, and social transformations which defined each era of German film and shows how a highly-politicised cinema often produced surprisingly apolitical films. Embracing popular traditions and other cultural legacies such as music, literature and prominent art movements like Expressionism, she explores the competing definitions of German cinema as art cinema, quality entertainment, political propaganda and rival of Hollywood.

Sabine Hake is Professor of German at the University of Pittsburgh. She is the author of *Passions and Deceptions: The Early Films of Ernst Lubitsch* (1992), *The Cinema's Third Machine: German Writings on Film 1907–1933* (1993), and *Popular Cinema in the Third Reich* (2002).

National Cinemas series
Series Editor: Susan Hayward

GERMAN NATIONAL CINEMA

Sabine Hake

London and New York

In memory of my father,
Günter Hake 1922–2000

First published 2002
by Routledge
11 New Fetter Lane, London EC4P 4EE

Simultaneously published in the USA and Canada
by Routledge
29 West 35th Street, New York, NY 10001

Routledge is an imprint of the Taylor & Francis Group

© 2002 Sabine Hake

Typeset in Galliard by
Keystroke, Jacaranda Lodge, Wolverhampton
Printed and bound in Great Britain by
Biddles Ltd, Guildford and King's Lynn

British Library Cataloguing in Publication Data
A catalogue record for this book is available from the British Library

Library of Congress Cataloging in Publication Data
A catalog record for this book has been requested

ISBN 0–415–08901–8 (hbk)
ISBN 0–415–08902–6 (pbk)

CONTENTS

ILLUSTRATIONS

ACKNOWLEDGEMENTS

In undertaking this enormous, and at times overwhelming, project, I have been exceptionally fortunate to write about German cinema during a time of fundamental changes in the political, social, cultural, and intellectual landscapes called 'Germany'. German unification has allowed cultural critics to think about central aspects of German culture, history, and national identity in ways that allow for a more differentiated approach to the continuities of German history and the changing meaning of 'the national' in relation to cultural productions, social practices, and representational modes. In film studies, the renewed interest in national cinema as a category of contestation has opened up new ways of thinking about European cinemas beyond the binaries of art versus entertainment, Europe versus Hollywood, the global and the local. The field of German film studies has profited greatly from these developments, whether through critical reassessment of the relationship between cinema, politics, and ideology; the rediscovery of neglected figures and periods of German film history; or the growing attention to popular tastes and hybrid traditions. As someone working on German cinema, I owe a particular debt to those scholars who have led the critical debates over the last two decades: Thomas Elsaesser, Anton Kaes, Marc Silberman, Eric Rentschler, and Barton Byg. In developing my own ideas about the processes and forces that constitute popular cinema, I have also profited immensely from the recent work of Alice Kuzniar and Gerd Gemünden.

Above all, I would like to express my deep gratitude to Susan Hayward, the series editor, for her undying patience and enthusiastic support. At Routledge, Rebecca Barden and Alistair Daniel helped to bring the project to fruition. Several colleagues shared their critical insights at various stages of the project, and I would like to thank them: Stephen Brockmann, Nancy Condee, Vladimir Padunov, Barton Byg, and Katie Trumpener. My work as a film scholar has profited immensely from critical exchanges with other film faculty at the University of Pittsburgh, especially Marcia Landy. The chair of my department, Sabine von Dirke, fought hard for the approval of an early sabbatical so that I could complete the project. Bozenka Goscilo did a fantastic job in editing out my Germanisms. An expert video technician, my mother Edeltraud Hake supplied me with an endless supply of German films on tape. Last but not least, I want to express my gratitude to Fred Nutt, who offered emotional support at a crucial turning-point and has been a welcome distraction ever since.

INTRODUCTION

This book offers the first comprehensive English-language account of German cinema from the beginning to the present. My goal on the following pages is to present filmic practices in relation to larger developments in society, to examine the cinema's position within popular culture, and to analyse the exchanges with other national cinemas and cultural practices. The remarkable ability of films to provide an archive of human fantasies and desires and to preserve the imaginary of the past within the present has influenced this project in manifold ways. However, the validation of film as an aesthetic object is not the main purpose of this overview. Instead special emphasis will be placed on the changing manifestations of cinema – as a mass medium, a social space, a public diversion, and a cultural institution – within the complicated history of twentieth-century Germany. Consequently, my analysis concentrates on the function of cinema as a public sphere defined by regional, national, and international influences and the importance of genre films in constructing social, sexual, ethnic, and national identities. Limitations of space have made it necessary to restrict this historical overview to mainstream cinema and feature film production. For the same reason, my critical approach privileges contextual rather than textual analysis and approaches film history as social history.

Within these constraints, I propose to move beyond symptomatic readings of a few canonical films and famous directors to pay closer attention to the elements of popular cinema – the genres, the audiences, and the stars – that constitute German cinema, and often in marked opposition to the demands of art cinema and political cinema. The main categories of analysis – national cinema, art cinema, and popular cinema – will be defined by the conflicts and contradictions that, especially in the case of German national cinema, have always sustained the problematic relationship between cinema and politics, on the one hand, and cinema and high culture, on the other. Concretely, this means that the category of national cinema cannot be discussed without acknowledging the foreign influences, international movements, and global developments and without recognising their relevance to the cultural paradigms – of integration, assimilation, cross-fertilisation, and hybridity – evoked as a threat to national culture. Similarly, the alliance between cinema and politics, including its ideological implications, cannot be discussed without reference to the models of entertainment and rituals of cultural consumption that are predicated

1

on the exclusion or suppression of the political. Last but not least, the programme of art cinema cannot be examined without considering its often antagonistic relationship to popular cinema, whether in the struggle over audiences or in competing approaches to the aesthetics and politics of representation.

Informed by these critical categories, this historical overview outlines the conditions of film-making in economic, political, social, and cultural terms and discusses the most famous, popular, and typical films through their respective contributions to changing definitions of genre, authorship, and film form. The seven chapters follow the standard historical periods that, in recognition of the centrality of politics to German cinema, are defined by world historical events, including two world wars and five regime changes. Technological innovations, artistic movements, social transformations, and cultural sensibilities appear as undercurrents and counter-currents in this highly politicised cinema that nonetheless produced surprisingly apolitical films. From the cinema of the Wilhelmine Empire (1895–1919), the Weimar Republic (1919–33), and the Third Reich (1933–45), the historical narrative moves on to the complicated divisions that define post-1945 Germany. The second part begins with the divided, but in many ways still unified cinema of the postwar period (1945–61) but then it continues with two parallel chapters about the German Democratic Republic (1961–89) and the Federal Republic (1962–89), only to conclude with post-unification cinema (1989–2000). Within this political framework, the individual subheadings of each chapter – organised around the terms 'popular cinema' and 'political cinema' – confirm German national cinema as a popular cinema that resisted easy integration into changing political systems and institutional structures; the same holds true for the traditions of art cinema that, whether through specific national forms and styles or the reception of international film movements, sustained a creative dialogue between films and film-makers across ideological divides and historical periods.

Throughout, the category of the national will be evoked as both a driving force behind, and as a desired effect of, mainstream filmic practices. Instead of subsuming everything under the normative category of national culture and, even more problematically, national character, the following chapters draw attention to the tensions among national, regional, and local traditions; among national, international, and global perspectives; and among cultural, economic, and political definitions of nation. The status of national cinema as a contested category will become especially evident in relation to foreign films, and the undisputed dominance of Hollywood in particular. But it also comes into view through the large number of foreigners working in the German film industry; the many co-productions with other European countries; and the continuous waves of emigration and migration of German film-makers to Hollywood and elsewhere. Finally, to move to aesthetic concerns, the inherent instability of the national as a function of cinema can be seen in the intense debates about so-called German styles; about the relationship between film and the other arts; about the place of popular cinema within the high and low culture divide; and about the use of film censorship, economic protectionism, and public subsidies in aligning the cinema with particular national

2

interests. All of these struggles and initiatives draw attention to the precarious nature of a national cinema striving for the kind of internal coherence and unity that, in fact, can and will never be achieved.

Defining German cinema through such conflicting forces necessarily expands the scope of the historical project and raises many questions about the relationship between film, politics, and society and the role of narrative film as a form of social history and national imaginary. On a methodological level, these questions complicate conceptual pairs like film versus cinema, film as history versus history of film, and history in cinema versus cinema in history. At the same time, the emphasis on German national cinema as a continuous compromise between art cinema and popular cinema opens up new perspectives. The emphasis on cinema as a cultural practice shifts the focus from individual texts to the contexts that define films within changing systems of production, distribution, and exhibition and that make them part of other aspects of public life and cultural consumption. Placing the cinema at the centre of modern mass culture draws attention to its affinities with urbanism, consumerism, tourism, and distinctly modern sensibilities, and it underscores its changing constellations with working-class culture, white-collar culture, and youth culture. Likewise, the attention to film as an integral part of modern life expands the terms of historical analysis in productive ways: from the canonical works to popular successes; from the formal characteristics of texts to changing modes of perception; from the social function of stereotypes and clichés to the psychological effects of transgressive pleasures and identifications. Last but not least, the place of narrative films in the popular imagination depends always on the creative exchanges with non-narrative forms such as documentary and experimental film-making; with established cultural practices such as literature, theatre, music, dance, and the visual arts; with the most advanced technologies of visuality and spatiality developed in architecture, photography, fashion, and design; and, finally, with competing mass media such as radio, television, and video.

The notion of national cinema as a category of contestation further complicates the understanding of film history as a continuous narrative with distinct periods and movements, continuities and ruptures, and cycles of rise and decline. Most frequently, the relationship between film and history is established on a number of levels: through the formal means, artistic styles, and directorial visions that link one film to other films; through the presumed homologies among filmic narratives, social experiences, and political processes; and through the necessary compromises among popular tastes, technological possibilities, and economical necessities. But what, for instance, is the function of the star phenomenon, the cult of authorship, the role of criticism and theory or, perhaps most difficult, the role of visual pleasures and emotional responses in the writing on film history? To continue with the more practical problems of historical writing, which of the available narrative models is most suited for the writing of national cinema? Can German national cinema be captured best in terms of social history, with everything from social and racial stereotypes to new cultural and political movements simultaneously reflected and prefigured in the cinema's prevailing stories, characters, and themes? Or are the qualities of this particular cinema more accurately described through aesthetic categories that reveal recurring visual and narrative conventions and identify innovative directorial styles and artistic movements? Is it more important for an understanding of twentieth-century German history to pursue a diachronic model that establishes relationships of cause and effect and that emphasises long-range developments in social mentalities and behaviours? Or can the problems in the relationship between cinema and modern life be made more transparent through a synchronic model that explores relationships of mutual exchange and pays closer attention to contemporaneous phenomena as they are worked out in different mass media and representational forms?

Even passing awareness of the different possibilities of writing film history is bound to bring into sharp focus the changing meaning of film history and national cinema within the present conjuncture, namely, the cultural landscape of Germany after unification. For instance, one might ask whether the revived interest in film history is fuelled by nostalgia for a modern mass medium increasingly marginalised by television, video, and the internet. One might wonder whether the renewed attention to national cinema marks the return of the national as a category of difference in, if not resistance to, the levelling effect of a global cinema culture ruled by Hollywood. In the particular case of Germany after 1989, the question of national cinema invariably draws attention to the much-discussed normalisation of German history and its direct and indirect impact on the available images of class, gender, race, and nation in the filmic traditions of self-representation. That feature films do play a crucial role in the making of national identities and the creation of a national imaginary is undeniable. On a less obvious level, the same holds true for film history. As the most important mass medium of the twentieth century, film not only continues to provide powerful stories and images but also uses its own historicity to convey a sense of cultural tradition and historical continuity. The debates about the national as a critical category in film studies and cultural studies have repeatedly confirmed this point (Higson 1989, Crofts 1993, Willemen 1994, Kaes 1995, Silberman 1996).

It is no coincidence that the narrative or feature film has come to dominate not only actual filmic practices but also the history of cinema. As historical documents, feature films offer unique insights into everyday life, illuminate the social imaginary, and show the formation of collective memory and national identity. As aesthetic products, feature films provide privileged access to the secret history of fantasies that are a reflection of, and a reaction to, the social and political conditions at a particular point in time. Promising spectatorial pleasure and emotional catharsis, feature films since the beginnings of cinema have exerted a powerful influence over everything from sexual behaviour and consumer choices to aesthetic preferences and political attitudes. Film genres, stories, and characters have done as much to give expression to social aspirations and anxieties as they have served as catalysts for political controversies and new cultural trends. However, using narratives in the reconstruction of historical periods or, worse still, collective mentalities remains problematic, for such an undertaking is predicated on certain assumptions about the mimetic nature of the filmic medium, its contribution to competing definitions of reality, and its psychological function both as an escape from, and a reflection of, the political and social conditions. Yet which forces actually organise the relationship between narrative, society, and nation? What is the 'real' of filmic narrative: social reality or the reality of desires? Does the feature film reflect social experience or does it represent that which is absent, denied, and ignored? Can films influence social processes or do they simply condense, displace, and magically resolve existing conflicts and contradictions? Must we link the emotional appeal of cinema to a pervasive need for illusion and escape or are even the most superficial films part of a continuous working through of fundamental problems and an authentic articulation of real lack? What is the relationship between narrative and sexual difference, and how are class, gender, and race configured differently in the dominant narrative forms and modes of address developed within German cinema?

How, then, should we define a national cinema? Are its characteristics determined by economic, political, or aesthetic forces? Does the national refer to actual practices, whether of film-makers or their audiences, or is it a function of promotional strategies, public policies, and the ideology of nationalism? Must we locate the meaning of national cinema in specific genres and styles, narrative themes and motifs, and more elusive definitions of social, sexual, and ethnic identity expressed through a highly codified national physiognomy and identified with particular actors and stars? Or is national cinema primarily a relational category, evoked only in opposition to other national cinemas and then most often through various strategies of resisting, excluding, and competing with Hollywood? Finally, in what ways does film engage the national differently, compared to other narrative traditions, such as folklore and literature, and other forms of public spectacle, such as opera and theatre? Establishing its sphere of influence through texts and contexts, the cinema – this quintessential mixed medium – has obviously succeeded like no other representational practice in incorporating diverse and often conflicting definitions of culture: high and low, national and regional, traditional and avant-garde, dominant and subversive, official and alternative. In providing a place of public assembly and in functioning as a public sphere, the cinema – this first truly democratic mass medium – has from the beginning provided an important forum for debates about culture, politics, and society, and it continues to serve as an instrument of innovation, provocation, and critical reflection. This function has been especially pronounced in relation to questions of national culture and identity.

All national cinemas are formed by these forces and influences, but every nation approaches the project of cinema differently within the existing structures for organising cultural production. Where, then, can we locate the specific, if not unique, qualities of German cinema? In the efforts by innovative directors, ambitious studios, and cinephile critics to lift cinema to the level of the other arts and infuse it with the kind of cultural relevance attributed to high literature and classical music as the privileged locus of German national identity? In the attempts by government agencies and political parties to control all aspects of image production and to turn film into a means of political propaganda and ideological indoctrination? Or in the difficult relationship of domestic audiences to their own filmic traditions and cinematic legacies? To phrase it differently, can we speak of a cinematic *Sonderweg* (special path) in ways suggested for modern German history? Or must we recognise the many similarities with other European cinemas, including Austria, France, Italy, and Russia? The following comprehensive overview of German cinema from the beginning to the present does not attempt to answer any of these questions. However, the individual chapters present a number of interweaving and overlapping narratives that open up a space for contemplating possible approaches.

1

WILHELMINE CINEMA
1895–1919

Until recently, little was known about films from the Wilhelmine period, that is, the cinema before 1919. Some of the reasons for such neglect apply to other national cinemas as well: the large number of films lost or in danger of disintegrating; the inaccessibility of film copies, stills, and print sources from the period; and the limited resources available for preservation. But a renewed interest in early cinema, which peaked during the 1995 centennial of the invention of film, has drawn scholars back to the archives. Cultural-studies-based approaches to film history have shed new light on longstanding controversies over not only the relationship between filmic texts and social, economic, cultural, and political contexts but also the contribution of cinema to modern mass culture and contemporary lifestyles. Moreover, because of its international orientation, early film-making has challenged the concept of national cinema and raised far-reaching questions about the circulation of cultural traditions in international markets and the enlistment of popular entertainment in the making of national identity.

Above all, the study of early cinema has allowed scholars to ask questions that reach beyond a particular historical period or national cinema and offer more general insights into modern mass media and the intricate connections among technology, entertainment, and consumer culture. For instance, which technological, economic, social, and cultural forces contributed to the invention of cinematography? Did the technology of film create new forms of diversion or was cinema an expression of, and a response to, dramatic changes in modern society? How does the cinema relate to other mass media (illustrated press, photography), advanced technologies of space (railway, telegraph), changing modes of visual perception, as well as to the interrelated processes of urbanisation, mechanisation, and industrialisation (Segeberg 1996, 1998, 2000)? Must we conceive of cinema as a radically new cultural practice or an eclectic mixture of popular traditions, established conventions, and modern mentalities? How did the rise of film affect literature and the other arts in their visual and narrative means as well as in their cultural and social significance? Where must we place early cinema in relation to proletarian culture, urban culture, bourgeois culture, ethnic culture, and popular culture? What is its contribution to the contemporaneous discourses of colonialism and nationalism? Did early cinema provide an alternative public sphere in which marginalised and suppressed voices found expression, or did it prepare the ground for both the commodification of culture described by Adorno and Horkheimer in their notion of the culture industry and the aesthetics of simulation evoked by many postmodern theoreticians? Finally, where can we locate the national, both as a political programme and an aesthetic category, within what seems like an irreversible trend towards the industrialisation of popular culture and the standardisation of fantasy production?

Addressing many of these questions, film historians have turned their attention to the beginnings of German cinema, both to fill considerable historical lacunae and to develop new methods of inquiry (Usai and Codelli 1990, Kessler et al. 1992). They have challenged earlier characterisations of Wilhelmine cinema as technically inferior and formally undeveloped on the grounds that the conventions of the classical Hollywood style had inappropriately served as the standard for all critical evaluation. Then, too, correcting the almost exclusive emphasis on Berlin as the capital and the centre of film production, scholarship on early cinema culture in other cities has shown regional influences working against the homogenising effect of the national in political debates and cultural practices (Paech 1988). Similar studies on small towns have documented how the cinema levelled the difference between city and country even where exhibition practices accommodated regional tastes (Warstat 1982). Feminist scholarship has shown the ability of early cinema to respond to the needs of women audiences, among other things through the heightened emotionality of the melodrama (Schlüpmann 1990). Finally, more detailed studies on local exhibition practices and early production companies have confirmed the socially integrative qualities of early cinema, especially during the transition from the short to the longer film, and thus offered an important corrective to the myths surrounding early cinema as a proletarian public sphere (Müller 1994).

However, there seems to be little agreement on the meaning of new historical knowledge and its impact on questions of periodisation and canonisation. Two basic models are available: one of continuous progression, the other with breaks and ruptures. Scholars either treat the cinema from 1895 to 1919 as a prehistory of the classical silent cinema or, conversely, see it as radically different in its approach to narrative continuity, psychological motivation, and modes of address. In the first case, the styles of the 1920s provide the normative standard for evaluating all earlier films. Within a comparative framework, such evolutionary models are often evoked to explain alleged instances of retardation in the German cinema before 1919. Accordingly, some critics have described expressionist cinema as the result of yet insufficiently developed filmic techniques (Salt 1979). Taking a different approach, other scholars have used early cinema and its presumed otherness to think about the formal shift from 'showing' to 'telling' as an abandonment of the subversive qualities identified with the greater emphasis on visual spectacle and the cult of attractions.

In any case, film-making before 1919 remains inseparable from the larger concerns of Wilhelmine culture and society, including modernisation and social reform and the rise of German nationalism. As an industry and a public diversion, the new mass medium emerged in a relatively young nation state forced to accommodate authoritarian and democratic tendencies and to incorporate reactionary and progressive positions on culture. From the founding of the Reich in 1871 to the collapse of the monarchy in 1918, citizens experienced dramatic changes in every aspect of public life, from belated industrialisation and urbanisation and the rise of a powerful working class to significant advances in social legislation and political representation. Germany under Emperor Wilhelm II entered a period of nationalist fervour and imperialist ambition. New industries and corporations acquired unprecedented powers. The culture of the *Gründerzeit* (literally: founding period) thrived on forms of historical eclecticism decadent in their formal and material excesses. In the educated middle classes, moral double standards ruled social interactions, and public debates exuded pretentiousness and hypocrisy. The provocation of naturalism and, later, expressionism only underscored the need for more fundamental changes in the existing power structures and the artistic practices that supported them. Around the turn of the century, new social and cultural organisations tried to overcome the sharp division between high and low culture and to improve the living conditions especially of the lower classes. Committed to the idea of social reform, these groups ranged from working-class cultural organisations to alternative lifestyle movements but also included radical activist groups fighting for better housing, sex reform, and women's rights.

Cinema:
a new technology, industry, and mass medium

Early cinema exposed the shortcomings of high culture and, through its close attention to contemporary problems, accelerated the process of democratisation. The strong resistance to cinema among members of the educated middle class suggests that their anxieties about the levelling effect of modern mass culture were fuelled by new social groups' demands for adequate representation on the screen. It was only after 1914 that cinema more directly began to support the interests of German nationalism and promote German cultural traditions against the threat of a global consumer culture, American style. At the turn of the century, however, cinema merely continued in the tradition of public diversions such as the variety, the circus, the fairground, and the panorama. Cultivating decidedly modern sensibilities trained in the big cities and at the new places of work, the cinema's attractions emerged as an integral part of everyday life and joined forces with other mass-produced forms of diversion such as illustrated magazines and trivial literature. But in contrast to the latter, cinema became a popular attraction through its double status as a technology in the narrow sense of machines and mechanisms and in the broader sense of producing and displaying illusions.

The experimental phase of cinematography took advantage of this convergence of perception and technology by exhibiting new optical devices (for example, Ottomar Anschütz's Tachyscope) and using their 'magic tricks' as a form of diversion. The move from scientific experimentation to public entertainment was completed when, from February to March 1895, Anschütz showed his 'living photographs' to a paying audience, thus also for the first time privileging collective over individual forms of reception. Max Skladanowsky, one of the many showmen and inventors from the period of early cinematography, usually gets credited with having organised the first public film screening as part of a variety show in the Wintergarten in Berlin on 1 November 1895. Emulating the variety format, the programme consisted of acrobatic acts, animal scenes, folk dances, and artistic presentations. A later series of Skladanowsky shorts from 1896 was more documentary-like and included street scenes from the neighbourhood around the Alexanderplatz. Both programmes were aesthetically and technically inferior to the actualities screened by August and Louis Lumière in Paris on 28 December 1895. With its high-quality products, the Cinématographe Lumière soon dominated European markets, whereas the German competition remained small and underfinanced.

Most technological advances during the following years were connected with Oskar Messter and Guido Seeber. Messter was a talented cinematographer who not only improved the mechanics of cameras and projectors but also marketed his inventions successfully (Kessler et al. 1994a, 1994b, Rossell 1998). The Maltese cross for flicker-free projection is his invention as are the popular *Ton-Bilder* (sound images) that, through a gramophone, synchronised sound and image for short musical numbers. Messter produced countless fictional shorts for Messter Film GmbH and, as early as 1897, began shooting regular newsreels after an initial short about the centennial of the birthday of Emperor Wilhelm I. After 1914, these newsreels appeared weekly as the famous *Messter-Woche*. Like Messter, Seeber combined business acumen and technological knowhow with an almost intuitive grasp of the camera's possibilities. Known for his innovative camerawork on *Der Totentanz* (1912, *The Dance of Death*) and other films by Urban Gad, Seeber specialised in trick photography and published the earliest manual on cinematography. Working for the Deutsche Bioscop, Seeber in 1912 also oversaw the construction of the Babelsberg studios, soon to become the famous Ufa-Stadt, the German Hollywood, on the south-western outskirts of Berlin.

In general, Wilhelmine cinema can be divided into three phases: the early years of emergence and experimentation (1895–1906), the period of expansion and consolidation (1906–10), and the process of standardisation identified with the longer film (1910–18). An accelerating as well as retarding factor in this development was the alignment of cinema with national interests during the First World War. During the years of travelling cinemas, which lasted until 1906 (and until 1915, in some rural areas), exhibitors either purchased or produced their own films and travelled from town to town to present their 'theatre of living photographs'. The programme usually included newsreels, nature scenes, humorous sketches, acrobatic acts, dramatic recitations, and shorts about local events. Two filmic styles, respectively associated with the names of Lumière and Meliès, prevailed: a realist style, with the camera recording the visible world and favouring a mode of representation located in the pro-filmic event; and a fantastic style that took advantage of the camera's ability to create new imaginary worlds and move beyond the limits of everyday perception. Newsreels and documentaries increased the audience's interest in the external world and confirmed to them the beauty of everyday life. By contrast, the *tableaux vivants* (staged group scenes) and the *féeries* (fairy-tales), as well as the popular shorts with musical numbers and acrobatic presentations, continued to adhere to the conventions of the proscenium stage, from the framing of the scenes to the frontal positioning of actors and performers. The celebration of an unabashedly sensationalist cinema modelled after the variety also extended to fantastic effects such as the symbolic use of colour (for example, blue for night, red for fire), which was achieved through tinting or toning. All of these influences contributed to the emergence of longer narrative forms in the 1910s and left a strong mark on the visual conventions of the early social drama and detective film.

Weekly changes in movie programmes and improvement of the exhibition spaces confirmed the cinema's growing popularity. Beginning in 1905, more and more storefronts, pubs, and coffee houses were converted into stationary cinemas, variously referred to as *Kino, Kientopp*, or *Kintopp*. With the increase in numbers – in Berlin, from 165 cinemas in 1905 to 206 in 1913 – came greater attention to comfort and luxury, as evidenced by spectacular movie palaces such as Berlin's Marmorhaus. Usually located in the downtown areas, on the large thoroughfares, and near railway stations and shopping districts, these new cinemas catered to various social groups, from workers, employees, and middle-class women to adolescents, artisans, and the unemployed. In the larger cities, screenings took place from eleven in the morning to ten o'clock at night, with patrons continuously entering the auditorium. Programmes lasted approximately fifteen minutes and always included piano or organ music accompaniment and, not infrequently, explanations by a commentator. Usually limited to the evenings, the *Kinobühnenschauen* (cinema stage shows) offered an entertaining mixture of short films and live acts; these programs remained popular until the late 1920s.

Movie audiences often came from the lower classes, but it would be misleading to characterise them as proletarian and think of early cinema only in class-based terms. Sociological studies from the period, including Emilie Altenloh's *Zur Soziologie des Kino* (1914, *On the Sociology of the Cinema*), described a very heterogeneous clientele, defined above all by their precarious position amidst social classes, ethnic groups, and different generations and brought together by shared experiences of discrimination and marginalisation. Nonetheless, the new medium was regularly discussed in the antagonistic terms of class, with writers and critics frequently denouncing the movies as a threat to bourgeois culture and society. As a potential source of social unrest, but also a thriving business and industry, the cinema obviously had to be controlled through various legal and administrative measures on the local, state, and national levels. Initially the police had been responsible for making preventive censorship decisions, a practice which allowed for significant variation. The introduction in 1906 of official pre-censorship, and the requirement of a censor's certificate after 1907, greatly simplified this process, with Prussia publicising its censorship decisions as a guideline for other federal states. Other new measures included admission monitoring for children and adolescents and the enforcement of city ordinances about safety standards and health codes. Eventually, municipalities found a workable compromise between controlling the cinema's presumably detrimental effect on public morality and profiting from its mass appeal through a local entertainment tax, a major source of revenues.

The cinema's rise from a small cottage industry to a national one – in 1913 alone, more than 350 new films were released nationwide – came about through the concentration of all resources (for example, financial capital, production facilities, technological knowhow) in the hands of fewer and larger companies. Additional factors included a more effective division of labour among film production, distribution, and exhibition; further specialisation in the film-related professions; and the move towards higher artistic standards and greater product differentiation. During these formative years, the founding of the Geyer printing lab in 1911 gave German companies some much-needed independence from their French competitors. Known for its lively cultural scene, Berlin quickly emerged as the centre of film-making, with the cafés and restaurants around Friedrichstrasse functioning as a kind of employment exchange, and with most of the studios located nearby in Tempelhof, Weissensee, and Babelsberg (Hanisch 1991). *Der Kinematograph* and *Die Lichtbild-Bühne*, the earliest trade papers, were founded in 1907 and 1908, respectively, to improve communication among the various branches of the industry and to offer advice on technological, economic, and legal questions. The first serious reviews in daily newspapers appeared around 1913 and were followed by extensive debates on the artistic merits of film in most mainstream publications.

Production companies from these early years include Jules Greenbaum's Deutsche Bioskop (1902) and Deutsche Vitascope (1909), as well as the first film producer who also functioned as a distributor, Alfred Duske's GmbH (1905). Exploring the possibilities of vertical integration, Paul Davidson first acquired a theatre chain in 1906, the ubiquitous Union-Theater, before creating the first German joint-stock film company, the Projektions-AG Union (PAGU), in 1909. Founded in 1915, Erich Pommer's DECLA company later contributed to the process of economic concentration by operating on a national level from the very beginning. Like Paul Davidson of PAGU, DECLA's Pommer belonged to a new generation of producers who believed in improving the technical and artistic quality of their products and in striving towards a broader social acceptance of the movies. In order to minimise their financial risks, some companies introduced short-lived practices such as the monopoly film. Thus the Asta Nielsen star vehicle *Abgründe* (1910, *The Abyss*) became the first film available through only one distributor. Practices such as blind booking and block booking had a similarly stabilising effect; so did advertising campaigns that made films part of other forms of cultural consumption. Commodity tie-ins appeared for the first time when the chocolate manufacturer Stollwerck & Co. in Cologne, distributor of the Cinématographe Lumière since 1896, installed vending machines in its theatres.

Responding to such developments, even political groups and public institutions discovered film's possibilities as a modern mass medium. The royal family turned to film as an effective promotional tool. Beginning with the grand opening of the Nord-Ostsee Canal in 1895, Wilhelm II repeatedly appeared in newsreels featuring military parades, victory celebrations, and manoeuvres of his beloved Royal Navy. To celebrate his twenty-five years as ruler, eight different production firms joined forces to produce *Der deutsche Kaiser im Film* (1912, *The German Emperor on Film*). The enlistment of cinema in the scenarios of German nationalism, militarism, and monarchism did not remain limited to the recording of public events. The *Deutsche Flottenverein*, a naval association, showed films celebrating German military might and glory in order to rally civilian groups and incite patriotic fervour. Colonial associations produced feature and non-feature films about South West Africa and German East Africa that took advantage of the widespread fascination with racial otherness to advance their racist and imperialist ideas.

Turning film into a marketable commodity and profitable entertainment required not only the institutionalisation of cinema as a social practice but also a further standardisation of filmic means. Between 1911 and 1914, the longer narrative film emerged as the most popular attraction at the movies. This process had a profound effect on the prevailing forms and styles. Inspired by the success of the so-called *Kinodrama* (film drama), the new multi-reelers introduced various new techniques related to camerawork, editing, and mise-en-scène. These included a greater variation in shot sizes, including close-ups and more narrative devices such as superimposition, fade-in/fade-out, cross-cutting, and masking (for instance, through iris and keyhole masks). In aesthetic terms, the creation of a film-specific language allowed film-makers to move beyond the influence of the other arts and explore the unique qualities of the medium. Yet in cultural terms, the emergence of the longer narrative film aligned the cinema also more closely with high-culture traditions (literature, theatre) and bourgeois tastes and morals (for example, the insistence on social relevance).

Above all, the longer film required a linear narrative within a clear time-space continuum, as well as consistent character development and psychological motivation. Within these constraints, there was still sufficient opportunity for cultivating national styles and sensibilities. Rejecting action-driven plots for psychological conflicts, the early German film dramas continued to privilege relations of contiguity over continuity – for instance, by treating the frame like a self-contained stage. Some scholars have explained the close attention to mise-en-scène at the expense of other filmic techniques as a belated or only partial adaptation of the conventions of storytelling. Yet it might also have derived from the greater influence of theatrical traditions or from a deliberate attempt at product differentiation, specifically, by creating a German alternative to the plot-driven, action-oriented Hollywood films. With these contradictory investments, the alleged backwardness of the films made possible the preservation of older forms of visuality and specularity. These remained an integral part of the cinematic apparatus and continued to assert their power against the increasingly conventional story lines and their underlying assumptions about gender, race, and class.

Sometimes the social and cultural provocation of early cinema found expression in mildly humorous stories about the filmic medium itself. From *Der stellungslose Photograph* (1912, *The Unemployed Photographer*) and *Wie sich das Kino rächt* (1912, *How the Cinema Takes Revenge*) to *Die Filmprimadonna* (1913, *The Film Prima Donna*) and *Wo ist Coletti?* (1913, *Where Is Coletti?*), films repeatedly thematised their conditions of production and reception and thereby drew attention to the cinema and its many pleasures (Hake 1992b). Confronted with relentless attacks by cinema reformers and literary critics, directors used these references to justify the cinema's integration into mainstream culture and, by emphasising the active qualities of spectatorship, to insist on film's cultural and social relevance. The pervasive need for cultural respectability and the underlying fear of social disintegration found expression in a particularly strong investment in the educational aspects and political possibilities of the new medium.

Firmly established by the late 1910s, the longer narrative film marginalised all other forms (documentary, animation), except the newsreel, and confirmed fictionality and illusionism as the dominant representational paradigm. From then on, the exploration of physical reality ceded to the imaginary relations that constituted the cinema as a popular diversion with clearly defined social and psychological functions. At the same time, the new conventions of genre cinema provided an important framework for fusing public and private desires and for mediating between the legitimating fictions of selfhood, whether defined in terms of class or nation, and the alternately transgressive and compensatory effects of sensation, suspense, romance, and fantasy. With the longer narrative film came more elaborate programmes that resulted in fewer daily screenings. This change allowed theatre owners to place more emphasis on the framework of presentation, which extended from motion-picture theatre architecture and design to rituals of attendance modelled on the bourgeois theatre.

Local, regional, and national differences notwithstanding, the European cinema of the prewar period remained international in orientation. The high degree of co-operation and collaboration and the relative lack of trade regulations kept film markets open until the early 1910s. The majority of films shown in Germany before the First World War were of foreign origin, with domestic productions usually taking a market share of 10 to 20 per cent. While French films, and the Pathé newsreels in particular, dominated programmes before 1910, Italian films became very popular after 1910, largely because of the success of monumental epics such as *Cabiria* (1914). The many Danish directors working in Berlin, including Ole Olsen, Benjamin Christensen, Stellan Rye, and Urban Gad, contributed to the great popularity of Scandinavian cinema (Behn 1994). During a period when questions of authorship were still considered irrelevant from an artistic and legal perspective, product differentiation was achieved primarily through the association of individual studios with specific genres. For instance, Nordisk was perceived as a company committed to address social problems, whereas Pathé and Gaumont became identified with ambitious literary projects. In aesthetic matters as well, a strong disregard for boundaries characterised the cinema's relationship to the other arts and made it the quintessential mixed medium. Film-makers creatively explored the possibilities of multimedial cross-fertilisation, introducing elements from the serial novel, making references to the operetta, imitating the theatre, and alluding to painting and photography. They also took advantage of the affinities among cinema, urbanism, tourism, and consumerism by, for instance, showing the dangers of urban living, exploring various social milieux, and venturing on imaginary journeys to exotic places.

Elements of a national cinema: stars, genres, directors

The emergence of the longer film and the codification of a filmic language would not have been possible without the enterprising businessmen, technicians, and performing artists who thrived in this volatile atmosphere of great economic risks and even greater opportunities. Aided by better cameras, lighting, and film stock, cinematographers such as Messter, Seeber, and the famous Karl Freund developed new visual techniques. Taking advantage of their background in theatre design, Rochus Gliese, Hermann Warm, and Paul Leni created beautiful mise-en-scènes through their alternately naturalistic, realistic, and illusionistic approaches to filmic space. Composers and musicians combined well-known repertory pieces and innovative original scores in practical cue sheets, thus starting a trend that culminated in the 1920 publication of Guiseppe Becce's *Kinothek*, a collection of mood music for movie accompanists.

Promoting their films as works with distinct artistic qualities, studios also relied increasingly on the notion of authorship and its claims about creativity and originality. Directors began to play a more significant role in the marketing of films and, like trademarks, became identified with particular genres (Wedel 1996). Thus Ernst Lubitsch and Max Mack acquired a reputation for comedies, Joe May for detective films, and Franz Hofer for melodramas. Even more important were the continuities established within genres through their stereotypical characters and formulaic story lines. Some studios designed their entire public image around specific genres, as did the Stuart-Webbs Film Co. with detective films. Others, such as the Mia May films, relied on the drawing power of the company's leading star. Serials and sequels turned out to be a most effective form for ensuring public interest and involvement; the same applied to publicity campaigns like the short-lived *Preisrätselfilme* (quiz films). Through serialisation in illustrated magazines as well as elaborate advertising campaigns, the cinema expanded its area of influence as a new public sphere and popular diversion with its aesthetic forms, cultural ambitions, and social rituals.

Above all, the star system established a structure for enlisting the psychological mechanisms of identification in the entire process from film production to reception. Closely identified with the prevailing social and sexual stereotypes and often associated with 'typical' German physical traits, the film star blurred the

15

boundaries between actor and role and created a much-needed sense of continuity among individual films and genres. The star phenomenon took advantage of the existing cult of celebrity but also opened up new possibilities for viewer identification through decidedly voyeuristic pleasures. What distinguished film acting in the silent era from other forms of performance was the strong sense of physical presence and, hence, of closeness and intimacy. Through their body types and facial expressions, film actors conveyed a unity of body and character not attainable on the stage. They gave new credence to older assumptions (for instance, taken from physiognomy) about outward appearance and inner self while at the same time promoting more fluid definitions of identity based on the modern notion of self-transformation. In problematising the body, actors played a key role in the construction of national identity, evoking the other as a temptation as well as a threat and defining Germanness in visual, narrative, and performative terms. Not surprisingly, the most famous stars became objects of mass admiration but drew fire from conservatives for inducing a most dangerous movie addiction.

These different qualities were often articulated along gendered lines. Male stars such as Albert Bassermann and Paul Wegener projected an image of traditional masculinity indebted to dramatic conceptions of character. By contrast, female stars inspired effusive claims about a new visual language, a superior form of communication located in the body. The first actresses to be perceived in this way were Asta Nielsen and Henny Porten. With her distinctive pageboy look and slender body, the Danish Nielsen brought an exceptional emotional intensity and erotic quality to the screen. She was idolised by an entire generation of intellectuals who saw her face as a symbol of the new poetics of film. Between 1910 and 1919, Nielsen made over forty films for Nordisk, often under the direction of her husband Urban Gad. Her greatest successes were social dramas that placed her on the side of the underprivileged and the oppressed in powerful demonstrations of female strength and self-determination. Nielsen's most famous films from the period were *Die arme Jenny* (1912, *Poor Jenny*), *Das Mädchen ohne Vaterland* (1912, *The Girl without Fatherland*), *Die Sünden der Väter* (1913, *The Sins of the Fathers*), *Engelein* (1914, *Little Angel*), and *Vordertreppe – Hintertreppe* (1915, *Front Entrance – Back Entrance*).

Whereas Nielsen was perceived as an almost disruptive presence in silent cinema, Henny Porten became identified with the normative force of traditional gender roles (Belach 1986). With her long blonde hair, plain features, and buxom figure, Porten personified traditional Germanic womanhood even when she appeared in rustic comedies that showed off her considerable comic talents. This first genuine German star had her greatest successes with melodramas in the literary tradition of Marlitt and Courths-Mahler. Her association with the maternal principle helped to placate widespread anxieties about women's emancipation and made her ideally suited for old-fashioned stories about female honour, duty, and sacrifice. At the same time, Porten used her talent and fame to draw attention to the most pressing issues of the time: working-class poverty in *Mütter, verzagt nicht!* (1911, *Mothers, Don't Despair!*), labour unrest in *Tragödie eines Streiks* (1911, *Tragedy of a Strike*), and unwed motherhood in *Abseits vom Glück* (1916, *Overlooked by Fortune*). The career women, bluestockings, and single mothers in these films often resisted male domination through moral rectitude and the renunciation of sexual pleasure. By incorporating such emancipatory elements, Porten emerged as the classical *femme forte* of early cinema who represented the problems of ordinary women more accurately than the cosmopolitan *femmes fatales* portrayed by Pola Negri and Mia May.

In the same way that the star system reflected dramatic changes in Wilhelmine society, including the emancipation of women and the rise of the working class, the most successful film genres responded to new lifestyles and sensibilities, but again with a detour through established popular traditions. Incorporating elements from rustic comedies, pulp novels, folk operettas, and fairy-tales, comedy and melodrama provided the most effective model for organising visual and narrative motifs and for linking them to specific configurations in modernity: the relationship between the individual and the masses; the conflicts among classes, sexes, and generations; the delayed process of urbanisation, the impact of new technologies, and the changing face of labour and industry.

This important function of genre as a narrativising of social experiences also extended to the representation of national differences. From the first screenings of foreign films, other national cinemas were regularly identified with specific genres and, by implication, mentalities: the Italian cinema with monumental epics, the French with literary adaptations, and Hollywood with slapstick comedies and Westerns. Making these associations an essential part of the ongoing negotiation of international and national influences, German film-makers adopted American styles in films with a stronger emphasis on action, movement, and suspense. Thus a short-lived series of Westerns imitated the successful Tom Mix films while also taking cues from the ever-popular Karl May novels and their decidedly German perspective on the American Wild West. The fascination with national difference found foremost expression in stereotypes and clichés that informed the conception of characters. The more problematic aspects of such stereotyping became apparent in the Jewish protagonists who, at the time, provided figures of identification for the large Jewish community of Berlin – often the inspiration for Ernst Lubitsch's early two- and three-reelers – but who, in the 1920s and 1930s, would also be enlisted in the discourses of anti-Semitism.

As a genre cinema, Wilhelmine cinema followed international trends but modified new narrative and visual conventions in accordance with familiar German tastes and traditions. Individual directors, producers, and studios took advantage of the inevitable tension between tradition and innovation, and often in very creative ways. Appropriating elements from the naturalist drama, the newspaper serial, and the pulp novel, the early melodramas translated social conditions into psychological processes, thus leaving their protagonists without the possibility of real change. Yet the stories also narrated individual experiences of discrimination, exploitation, and oppression and, in so doing, acknowledged the reality of human desire. Fantastic films incorporated visual and narrative motifs from romantic painting and literature, as well as from the popular Gothic novels, to simulate the effects of what might be called the modern uncanny. The historical epics, sometimes also called costume dramas or period films, displaced political events into the material splendour of set and costume design and resolved questions of historical agency through the vacillation between individual heroism and collective destiny. Yet in their insistence on visual pleasure without regard for psychological motivation or historical accuracy, the elaborate costume dramas at least preserved some of the anarchic qualities of early *Kientopp*.

Meanwhile, detective films and suspense thrillers played with national stereotypes without necessarily promoting nationalistic sentiments. British crime fiction served as a model for Joe May's Stuart Webbs series with Ernst Reicher, as well as for the Joe Deebs series with Max Landa. The fascination with British rationality and pragmatism stood behind Richard Oswald's heavy reliance on the Sherlock Holmes figure and inspired a surprising number of stories with smart women detectives like Nobody and Ellen Grey. Started by Louis Feuillade in 1913, the *Fantômas* series exerted a strong influence on conventional mysteries such as *Der Bär von Baskerville* (1915, *The Bear of Baskerville*) as well as on the more innovative Fritz Lang thrillers from the early 1920s. American action adventures inspired the work of actor-director Harry Piel, the 'German Douglas Fairbanks', who performed his own stunts in adventure films until the 1950s.

The detective films contributed to the emergence of a distinct filmic style through their fast-paced stories and dramatic situations, their colourful characters from different backgrounds, and their unusual locations and exotic settings. More important still, establishing narrative continuity across time and space and building suspense through framing and editing proved essential to such key moments as the chase, the cliffhanger, and the last-minute rescue. All of these narrative elements provided an opportunity for individual directors to develop a signature style. Thus Joseph Delmont's *Der geheimnisvolle Club* (1913, *The Mysterious Club*) stood out through the use of real locations, whereas *Der Steckbrief* (1913, *The Wanted Poster*) by Franz Hofer, a rediscovered early auteur, convinced through poetic mise-en-scènes. Contributing to the strong female presence in the detective genre, Hofer favoured beautiful heroines who, as in *Die schwarze Natter* (1913, *The Black Snake*) and *Die schwarze Kugel* (1913, *The Black Ball*), managed to solve all problems with intelligence and determination.

Early film comedies engaged social conflicts and problems more directly, and often with far-reaching implications for the alignment of cinema with dominant ideology. Comedies from the Wilhelmine period covered the entire range from the grotesque to the silly and crude. What distinguished them from Weimar film comedies was their close attention to local and ethnic milieus, an irreverent play with gender roles, and a marked penchant for sadistic pleasures and nihilistic attitudes. Laughter served two distinct functions: to provide release from the pressures of everyday life – for instance by showing its absurdities – and to affirm one's group identity against other social classes and ethnic communities. The tacit assumptions about shared values and beliefs made many of these comedies ill-suited for exportation but contributed to their success as simultaneous fantasies of transgression and acts of accommodation. Taking a very conciliatory approach, rustic comedies presented the country folk as the embodiment of old-fashioned gullibility and a more innocent past. The many mistaken-identity plots in the sophisticated comedies made the personal problems caused by social mobility and the redrawing of class boundaries the source of an ultimately affirmative humour. In many cases, the involvement of individual actors determined a film's critical possibilities. Karl Valentin, for instance, revealed the absurdities of everyday life in numerous ethnic comedies from *Valentins Hochzeit* (1912, *Valentin's Wedding*) to *Mysterien eines Frisiersalons* (1922, *Mysteries of a Barber's Shop*), a later collaboration with Bertolt Brecht and Erich Engel. Working in the tradition of the Bavarian folk play, Valentin deconstructed social conventions and regional traditions through an aggressive, and very cerebral, form of physical humour. Introducing slapstick elements into ethnic milieus, Lubitsch focused on the Jewish clothing-manufacture in *Der Stolz der Firma* (1914, *The Pride of the Firm*) and *Schuhpalast Pinkus* (1916, *Shoe Emporium Pinkus*). His exploration of gender roles found expression in provocative stories of desire and deception, from the debunking of male chauvinism in *Don Juan heiratet* (1909, *Don Juan Gets Married*) to the gender confusion caused by female cross-dressing in *Ich möchte kein Mann sein* (1918, *I Don't Want to Be a Man*).

The early melodramas, and the social dramas even more critically, addressed the problem of female self-determination within a discernible social setting and with close attention to the performative aspects of femininity. Films such as *Mutterliebe* (1909, *Mother Love*), *Grausame Ehe* (1910, *Cruel Marriage*), and *Ich will keine Stiefmutter* (1911, *I Don't Want a Stepmother*) offered sustained reflections on modern marriage and motherhood and addressed social problems without the usual moralising tone. Aesthetically, the melodramatic approaches remained indebted to social realist aesthetics and a firm belief in the visibility of social structures. By mapping the psychological dimensions of the bourgeois interior, the social dramas with Nielsen and Porten validated the emotionality of women and the contribution of the private sphere. The translation of social relations into spatial created the highly symbolic mise-en-scènes that gave rise to the artistically more ambitious sub-genre of melodrama, the *Kammerspielfilm* (chamber play film), which explored the claustrophobic interiors of bourgeois and petty-bourgeois life in greater detail. After the war and in the context of expressionism, the chamber play film began to privilege male over female perspectives and abandoned the critique of gender and family relations for psychological introspection.

Whereas the unjustly maligned melodrama staged the problem of femininity by taking advantage of popular traditions, the artistically more ambitious fantastic film addressed the crisis of masculinity through the literary and artistic forms of the nineteenth century. Melodramatic modes were considered most suited for representation of the domestic sphere, yet the fantastic with its precarious sense of reality proved ideal for articulating the problem of male subjectivity. The effects of the uncanny found paradigmatic expression in the performances of Albert

Bassermann, Olaf Fönss, Conrad Veidt, and Bernhard Goetzke, all of whom acted out traditional assumptions about male character within increasingly unstable configurations of identity, power, and desire. Most filmic variations on the fantastic approached this modern uncanny as an experience of boundaries: between the animate and inanimate world, between awaking and dream, between the self and the other. This experience was often articulated in terms of visual perception, which explains the recurring motif of blindness and the frequent use of mirrors and doubles. The preoccupation with looking, and the underlying struggle for control, revealed a deep fear of losing oneself in the confrontation with women, workers, and foreigners – in short, with the vilified, demonised, and ostracised representatives of German modernity.

Fantastic films alluded to the tradition of the fairytale and achieved the visualisation of the marvellous in elaborate dream sequences – like the ones from *Rübezahls Hochzeit* (1914, *Rübezahl's Wedding*). References to German romanticism appeared in Richard Oswald's *Hoffmanns Erzählungen* (1916, *The Tales of Hoffmann*), whereas a distinctly Gothic style prevailed in one of the earliest filmic reflections on the relationship between man and machine, *Homunculus* (1916) with Otto Rippert. More troublesome affinities between cinema and dream were first explored in Stellan Rye's *Der Student von Prag* (1913, *The Student of Prague*), with the demonic Wegener in the title role. Written by Hanns Heinz Ewers, a prolific writer who specialised in the fantastic, the film translated elements of the romantic imagination (the figure of the double, the pact with the devil) into filmic and, therefore, profoundly modern terms (Keiner 1987). *Der Golem* (1914, *The Golem*), the first in a number of films about the eponymous mythological figure, used the fascination with medieval life and cabalistic ritual to evoke familiar Jewish stereotypes and to reflect on the history of anti-Semitism. With their focus on pre-industrial societies, traditional folk culture, and small-town living, the fantastic films provided contemporary audiences with a framework for expressing their ambivalence towards modern life. On-screen, the allusions to myths and fairytales helped to displace the shock of technology into eternal times and archetypal situations. At the same time, the romantic figure of the double gave expression to an urgently contemporary sense of dissociation and alienation. Firm believers in the artistic possibilities of film, both Wegener and Ewers promoted the fantastic as an authentically German tradition that combined old thematic preferences with new technological possibilities. In so doing, they established a model for reconciling modern and premodern elements and for eliminating the high/low-culture divide through the imaginary worlds provided by film.

The controversies over silent cinema's allegedly negative impact on cultural practices were most obvious in its relationship to theatre and literature. Central to the formation of national identity since the late eighteenth century, the theatrical establishment felt threatened by the growing competition for audiences and feared loss of its historical role in constituting the bourgeois public sphere. From Georg Lukács to Herbert Tannenbaum, critics contemplated the formal differences between cinema and theatre and formulated an aesthetic of cinema out of its inherent limitations, beginning with its 'muteness'. Writers speculated about the diminished role of literary culture in constituting Germany as a *Kulturnation*, that is, a nation defined more through its cultural traditions than its social and political accomplishments. The cinema's assault on the values represented by literature, including such cherished notions as the autonomy of art, was seen as symptomatic of a deeper crisis of bourgeois individualism.

Such principled opposition notwithstanding, the cinema offered many career opportunities for writers, actors, and artists. The so-called *Autorenfilm* (authors' film) helped to create a cinema of quality that, because of the contribution of well-known writers, earned middle-class respectability and cultural legitimacy. Inspired by the French *film d'art* and its acclaimed adaptations of classical authors, the *Autorenfilm* actively promoted contemporary writers. Under the motto 'Films of famous authors are the future of cinema!' production companies secured the film rights to the dramatic works of Gerhart Hauptmann, Hermann Sudermann, Max Halbe, and Arthur Schnitzler. While polemicists were still arguing whether or not film would ever be art, Kurt Pinthus published *Das Kinobuch* (1914, *The Cinema Book*), with scenarios by several expressionist authors who explored the medium's affinities with the fantastic, the supernatural, and the grotesque. Like the film star and the director, the famous writer functioned as a link between individual films and, through the notion of creative authorship, elevated the cinema to the level of the other arts. After Bassermann's screen debut in the Max Mack adaptation of Paul Lindau's *Der Andere* (1913, *The Other*), a variation on the Jekyll and Hyde motif, a growing number of stage actors began to appear regularly in films, attracted by the high pay and the promise of instant celebrity. Respected theatre producers like Max Reinhardt and Leopold Jessner soon followed suit. Envisioning a new theatre for the masses, Reinhardt in the early 1910s adopted some of his stage productions to the screen and even directed two films that skilfully mixed fantastic and romantic motifs, *Die Insel der Seligen* (1913, *The Isle of the Blessed*) and *Eine venezianische Nacht* (1914, *One Venetian Night*).

Whether perceived as a threat or a salvation, the cinema provided the educated middle class with an opportunity to affirm the place of literature in modern culture and to appreciate new filmic techniques from the perspective of literary modernism; these debates have become known as the *Kino-Debatte* (Heller 1984, Hake 1992a). The literary and artistic avant-gardes either tried to rescue the project of high culture from the dangers of commodification, or they proposed to change the relationship between art and life in fundamental ways. Writers as diverse as Alfred Döblin, Thomas Mann, and Else Lasker-Schüler engaged in a passionate debate for and against the cinema that lasted until the late 1920s and affected all literary forms and institutions (Kaes 1978, Güttinger 1984a and 1984b). Initial curiosity and disdain soon gave way to a more systematic involvement with a new art form simultaneously described as dramatic, epic, and poetic, and variously compared to theatre, music, and pantomime. To contain the cinema's disruptive force, the proponents of high culture often evoked traditional poetic categories. Throughout, the debater's preoccupation with new audiences betrayed deep anxieties about the disappearance of the traditional bourgeois public sphere where intellectuals played a privileged role as the final arbiters of taste. In some cases, these controversies gave rise to utopian dreams of cinema as a solution to the crisis of language. Through the cinema, many critics hoped, audiences could reclaim the unity of experience in the very act of looking. Whereas literature and the other arts seemed weighted down by problems of mediation, the new medium conjured up an imaginary space of lifelike representations and immediate pleasures; hence Hugo von Hofmannsthal's and Ernst Bloch's enthusiastic comments on the close affinities between cinema and dream.

The debates about the corrupting influence of cinema took a decidedly political turn in the polemical writings by educators, lawyers, administrators, and religious leaders. These cinema reformers fell into two groups: those primarily concerned with social reform and public health, and those interested in the cinema as a tool of German nationalism and cultural renewal. Thus, on the one hand, in numerous articles and books, Konrad Lange attacked the trashy film (*Schundfilm*) with moralistic arguments adopted from late nineteenth-century debates on trivial literature. On the other hand, Hermann Häfker and his associates from Bild und Film (*Image and Film*), a Catholic media organisation founded in 1912, emphasised film's pedagogical uses and promoted the so-called *Kulturfilm* (cultural film), a form of documentary committed to idealised representations of nature, country, and native people (Diederichs 1986). Focusing on the social relevance of cinema, the reformers advanced psychological theories of spectatorship and contributed to an early sociology of film. They investigated the relationship between cinema and ideology through their close attention to the mechanisms of mass manipulation and considered its contribution to future public policies, education reforms, and media initiatives. But above all, the cinema reformers rallied against the emotional excesses of cinema that, in their view, were destined to contribute to the collapse of Wilhelmine society.

German cinema and the First World War

While the prewar years saw the emergence of a popular cinema with strong international ties, the propagandistic uses of film during the First World War aligned the cinema with the goals of German nationalism. The war forged a powerful bond between the industry and the state and left an indelible mark on the cinema not only through censorship practices and quota laws but also through the enlistment of film in political propaganda (Barkhausen 1982, Mühl-Benninghaus 1997). Reflecting the growing concern with national differences and boundaries, films became part of the aggressive campaigns that, after 1919, would continue – of, course under different conditions – in the economic and cultural realm. In many ways, the declaration of war in 1914 completed the consolidation process in the film industry. Once the films by the enemy nations were no longer in distribution, German companies encountered little other competition and expanded aggressively to meet the demands of an increasingly war-weary populace. Larger discretionary incomes and a greater need for escapist fare made moviegoing more attractive for larger segments of the population. Between 1914 and 1919, almost seven hundred new cinemas opened. The number of films produced in Berlin quadrupled, with countless smaller firms specialising in cheaply made sentimental dramas and comedies. Finally, German firms saw a chance to escape the French dominance and divide domestic markets among themselves. Hollywood films continued to be shown until 1916; Nordisk also remained a strong presence, because of the close ties between German and Danish companies.

The cinema's contribution to the war effort and to the survival of the monarchy dramatically changed the economic and political status of the film industry. Granted, production companies lagged behind the British and the French in their use of propaganda as an ideological continuation of war. German films never achieved the kind of emotional effects attributed to the British *The Beast of Berlin*, which portrayed the enemy as blood-thirsty Huns. However, concerted efforts to introduce national perspectives into the cinema, both on the institutional and ideological level, resulted in a fundamental redefinition of popular culture and had far-reaching implications for the postwar years. The cinema's nationalistic awakening began with the organisation of patriotic film days and screenings at the front. Military farces and sentimental dramas helped to strengthen the bond between the soldiers and their families back home. Animated films (for example, those of Julius Pinschewer) relied on humour to promote the sale of war bonds. In *Hurra! Einquartierung!* (1913, *Hurrah! Quartering!*) and *Weihnachtsglocken* (1914, *Christmas Bells*), Hofer used elements from rustic farce and social drama to offer assuring glimpses from the home front. Paul Leni's story of an army physician, *Das Tagebuch des Dr. Hart* (1917, *The Diary of Dr Hart*), stood out through a surprising realism in its presentation of daily life in the military. Such exceptions notwithstanding, the majority of films produced between 1914 and 1918 carefully avoided all references to the war and completely ignored the problems that caused the fall of the monarchy and fuelled the revolutionary energies in 1918 and 1919.

Through the division between aggressive propaganda and conventional entertainment, the cinema became part of a pervasive militarisation of culture. From the heavy reliance on mass media in reports from the front to the promotion of a more pernicious warfare through fictional images and stories, the First World War emerged as the first truly modern media war. It radically redefined the relationship between representation and reality. An important function of the newsreels was to disperse rumours about the horrors of trench warfare and to maintain patriotic spirit and public morale. In order to do so, *Eiko-Woche* and *Messter-Woche* abandoned the traditional tableaux format of battle panoramas for the shifting points-of-view normally found in feature films. Interested less in documentary accuracy than in emotional effects, these war newsreels often adopted a distinctly narrative style (for instance, by including staged scenes from the trenches). Moreover, the use of photography and cinematography in reconnaissance established aviation and cinema as compatible forms of visual control. Early ballistic studies (for example, Anschütz's camera gun) had relied on very similar technologies of vision and confirmed simulation as an integral part both of advanced warfare and of modern consciousness. Through the technologies of war, the filmic interventions into the real gave rise to a newly constituted unreal (for example, the disembodied enemy), a process predicated on the growing distance between man and machine and the replacement of cause and effect by more elusive definitions of agency.

Two organisations closely identified with the military-industrial complex became instrumental in mobilising early cinema in the service of German nationalism. The Deutsche Lichtbild Gesellschaft (DLG, German Society for Visual Media) was formed in 1916 by Ludwig Klitzsch and Alfred Hugenberg as a promotional tool for German heavy industries pursuing expansionist plans in the Balkans and the Near East. Similar interests stood behind the Deutsche Kolonial-Filmgesellschaft (DEUKO, German Colonial Film Society), founded in 1917 to propagate the colonial idea. The DLG, which after the war became the Deulig, produced countless documentaries and contributed significantly to the rise of the cultural film. In 1917, the German High Command under General Erich Ludendorff created its own propaganda unit, the Bild- und Filmamt (BUFA, Office for Photography and Film), for the explicit purpose of supporting the war effort through photographic and filmic means and of co-ordinating all official media activities in one central agency. Ludendorff's proposals for a large film company financed by the Reich extended these activities into an uncertain future. As all hopes for a military victory vanished and the fall of the monarchy became inevitable, government control over the production of images – and, by implication, the masses – seemed all the more important.

The Universum Film-AG (UFA), the legendary film studio that still looms large in the German imagination, was the product of such political calculations. Founded on 18 December 1917 with a starting capital of RM25 million, of which the Reich alone contributed RM7 million, the UFA brought together the government, represented by the War Ministry under Ludendorff, with major industries and financial institutions, including Deutsche Bank (whose director Emil Georg von Stauss became chairman of the board), the electrical giants AEG and Bosch, and the Hamburg-America Line, to name only a few. As the director of the Krupp concern and a representative of the Rhine–Ruhr industrial complex, Alfred Hugenberg played an important role in co-ordinating corporate interests and right-wing politics over the next decade; so did Ludwig Klitzsch, who, as director of the Scherl publishing conglomerate, participated actively in the restructuring of UFA during and after the war. Quickly establishing its influence in film production, distribution, and exhibition, UFA bought the German sister companies of Nordisk, as well as the Messter and Union studios in Berlin Tempelhof, and acquired large shares of PAGU. Wielding almost monopolistic power, this powerful vertically integrated concern would have a decisive influence on every aspect of cinema culture during the 1920s. Even when the Reich sold its shares to Deutsche Bank in 1921, Ludendorff's project of nationalistic propaganda through mass entertainment was far from finished; it simply continued in the economic terms established by the ambitious plans for Film Europe and the cultural analyses offered in later debates on Americanism. Following the abolition of the monarchy in 1918 and the adoption of a democratic constitution in 1919, the close ties between state and industry continued to haunt the German cinema for decades to come.

2

WEIMAR CINEMA 1919–33

The years of the Weimar Republic have played a key role in the writing of German film history and contributed greatly to the recognition of film as an essential part of twentieth-century German culture. The signing of the constitution ushered in a period of dramatic change that, in the popular imagination, has become identified with the liberal, urban, and cosmopolitan atmosphere of the 'golden twenties'. The new government established parliamentary structures and improved civil rights, including women's right to vote; other reforms concerned workers' housing, labour conditions, reproductive rights, and freedom of speech. The literary and artistic avant-gardes gave rise to a progressive mass culture committed to experimentation, innovation, and social change. However, the difficult conditions under which the various short-lived governments introduced democratic traditions also revealed the persistence of pre-war authoritarian power structures. The new political and cultural elites tried to move beyond the postwar atmosphere of disillusionment, cynicism, and resentment. After a brief period of stabilisation, in which cultural life flourished, the waves of unemployment, hyperinflation, and, finally, the worldwide economic depression contributed to the destruction of the young republic by the combined force of traditional conservative and rightwing parties and new political movements defined by a fanatical anti-Bolshevism and anti-Semitism.

As in the case of Wilhelmine cinema, scholars distinguish three phases: the years from 1919 to 1924, which saw the rise of the expressionist film out of the lost war, the failed revolution, and the rampant inflation; the years from 1924 to 1929, which brought economic stability and more realist approaches in the style of New Objectivity; and the years from 1929 to 1933, which began with the restructuring of the industry after the introduction of sound and ended with an intense politicisation of cinema before the Nazi takeover. Although only 10 per cent of the films have survived, the cinema of the Weimar Republic has inspired a wide range of socio-psychological, art historical, and cultural-studies analyses. During the last decade in particular, Weimar cinema has provided a critical model for problematising the notion of autonomous art with regards to new technologies of mechanical reproduction and mass consumption; for mapping the complicated relationship between art and politics, popular cinema and dominant ideology; and for exploring the larger configurations of cinema, urbanism, and modernity. The most famous films have served as reference points in the revisions of German cinema from the 1950s to the 1990s and have allowed film-makers to establish aesthetic and critical traditions across the cultural divide marked by the Third Reich.

However, the study of Weimar cinema has also raised many questions relevant not only for a better understanding of the period but also for all of German cinema and its precarious position between art, politics, and entertainment. To begin with, was Weimar cinema an art cinema unloved by the masses or a popular cinema with artistic ambitions? Do the feature films made between 1919 and 1933 offer an accurate reflection of the dramatic changes in German society, from the traumas of war and inflation and the freedom of the 'golden twenties' to the world economic crisis and the rise of fascism? Are the films more adequately described through the formal categories of art history or through the social function of modern mass media, including the phenomenon of Americanism? Is the history of Weimar cinema to be understood in the context of new technological developments and their inflection by specific institutional constraints? Or would it be more appropriate to focus on the cinema as a public sphere with changing alliances to the goals of high culture, mass entertainment, and social and political change? Can the historical trajectory be described in terms of artistic decline, with the expressionist film of the early 1920s as the high point, or as a series of missed opportunities that began with various initiatives for the quality film and that ended with the aesthetically advanced social realist films of the early 1930s? Is the end of Weimar cinema marked by the introduction of sound or the rise of National Socialism?

Two famous studies, both written in the aftermath of the Third Reich, have profoundly influenced the scholarly reception of the period. First, in *From Caligari to Hitler: A Psychological History of the German Film* (1947), Siegfried Kracauer examined the films for the 'psychological dispositions or tendencies as prevail within a nation at a certain stage of its development' (1974: 6), in this case, Germany after the First World War. Focusing on recurring thematic preferences and narrative motifs, Kracauer saw the vacillation between anxiety and aggression, and revolt and submission, as an expression of the German national character and its foundation in authoritarian social structures. Accordingly to his socio-psychological reading, Weimar films reveal hidden pre-fascist tendencies that make the rise of Hitler seem almost inevitable. Concentrating on the expressionist movement, Lotte Eisner in *The Haunted Screen* (1952) used stylistic categories to conclude that 'the German cinema is a development of German Romanticism, and that modern technique merely lends visible form to Romantic fancies' (1977: 113). The body of work thus constituted must be regarded as both profoundly anti-modernist in its cultural sensibilities and self-consciously German in its preoccupation with problems of identity and the metaphysics of space.

Critics have responded to Kracauer's teleological construction of Weimar cinema as pre-fascist cinema through a number of detailed historical studies: about the slow emergence of a leftist film culture (Murray 1990); the economic and cultural predominance of Hollywood (Saunders 1994); the critical reception of films in the last years of the republic (Korte 1998); and the corporate, legal, and institutional battles surrounding the new sound technology (Mühl-Benninghaus 1999). Kracauer's socio-psychological approach has been modified through closer attention to the techniques and modes of spectatorship that constitute modern subjectivity in relation to questions of gender, class, race, and national identity. Some studies have used the problematic of a subjectivity in crisis to examine the visual and narrative strategies that constitute Weimar cinema as a modernist cinema (Elsaesser 1984 and 2000b). But the question of spectatorship has also been explored from a feminist perspective, especially as regards the importance of melodramatic forms in addressing women audiences and offering alternative models of female spectatorship (Petro 1989). Under the influence of German cultural studies, Weimar cinema has been re-examined as an integral part of Weimar culture, from the many overlaps with urbanism and consumerism to the psychological effects of war and inflation. Greater attention to the affinities between war, modernity, and visual perception, as captured in the notion of shell shock, has also allowed scholars to think of Weimar cinema not just as pre-fascist but also as postwar cinema (Kaes 1995 and 2002).

Weimar cinema as art cinema

Robert Wiene's *Das Kabinett des Dr. Caligari* (1920, *The Cabinet of Dr Caligari*) occupies a central place in assessments of Weimar cinema (Prawer 1980, Budd 1990, Jung and Schatzberg 1999). Often described as the quintessential expressionist film, *Caligari* has become famous for its painted backdrops, skewed angles, dark shadows, and claustrophobic interiors designed by Hermann Warm, Walter Reimann, and Walter Röhrig. The haunting story of the mysterious Caligari and his medium, the somnambulist Caesare, has been read as symptomatic of the unstable social and political situation after the First World War. Stylistically, the film combined elements from German romanticism and Gothic literature, including the device of the unreliable narrator, with the staging and acting conventions of expressionist theatre and early film melodrama. Yet historically, *Caligari* was also a product of the transition between the so-called primitive cinema and the classical silent cinema. And economically, the film established an important model for using style as a form of product differentiation on domestic and foreign markets.

The critical and popular success of *Caligari* paved the way for German art films distinguished through their highly stylised sets, dark characters, and bizarre stories. The subsequent emergence of a recognisable expressionist style was primarily the work of set designers such as Robert Herlth, Kurt Richter, Erich Kettelhut, and Hermann Warm who, often with no more than plaster, paper, and paint, created what some might call a mise-en-scène of the national unconscious. The famous screenwriter Carl Mayer, who often collaborated with Friedrich Wilhelm Murnau, translated the haunting stories of desire, death, and destruction into uniquely filmic effects. Known for his masterful use of atmosphere, or *Stimmung*, to use the German word, Mayer emerged as the unifying force behind film expressionism. While expressionist elements can be found in a number of genres and oeuvres, only a few films aimed at a radical transformation of the visible world, a projection of psychological states into highly constructed filmic spaces. These films include Robert Wiene's *Genuine* (1920), *Raskolnikow* (1923), and *Orlacs Hände* (1924, *The Hands of Orlac*); Karl Heinz Martin's *Von morgens bis mitternachts* (1920, *From Morn to Midnight*), based on the well-known Georg Kaiser play, Arthur Robison's *Schatten* (1923, *Warning Shadows*), Paul Leni's *Das Wachsfigurenkabinett* (1924, *Waxworks*). *Der Golem: Wie er in die Welt kam* (1920, *The Golem: How He Came into the World*), by and with Paul Wegener, and Henrik Galeen's *Der Student von Prag* (1926, *The Student of Prague*), a remake of the original featuring Conrad Veidt, are often included in the expressionist canon but actually stand closer to the tradition of the fantastic from the prewar years.

The expressionist film is notorious for the way it resists definitions, and comparisons to expressionism in theatre and the visual arts have done as much to obscure as to clarify expressionism's own transitional moments (Barlow 1982, Kasten 1990). Important literary and artistic influences include romantic painting (Friedrich, Spitzweg) and literature (Hölderlin, Novalis, E. T. A. Hoffmann). Yet the partiality for the unreal and the interest in the uncanny also introduce more contemporary anxieties, beginning with the thematisation of new visual technologies in the intense preoccupation with looking. Expressionism in the cinema must therefore be approached on two levels: as a cluster of formal characteristics and narrative elements and as a particular atmosphere, a mood, that points to a profound crisis of identity in modern mass society. In the first sense, the expressionist film shares much with the expressionist drama, such as the preoccupation with father–son conflicts and the dangers of female sexuality; the preference for familiar social types rather than psychologically developed characters; and the fascination with chaos, madness, and rebellion. Artistically ambitious films from the period tend to portray the crisis of identity in its larger social and political implications. This approach is not always free of racial stereotyping; consider under this aspect the almost compulsive evocation of the other (e.g., in *Nosferatu* and the *Golem* films) through the negative depiction of Jewish characters and the fixation on typical 'Jewish' features and qualities.

In the second sense, the expressionist film is primarily a visual phenomenon, a mise-en-scène of fear and desire. Internal conflicts and desires are projected onto an external world that has become foreign and strange, a process that finds expression in the destabilisation of the subject at the centre of the narrative; hence the close ties to the horror film (Coates 1991). Often created entirely in the studio, these films rely on a psychological conception of space that foregrounds the medium's affinity with intermediary states such as dream, intoxication, and insanity. The fact that modern techniques are turned into effective means for escaping into pre-industrialist, premodernist worlds makes the expressionist film a powerful symbol of the precarious position of cinema between myth and modernity. Incorporating elements from expressionist architecture and painting, the set designs reject the ordered geometrical world for the kind of symbolic investments achieved through oblique angles, flat surfaces, skewed perspectives, and chiaroscuro lighting.

This metaphysics of space extends from landscapes and buildings to objects of everyday use and includes a theatricalisation of performance through exaggerated gestures, dramatic costumes, and heavy makeup. Of equal importance to the understanding of film expressionism are certain recurring plot structures and narrative motifs: the relationships of power and dependence, domination and subordination; the fixation on the burdens of the past and the troubles of the future; the spectacle of female sexuality and the pitfalls of male desire; the promises and threats associated with industry and technology; and the dangers and attractions of the modern metropolis. Adding to these thematic patterns, these experiences are often re-enacted through an almost obsessive concern with visual relations, modes of spectatorship, and problems of perception, which explains the emphasis on frame composition and the relative disregard for narrative continuity.

Many members of the film industry had welcomed the idea of national cinema during the war years and either turned film into a means of political propaganda or strengthened its ties to Germany's cultural legacies. Yet after 1918, the further processes of concentration set into motion by the founding of UFA were motivated primarily by economic concerns and focused almost exclusively on film as art and entertainment. National styles and traditions were enlisted as aspects of the commodity in an increasingly competitive international marketplace. Striving for greater influence, UFA acquired the Messer and Union studios in Berlin, built more first-run cinemas, and began to publish film books and magazines in an attempt to control all areas of cinema culture. DECLA and Bioscop first merged in 1920 to become the second largest film studio and then joined forces with UFA in 1921. In the same year, the Reich sold its UFA shares to the Deutsche Bank and thereafter exerted its influence most effectively through political measures. By expanding and diversifying, the UFA studio during the 1920s pursued a double strategy: to protect its domestic interests against the growing influx of American films and to contribute to the development of a European alternative to the feared American cultural hegemony. This strategy included building the elaborate distribution and exhibition networks that, by the mid-1920s, made UFA the only serious competitor for the Hollywood majors on European markets.

Classic silent cinema began as an inflation cinema that was able to realise its aesthetic ambitions because of the power vacuum created by economic, social, and political change. During the first years after the war, the devaluation of the currency and the low production costs, including the availability of cheap labour, contributed to an unhealthy hyperactivity and expansionist frenzy. In the absence of foreign competitors, countless smaller firms flooded the market with mediocre products made for quick consumption. Leading studios such as UFA invested in big historical spectacles and ambitious art films that improved the reputation of the German film abroad and, in so doing, provided a valid business strategy for the entire next decade. The international success of *Caligari* confirmed that films with 'typical' German styles could be profitable and, moreover, that only the emphasis on the national would make German companies competitive internationally. Hailed as an artistic novelty after its 1921 New York premiere, *Caligari* was part of a brief export wave that started in 1920 with *Passion* (the American title of Lubitsch's *Madame Dubarry*) and also included *Carmen* (1918) and *Sumurun* (1920). The positive reception of these films in the United States provoked fears of a 'German invasion' and prompted several studios to eliminate the unwanted competition by inviting some of the major players to Hollywood: Lubitsch and Negri as early as 1922, and Murnau in 1926.

The passing of the *Reichslichtspielgesetz* (Reich Film Law) in 1920 confirmed the influence of prewar institutions and debates, including the early reform initiatives against 'trash and smut'. These calls for stricter censorship laws responded to a wave of *Sittenfilme* or *Aufklärungsfilme* (sex education films) about brothel life, prostitution, venereal diseases, and back-alley abortions (Hagener 2000). These films took advantage of the changing attitudes towards sexuality that, in the immediate postwar years, found expression in an almost desperate lust for life that contributed to rising insecurities about new gender roles. But as in the sensationalist dramas about drug addiction – *Opium* (1919) with the sexually ambiguous Conrad Veidt would be a good example – the taboo subject matter usually provided little more than titillation and excitement. A rare exception, Richard Oswald's controversial *Anders als die andern* (1919, *Different from the Others*) provided a platform for Magnus Hirschfeld, the founder of the Institute for Sex Research, to speak out against Clause 175, which criminalised homosexuality. In response to dramatic changes in public morality but equally concerned with other, more fundamental threats to law and order, the new federal law unified and clarified censorship practices. After 1922, a film could be censored if it threatened the vital interests of the state or endangered public safety, if it damaged the image of Germany abroad or its relationships with other nations, and if it violated religious standards or had a brutalising effect on children. To preserve the freedom of speech, a clause was added to protect all films with an artistic, religious or philosophical message – a provision frequently ignored in actual censorship practices.

Film's precarious position between art and commodity reached a productive compromise in the concept of quality film advocated by the most famous producer of the Weimar period, Erich Pommer (Jacobsen 1989, Hardt 1996). The founder of DECLA and head of DECLA-Bioscop since 1920, Pommer took over production at UFA in 1923. He created a trademark style for the studio by promoting innovative set design and by demanding superior artisanship and technical expertise. His manufacture-based approach has been compared to the guild system of the medieval building associations. Beginning with *Caligari*, Pommer supervised the production of big-budget films that included such classics as *Der letzte Mann* (1924, *The Last Laugh*), *Varieté* (1925, *Variety*), *Ein Walzertraum* (1925, *A Waltz Dream*), and *Metropolis* (1927). Bringing together a remarkable group of professionals, the Babelsberg studios set the highest technical and artistic standards in Europe. Film architects such as Walter Röhrig, Otto Hunte, Erich Kettelhut, Robert Herlth, and Rochus Gliese lent their great expertise to the imaginary worlds of myth and fairy-tale, the monumentalism of historical spectacles, and the sleek elegance of modernist city films. Cinematographers Fritz Arno Wagner, Günter

Anders, and Günther Rittau gave the filmic images brilliance and depth, and Carl Hoffmann created an expressive, anti-naturalist look through his dynamic use of light and shadow (Esser 1994). For his experiments with free camera movements in *Der letzte Mann*, Karl Freund built the famous 'unleashed camera', whereas Eugen Schüfftan used semi-permeable mirrors to introduce models into large-scale scenes for the futuristic city of *Metropolis*. Though not always commercially successful, Pommer's quality productions with their collaborative spirit offered an important alternative to traditional notions of individual creativity. More important yet, his definition of quality resided in a concept of national culture still uncontaminated by nationalist politics. Unfortunately, with *Metropolis* alone costing more than six million RM, UFA experienced growing financial difficulties in the late 1920s and, as a result, fell under the influence of right-wing ideologues with considerable financial means and political ambitions.

The structural problems in the film industry became apparent after 1924, when the introduction of a new currency, the Reichsmark (RM), stabilised the economy. The Dawes plan channelled foreign capital back into Germany and opened up the market for new investors. Known as the stabilisation period, the years from 1924 to 1929 brought greater economic and political stability for society as a whole. The consolidation process within the industry proved crucial for developing further the generic traditions and stylistic models of the prewar period. In trying to control the influx of American investment capital and to limit the foreign competition, the government passed stricter protective laws. Import licences were given proportionally to distributors of American films who, in turn, circumvented the new regulations by producing so-called quota quickies or contingency films – inexpensive, low-quality films that ensured the continuous presence of the Hollywood majors on German and European markets. Under the contingency system, the percentage of American films dropped from approximately 44 per cent in 1926 to 28 per cent in 1931. During the same period, the numbers of French films increased from 4 to 11 per cent, largely owing to the joint ventures and co-productions started under the heading of Film Europe. Nonetheless, the fact that the market share of domestic products increased from 39 to 58 per cent did not translate into economic health, for such an increase had little to do with actual box office receipts. In fact, UFA was almost brought to the brink of financial ruin by its expensive prestige productions. Thus, in exchange for a ten-year loan of four million dollars, the studio in 1925 entered into a profitable agreement over distribution rights with Metro-Goldwyn Mayer and Paramount, known as the Parufamet agreement, which gave the Hollywood majors access to UFA's prestigious first-run cinemas. Other film companies signed similar contracts, including, for instance, Terra-Film with Universal and Phoebus with MGM.

After 1924, each year witnessed the release of an average of four to five hundred domestic and foreign films. For the German studios, the rising investments – the average cost per film increased from RM12,000 in 1920 to RM175,000 in 1928 – rarely translated into higher profits. Increasingly, film distribution was used to offset financial losses in production; soon the larger production companies also controlled the distribution networks. The exhibition sector, for the most part, remained decentralised, and that despite the fact that several major studios began to acquire national theatre chains, with the UFA theatres and UT theatres a ubiquitous presence in most major cities. The studios' growing dependence on international investment capital was another matter, as were the new alliances between conservative and right-wing parties and big industrial corporations. The power of banks and corporations over film production became glaringly obvious when the publishing house and media concern Ullstein sold the Terra studio to IG Farben, the chemical giant. In 1928, Emelka bought Phoebus-Film, which had secretly received government financing – a fact that, when it was made public, caused a political scandal, but also seemed symptomatic of the ongoing politicisation of cinema on an institutional and ideological level.

Precisely by confronting such economic and political difficulties, the German film industry in the 1920s gave rise to an innovative art cinema identified with famous directors such as Ernst Lubitsch, Fritz Lang, Friedrich Wilhelm Murnau and, to a lesser extent, Georg Wilhelm Pabst. They moved beyond the conventions of genre to impose their unmistakable styles on the established forms. As a result, their films can be described less through a fixed set of themes or motifs than through the articulation of a particular problematic across narrative and visual conventions. To begin with the earliest member in this distinguished group, Lubitsch continued to celebrate the enlightened eroticism and irreverent materialism that already distinguished his early one- and two-reelers. Yet increasingly, these humorous effects were achieved through uniquely filmic devices such as point-of-view shots, shot/counter shots, and parallel editing. Through his calculated use of doors, windows, and mirrors, the director explored the power of the gaze and revealed the social and psychological obstacles to the fulfilment of individual ambition and desire. The rustic comedy *Kohlhiesels Töchter* (1920, *Kohlhiesel's Daughters*), with Henny Porten in the double role as the pretty and ugly sister, still relied on the frontal staging and acting conventions known from the theatre. Romantic comedies such as *Die Austernprinzessin* (1919, *The Oyster Princess*), *Die Puppe* (1919, *The Doll*), and *Die Bergkatze* (1921, *The Mountain Cat*) presented the pitfalls of female desire through a highly filmic mixture of fairy-tale elements, slapstick humour, and narrative irony. The relationship between the material excesses of power and the fickleness of love was played out with more fatal consequences in *Madame Dubarry* (1919) and *Anna Boleyn* (1920), two period films whose stories moved effortlessly between the micro-politics of desire and the grand scales of history. What made Lubitsch so important for UFA marketing strategies and what brought attractive offers from Hollywood was his uncanny ability to combine artistic quality with popular appeal and to make films that were innovative, provocative, and conventional in the best sense of the word.

Equally competent in urban comedies and historical spectacles, Lubitsch was the first director to use the camera as an instrument of ironic commentary. Maintaining his distance from the narrative through uniquely filmic means, he conveyed both a fundamental scepticism about human nature and a deep understanding for individual vanities. While making Jannings and Negri major stars, Lubitsch was never an actor's director and cared little about psychological complexities. Instead, he relied heavily on objects in mediating between the inner reality of the characters and the visible world depicted on the screen. Precisely this difference gave rise to the sympathetic views on human failings that later became known as the 'Lubitsch touch'. Whether in historical, contemporary or fantastic settings, with melodramatic or comic overtones, Lubitsch always returned to this particular tension between appearance and truth in order to confirm the power of the gaze, and of surface phenomena, in sustained reflections both on the nature of human desire and on the cinema's visual attractions. Reaching the high point of his German career during the transition towards narrative integration, Lubitsch remained indebted to the pleasures and sensations of early cinema. He mocked moral rectitude and high-mindedness and debunked cherished notions such as love, honesty, responsibility, and integrity; hence the frequent characterisation of his period films as 'history from the keyhole perspective'. Yet his scorn for ideas and ideals also betrayed a deeply cynical view of gender relations, social structures, and political processes; in that sense, Lubitsch remained a profoundly conservative director (Prinzler and Patalas 1984, Hake 1992b).

Fritz Lang appropriated popular, classical, and avant-garde traditions for a highly original vision that covered a wide range of themes and topics and that found expression, after 1933, in his contribution to American film noir. Some critics have interpreted Lang's interest in power relations as a premonition of pre-fascist tendencies and read his heavy reliance on set design as a symptom of social paralysis. Eclectic in the use of literary, mythological, philosophical, and contemporary references but consistent in the emphasis on stylisation, Lang worked primarily in two genres, the monumental epic and the urban thriller. Both are structured around a fixed set of elements: the helplessness of the individual in the face of evil; the will to power and the need for reconciliation; the fascination with death and destruction; and, most importantly, the inescapable forces of fate and destiny. Whether in the oriental episodes of *Der müde Tod* (1921, *Destiny*), the epic settings of *Die Nibelungen* (1922–24, *The Nibelungs*) or the social dystopias of *Metropolis* (1927), architecture provided the director with both a metaphor of modern society and a model of filmic space through which to study the movements of the individual and the masses. His obsession with mass choreography found expression in the pictorial quality of historical, contemporary, and futuristic settings and gave rise to the pessimistic, fatalistic, and defeatist social imagination that sustained them. The eclectic approach taken by Lang and his favourite designers Hunte and Kettelhut found its narrative equivalent in the screenplays by Thea von Harbou, who combined the trivial and the profound with a similar awareness of their sensationalist qualities (Keiner 1991, Schönemann 1992, Bruns 1995). All of these disparate influences came together in *Metropolis* which, together with *Caligari*, has assumed almost mythical stature as a metaphor of German modernity and an allegory of Weimar society (Minden and Bachmann 2000, Elsaesser 2000a).

The thrillers and detective films address similar concerns about power but examine its consequences in smaller, more contemporary settings. These filmic reflections on urban life, crime, money, technology, and modern mass media all hinge on the growing relevance of vision and visuality in the struggle over narrative and, by extension, discursive authority. The anti-humanism that in the monumental films gives rise to a populist mythology with not unproblematic political references becomes in the thrillers an instrument of critical analysis. With these wider implications, the Weimar thrillers stage the fundamental alienation of modern man, his struggle with anonymous power structures, and his fear and paranoia through distinctly filmic ciphers. These second-hand images, in turn, are mediated by other systems of representation such as photographs, recordings, writings, mirror reflections, and so forth. Translating these representational inquiries into social and political terms, the two-part *Dr. Mabuse, der Spieler* (1921–2, *Dr Mabuse, the Gambler*) and its sequel, *Das Testament des Dr. Mabuse* (1933, *The Testament of Dr Mabuse*), which was banned by Goebbels, evoked the pathologies of Weimar society with sensationalist flair and uncanny foresight. Through the confrontation between the representatives of law and order and the criminal organisation of its mad mastermind, the famous series revealed the interdependencies between legality and illegality, rationality and irrationality, and drew attention to the power of new technologies of communication and surveillance within a society slowly destroyed by disorientation, dissatisfaction, and disorganisation. This diagnosis of a complete breakdown in the available models of interpretation stood behind the financial intrigues and market manipulations depicted in *Spione* (1928, *Spies*) and gave contemporary urgency to the story of the child murderer in *M* (1931), Lang's first sound film and a brilliant continuation of his filmic inquiries in the acoustic and auditory realm (Kaes 2000).

While the work of Lubitsch and Lang is usually examined in the context of larger social developments, the films of Friedrich Wilhelm Murnau tend to invite close readings that emphasise the formal qualities of mise-en-scène, lighting, framing, and editing (Eisner 1979). His explorations into the poetics and metaphysics of filmic space place Murnau both at the centre and on the margins of Weimar art cinema. The director often adapted canonical literary texts and developed his visual strategies around established iconographies, above all those of nineteenth-century romantic painting. This influence is most profound in *Nosferatu* (1922), based on the Bram Stoker novel *Dracula*, and *Phantom* (1922), an adaptation of the Gerhart Hauptmann novella, two fantastic films that have received the convenient but misleading label 'expressionist'. Combining authentic outdoor settings and stylised studio interiors, the films in fact produce, or rather reproduce, dreamlike images that emerge from the unconscious of desire and the visual imagination. Yet even the more contemporary settings are organised around imaginary thresholds that blur the boundaries between past and present, nature and culture, and, most importantly, fantasy and reality. The most famous example for the latter is *Der letzte Mann* (1924, *The Last Laugh*), the director's most explicit commentary on social mobility and its victims, in which he presents the title figure's humiliating demotion entirely through filmic effects and without any intertitles.

35

Murnau's poetic realism thrives on powerful dichotomies between interiority and exteriority, temporality and spatiality, and subjectivity and objectivity that resist easy integration and mediation. These polarisations stand behind his fascination with extreme states (blindness, madness, dream) and liminal places (deserted castles, remote estates); even his subtle exploration of homoerotic attractions revolves around the overcoming of distances in the act of looking. In his filmic oeuvre, the idylls of small-town Biedermeier culture and the fashionable settings of Weimar modernity alternate with deceptively beautiful landscapes that, each in their own way, conjure up an uncanny atmosphere, and awareness of the sublime, that has been called quintessentially German (Gehler and Kasten 1990a). The blurring of boundaries even extends to the competing formal influences within the films themselves. This dynamic finds expression in highly stylised rural melodramas such as *Der brennende Acker* (1922, *The Burning Earth*) and imaginative literary adaptations like *Tartüff* (1925, *Tartuffe*), inspired by Molière, and *Faust* (1926), UFA's prestige production of Goethe's most famous drama. During the 1920s, Murnau exerted a strong influence on his contemporaries through his creative contribution to the chamber play genre. Yet in the end, his filmic sensibility remained the exception in an art cinema struggling to strike a compromise between convention and innovation. While Lubitsch and Lang enjoyed long and distinguished American careers, the one with sophisticated comedies, the other with crime thrillers, Murnau completed only two projects in Hollywood: *Sunrise* (1927) and *Taboo* (1931) before his premature death.

Directing most of his films during the stabilisation period, Georg Wilhelm Pabst is often associated with New Objectivity and its celebration of technological progress and its willing acceptance of the *status quo*. The absence of a recognisable thematic or problematic has resulted in conflicting judgements about Pabst's status as an auteur (Rentschler 1990). His films deal with such diverse problems as war, inflation, prostitution, labour struggles, marital problems, and revolutionary politics. Significantly, the same principle of detached enchantment guides the visual representation of women, interiors, and the objects of everyday life. Yet the realism that distinguishes Pabst's approach to camerawork and mise-en-scène also accommodates more voyeuristic and fetishistic scenarios. From the social criticism of the inflation drama *Die freudlose Gasse* (1925, *The Joyless Street*) and the psychological subtleties of *Geheimnisse einer Seele* (1926, *Secrets of a Soul*), the first film to explore the relationship between psychoanalysis and cinema, to the engaged humanism of the anti-war film *Westfront 1918* (1930), Pabst registers the individual gestures of resistance, surrender, and compliance with the same formal brilliance and technical perfection. His films with Louise Brooks, *Tagebuch einer Verlorenen* (1929, *Diary of a Lost Girl*), the account of a young girl's descent into prostitution, and *Die Büchse der Pandora* (1929, *Pandora's Box*), based on Frank Wedekind's famous Lulu plays, move beyond the objectification of the female body to create an eroticism of the filmic image. His mastery of the new sound technology allows Pabst to present the German–French encounter in the mining drama *Kameradschaft* (1931, *Comradeship*) through a veritable cacophony of languages, voices, and sounds. While committed to the progressive spirit of the stabilisation period, his films resist metaphysical investments in favour of the beauty of appearances. By creating such surface effects, Pabst during the Weimar period contributed to the new style of objectivity and factuality that was both provocatively materialist and profoundly consumerist in orientation.

The development of a distinct filmic style beyond the literary ambitions of the early *Autorenfilm* also involved other directors whose names are usually, and often incorrectly, connected to specific genres. Known for his early sex education films, Richard Oswald became a specialist for costume films and melodramas. He demonstrated his dramatic skills in an adaptation of the successful Vicki Baum novel, *Feme* (1927, *Assassination*), one of the few films from the period that alluded to the problem of political violence – in this case, the assassination of Foreign Minister Walter Rathenau by a right-wing group. Ewald André Dupont, who was repeatedly drawn to circus settings after the international success of *Variety*, applied his talent for precise observation also to other social milieus, including traditional Yiddish life in *Das alte Gesetz* (1923, *The Old Law*). Henrik Galeen, whose mastery of the Gothic style found expression in *Der Golem* and *Alraune* (1928, *Mandrake*), had much more commercial success with sophisticated comedies set in the upper class. And Gerhard Lamprecht, who was well known for social dramas with a critical agenda, demonstrated his contemporary sensibilities in several successful literary adaptations, including *Emil und die Detektive* (1931, *Emil and the Detectives*), based on Erich Kästner's famous children's book.

The quality work of these directors contributed to the profitable rapprochement between film and the other arts that transformed cinema into a middle-class diversion and dissolved the hierarchies between high and low culture. Moving more freely between stage and screen, actors developed a greater range of styles, from the heightened theatricality of Krauss and Jannings to the nuanced psychological performances of Veidt and Kortner. After the commercial success of *Hamlet* (1921), which featured Asta Nielsen in the title role, studios began to search nineteenth-century and twentieth-century literature for suitable story material. Responding to the crisis in the literary public sphere, Béla Balázs, Rudolf Leonhardt, and countless other writers turned to film criticism and scenario writing. Gerhart Hauptmann, whose account of a transatlantic voyage in *Atlantis* was brought to the screen as early as 1913, inspired numerous adaptations, including one of his most famous naturalist dramas, *Rose Bernd* (1919) and *Die Weber* (1927, *The Weavers*). Critically acclaimed films such as *Die Hose* (1927, *The Pants*), based on the play by Carl Sternheim, and *Heimkehr* (1928, *Homecoming*), based on the Leonhard Frank novella, demonstrated that literary sources did not necessarily preclude an adequate filmic treatment. Contributing to the proliferation of intertextual, multi-media effects, conglomerates such as Ullstein and Scherl began to novelise famous films in elaborately designed books. They used illustrated magazines to promote rising stars and published newspaper serials to advertise new films in production, a practice repeatedly chosen in the promotion of Ullstein success author Vicki Baum.

The close connections between film and literature did not only change the mechanisms of cultural production and consumption; these exchanges also brought into focus the formative influence of the cinema on other art forms. There was a clear trend in mainstream films towards narrative continuity, psychological motivation, and the appearance of verisimilitude. This seamless text was modelled on the nineteenth-century realist novel, including its more trivial forms, and resonated strongly in contemporary fiction, especially the so-called *Zeitroman* (topical novel). At the same time, innovative literary authors and theatre producers took elements from film – the approach to montage and mise-en-scène, the affinity for the quotidian and the ephemeral – to incorporate contemporary perspectives into their own work. The rather conventional screen adaptation of Alfred Döblin's famous novel, Piel Jutzi's *Berlin Alexanderplatz* (1931), showed that modern literature could be more radical than its celluloid counterpart in exploring modernist techniques, including those inspired by film. Moreover, the wave of literary adaptations and the inevitable artistic and legal problems drew attention to the differences among competing definitions of authorship under conditions of industrial production and mass marketing. In a polemical treatise about his law suit against Nero-Film, the company that had produced the disappointing screen version of *Die Dreigroschenoper* (1931, *The Threepenny Opera*), Bertolt Brecht analysed the inherent contradiction between the conservatism of the film industry and the revolutionary potential of the filmic medium to draw more general conclusions about the conditions of film-making under capitalism.

While marginalised by the overwhelming trend towards narrative and verisimilitude, formal experimentation continued to thrive in avant-garde practices. Unlike the documentary, which used non-narrative forms for clearly defined purposes, the abstract or absolute film cultivated the free play with movement, rhythm, light, contrast, and form and maintained strong links to modern painting and photography. Lotte Reiniger remained one of the few to combine the possibilities of animation and storytelling in beautiful silhouette films such as *Die Abenteuer des Prinzen Achmed* (1926, *The Adventures of Prince Achmed*). For the most part, encounters between film and art remained limited to a purist approach to the medium that avoided narrative forms. Viking Eggeling in *Diagonal-Symphonie* (1923, *Diagonal Symphony*) worked with painted scrolls, while Oskar Fischinger developed elaborate graphic systems to explore the synaesthetic relationship between music and image, an interest that continued in his reflections on colour and form in the later *Komposition in Blau* (1934, *Composition in Blue*). By contrast, Hans Richter moved from formalist studies such as *Rhythmus* (1921–25, *Rhythm*) to the social commentary found in experimental shorts like *Inflation* (1928). His belief in formal experimentation as the foundation of progressive politics inspired an early avant-garde pamphlet, *Filmfeinde von gestern – Filmfreunde von morgen* (1929, *Enemies of Film Yesterday – Friends of Film Tomorrow*), and stood behind later calls for a socially responsible film in *Der Kampf um den Film* (1939, *The Struggle for the Film*).

During the 1920s, abstract film-makers often found employment, and an outlet for their creative ideas, in movie-theatre advertising, which used the most advanced animation techniques to sell sweets, drinks, and cigarettes to audiences. Film-makers with a background in photography resorted to similar strategies when making cultural films and industrial films. These films were influenced by art movements such as New Vision and New Photography and associated with the names of Albert Renger-Patzsch and László Moholy-Nagy, respectively. Both treated the camera as a powerful instrument for representing, or reinventing, the visible world. In the work of Walter Ruttmann, this convergence of painterly, photographic, and filmic influences can be traced from the abstract quality of the *Opus* films (1918–23) to the celebration of urban life in *Berlin, die Symphonie der Grossstadt* (1927, *Berlin, Symphony of the Big City*), which provided an inspiration for many later city films (Goergen 1989). Whereas Ruttmann relied on the principle of cross-section, Alexis Granowsky in *Das Lied vom Leben* (1931, *The Song of Life*) used montage and its affinities to machine cult aesthetics to celebrate technology as the foundation of modern life. Towards the end of the New Objectivity period, the growing awareness of social reality as a construction produced a number of innovative films that combined narrative, documentary, and avant-garde techniques. Examples include Ernö Metzner's dreamlike studies about the dangers of big-city life, *Polizeibericht Überfall* (1928, *Accident*), and a filmic collaboration by Robert Siodmak, Edgar Ulmer, and Billy Wilder, *Menschen am Sonntag* (1929, *People on Sunday*), which shows young Berliners at their typical weekend activities and diversions. Combining narrative and non-narrative elements and enlisting documentary styles for social observations, these films offered an important model for leftist film-makers trying to develop a self-consciously proletarian cinema during the early 1930s.

Weimar cinema as popular cinema

Weimar cinema is frequently portrayed as an innovative art cinema that eschewed generic traditions and resisted the formal conventions of an emerging classical cinema. However, a closer look at the entire production, especially from the period between 1924 and 1929, points to the prevailing influence of popular genres developed during the Wilhelmine period. As a system for organising meanings, genre proved especially effective in responding to social and political problems and in giving expression to experiences of uncertainty, instability, and radical change. The established modalities of humour, drama, action, and adventure could at once articulate and contain the underlying conflicts and contradictions. Contemporary figures such as the war profiteer, the society lady, the class-conscious worker, and the pretty salesgirl offered spectators multiple positions for identifying with the infinite new stories of big city life and for experimenting with optimistic, materialistic, idealistic, and cynical attitudes. Dreams of social advancement and financial gain, the rivalries between old money and new money, the lure of the criminal underworld, conflicts among the generations, romance in the work place, marital crises and infidelities, high-spirited sparring between the sexes – these are only some of the themes that sustained the effective mixture of social commentary and escapist fantasy in most comedies and dramas with a contemporary setting.

These popular traditions resonated even in the famous art films from the period, beginning with *Caligari* and its undeniable debt to the fantastic. From Pabst's social dramas, which introduced melodramatic themes into cool modernist settings, to Lang's Mabuse series, which experimented with elements from the detective genre and the suspense thriller, even the most ambitious directors relied extensively on stereotypes, clichés, and formulas. Genres provided a framework for engaging with social conventions and, even more than in the Wilhelmine period, for introducing new artistic and critical perspectives. Directors working almost exclusively in this fashion included Ludwig Berger, who cultivated a fondness for romantic fairytale motifs, Wilhelm Thiele, who was known for his light comic touch, and Richard Eichberg, whose name became synonymous with action-driven, effect-filled plots.

Formal innovation, social commentary, and popular appeal also came together in two genres often considered part of expressionist cinema: the *Kammerspielfilm* (chamber play film), whose origins lay in the early 1910s, and its more contemporary manifestation in the *Strassenfilm* (street film). These sub-genres of the melodrama projected psychological conflicts on to spatial configurations and presented their characters within highly codified spaces: in the first case, the interior with its protective and oppressive qualities and, in the second, the street as a symbol of the big city with its dangers and attractions. Like the social dramas from the prewar period, the chamber play film and the street film used a limited number of protagonists and locations, preferred slow editing and constructed mise-en-scènes, and paid close attention to psychological details and nuances. Whereas the early expressionist films relied on fantastic and mythological elements, the later chamber play films and street films focused on contemporary settings to make visible the German middle class's deepening sense of alienation, disorientation, and disengagement.

The chamber play film expressed conservative attitudes especially in its opposition to the big city and its affirmation of traditional family values. In *Scherben* (1921, *Shards*) and *Sylvester* (1923, *New Year's Eve*), the petty-bourgeois interior provided Lupu Pick with an opportunity for testing naturalist milieu theories and applying them to the psychodramas of petty-bourgeois life. These and similar cautionary tales about the contested spaces of modern subjectivity typically articulate experiences of oppression, transgression, and final resignation in gendered terms and through the aesthetic registers of the modern uncanny. Furthermore, they project social conflicts into sexual relations and translate suppressed desires into the unstable terms of visual perception. Taking inspiration from the oedipal family drama, most stories feature stock characters such as the rebellious son, the weak father, the maternal wife, and the seductive *femme fatale*. Typically the male characters respond to the comforts of the bourgeois home with claustrophobia. Yet the brief sojourns into the world of freedom and adventure symbolised by the street invariably end with the man's remorseful return to the family. Obviously, both the private and the public sphere have become places dominated by women, and the male characters fight this perceived loss of authority through a mixture of resentment, dread, and self-pity that often culminates in the symbolic punishment of the sexually threatening woman.

Following in the tradition of the social drama, the street film concentrates more directly on the conflict between the upper and lower classes and addresses typical urban problems such as bad housing, poverty, unemployment, violence, and discrimination. In Karl Grune's prototypical *Die Strasse* (1923, *The Street*), the street facilitates new social experiences and enables the protagonists to reflect critically on their living conditions, a tradition that continues in the social realist films of the late 1920s and early 1930s. When these stories are told from the female perspective – Leopold Jessner's *Hintertreppe* (1921, *Backstairs*) with Henny Porten is a good example – the most common solution to personal problems seems to be delirium and insanity. *Dirnentragödie* (1927, *Tragedy of a Prostitute*), with Asta Nielsen, confirms the frequent identification of a liberated female sexuality with criminality (for instance, in the figure of the shrewd prostitute) and its equally common neutralisation through maternal qualities (for instance, in the figure of the motherly whore). Nonetheless, these women characters are often portrayed with surprising psychological complexity, which explains the genre's special appeal to female audiences who identified with the emotional excesses of the melodramatic form (Wager 1999). Popular throughout the 1920s, the genre of the street film covered the entire range from conventional melodramas with strong doses of Wilhelmine morality to sleek city symphonies with a more pragmatic, and occasionally also more cynical, attitude towards love and sexuality. Joe May's *Asphalt* (1929) brought together both sides – the sentimentality of modern love and the fascination with surface phenomena – in what would be a final demonstration of the genre's visual possibilities before the introduction of sound.

Although postwar German cinema built its artistic reputation on the contribution of expressionism, its greatest commercial successes came with big-budget period films, sometimes also referred to as historical dramas or costume films. These productions changed the public perception of cinema as a cheap diversion and contributed notably to product differentiation at UFA and other leading studios. Moreover, the staging of the past and the attention to its 'universal' messages provided an important vehicle for working through contemporary problems, from the deprivations of the war years and the 'shameful peace of Versailles' to the challenges faced by a modern democracy. The popularity of historical spectacles peaked around 1919, indicating a widespread desire both for escapist fantasy and material excess and for adequate representations of the modern masses, if only as extras in historical costumes. The work of Griffith and DeMille proved very influential in the development of the genre, as did the eclectic styles of late nineteenth-century painting and architecture and Max Reinhardt's spectacular theatre productions with their dynamic mass choreography. Rejecting the intimate formats associated with artistically more ambitious genres, the period films presented their tragic love stories on the grand scales of history and with heavy loans from the iconography of historicism. Significantly, the use of monumental sets, spectacular costumes, and numerous extras was often counterbalanced by a highly personalised view of history that affirmed the individual at the centre of the narrative.

Two directors were largely responsible for the commercial success of the period film. After *Veritas vincit* (1918), an episodic film reminiscent of *Intolerance* (1916), Joe May perfected his sensationalist formula in *Die Herrin der Welt* (1919, *The Mistress of the World*), an eight-part epic starring his wife Mia May. He also directed *Das indische Grabmal* (1921, *The Indian Tomb*), the first of many screen adaptations of von Harbous's famous oriental fantasy of love, death, and tyranny. May convinced through the enormous scale and sheer volume of his productions and exhibited an unmitigated penchant for exotic settings and characters, whereas Lubitsch infused his dynamic mass choreographies with more suspicious glances at the relationship between public power and private desire. Whether in the revolutionary Paris of *Madame Dubarry* or the Tudor London of *Anna Boleyn*, the historical settings provided Lubitsch with a convenient framework for reflecting on the libidinal forces behind political movements and decisions. Both filmic approaches to the past, May's monumental spectacles and Lubitsch's intimate vignettes, were eventually absorbed into the more politicised approaches to German history that dominated in the late 1920s.

During the stabilisation period, some directors explored more idealised views of history that included explicit and implicit contemporary references. Thus several films about the French revolution, from Buchowetzki's expressionistic *Danton* (1921) to the Kortner vehicle *Danton* (1931), concetrated on the figure of the revolutionary hero, an allusion to the failed German revolution of 1919. Meanwhile, the Prussian films offered nostalgic views of Prussia under Frederick the Great and, again with obvious compensatory functions, depicted this period of aggressive expansionism as a rare moment of greatness for the German nation. Adding to Prussian history's appeal for new fantasies of nation and empire, the actor Otto Gebühr became closely identified with the figure of the king after the influential four-part *Fridericus Rex* series produced by Arzen von Cserépy between 1922 and 1923. Most films about the period of Frederick the Great celebrated the authoritarian, paternalistic relationship between leader and nation and confirmed all-male groups as the true foundation of society. Later Prussian films also explored other, equally problematic aspects of the Prussian myth, including the renunciation of personal happiness for the good of the state and the role of the military as a binding model for private and public life.

Another popular genre, the *Bergfilm* (mountain film), is often identified with a similar cult of heroic masculinity. However, with its modernist qualities, the mountain film occupies a much more precarious position between the symbolic investment of archetypal landscapes and their enlistment in the national imaginary. In terms of aesthetic sensibilities, the genre's leading practitioners stand closer to the realist aesthetics of New Objectivity, the documentary tendencies in New Vision photography, and, of course, the non-narrative ethos of the cultural film. All influences find expression in the remarkable technical tricks and physical stunts performed by the genre's leading cinematographer, Hans Schneeberger. The enthusiastic embrace of cinema as a technology of conquest and discovery and the preference for a camera aesthetic determined by the pro-filmic event confirm these films as modernist works, whereas the glorification of primordial nature, the metaphysics of place and belonging, and the idealisation of pre-industrial communities reveal the genre's debts to the discourses of right-wing nostalgia and negative utopianism. Resisting any simplistic equation with (pre)fascism or reactionary modernism, the mountain films participated in the dialectics between modernity and myth that contributed to the proliferation of various irrationalisms and nationalisms towards the end of the Weimar Republic (Rentschler 1990).

The best-known representative of the genre during the 1920s, Arnold Fanck demonstrated in *Der heilige Berg* (1926, *The Holy Mountain*) and *Die weisse Hölle vom Piz Palü* (1929, *The White Hell of Piz Palu*) how to combine melodramatic and documentary elements to great effect. By acknowledging the overdetermined place of mountains in the national imagination, the director found a productive balance between the apotheosis of man, the cult of technology, and the poetics of cinema. In contrast to Fanck, whose contemporary sensibilities included extensive references to mass tourism, other directors exploited this uniquely German genre for more essentialising positions of nature and culture that combined anti-capitalist arguments with folk mythology and ethnic stereotyping. Contributing to this trend, Leni Riefenstahl in her first directorial effort, *Das blaue Licht* (1932, *The Blue Light*), turned the mountains into an overdetermined symbolic space that gave rise to the singular individual; in this case: a young mountain girl played by the director herself. Riefenstahl worked again for Fanck in *S.O.S. Eisberg* (1933, *S.O.S. Iceberg*), the story of a heroic Arctic rescue expedition, which took them to the eternal landscapes of ice and water – just when momentous events were taking place in Germany.

All of the problematic elements of the mountain film came together in the career of the Tyrolian alpinist, actor, cameraman, and director Luis Trenker, whose name, beginning with *Der Rebell* (1932, *The Rebel*), has come to personify both the genre's inherent tension between rebellion and authoritarianism and its changing political alliances from the 1920s to the 1980s. To what degree the mountains of Weimar cinema offered both a model and a counter-model of modernity could be seen in the famous dissolve from the Dolomites to the Manhattan skyline from *Der verlorene Sohn* (1934, *The Prodigal Son*), the film that carried this metaphysics of form into more difficult political times. The later films by these early proponents of the mountain film confirmed the apotheosis of physical beauty and strength in the figure of the solitary hero as a prefiguration of the mixture of cold idealism and sentimental megalomania that, after 1933, would characterise much of official Nazi art.

Through their association with certain roles and performance styles, the leading stars of Weimar cinema played a central role in the development of a national physiognomy (Hickethier 1986). Famous actors and actresses established continuities between pre- and postwar cinema and defined the conditions under which specific body types could be equated with specific character traits. From Nielsen and Porten to Wegener and Goetzke, many stars from the prewar years reached the height of their fame during the 1920s by cultivating a more economical, though not necessarily more subdued, acting style. While lacking the glamour of the Hollywood stars, young UFA actresses covered the entire range of modern femininity from the classical *grandes dames, demimondaines,* and *ingénues* of the stage to the emancipated New Woman who, whether as a working girl or a society wife, stood out through her fashionable look and her liberal attitude towards love, romance, and sexuality. Brunettes such as Mia May and Lil Dagover were usually cast as seductive *femmes fatales* in melodramas and sophisticated comedies. As portrayed by Lilian Harvey, Dolly Haas, and Käthe von Nagy, the contemporary type of the *Girl* became identified with a more uncomplicated approach to erotic matters. By contrast, Brigitte Helm and, later, Marlene Dietrich acquired a reputation for introducing a touch of danger into the relationships between the sexes. As the embodiment of modern androgyny, including its affinities with hysteria and neurasthenia, the celebrated theatre and film actress Elisabeth Bergner emerged as the object of adoration for an entire generation of moviegoers.

Compared to actresses, whose contributions remained limited to the problem of femininity, male actors covered a much wider range of dramatic possibilities. The large number of character actors from the theatre gave credence to the cinema's artistic ambitions and brought with them the conventions, first written for the classical stage, that defined the dominant models of masculinity through specific physical types, facial expressions, and gestural codes. The portrayal of male authority remained the prerogative of older, larger-than-life character actors who, quite literally, filled the screen with their enormous bodies. The dynamics of domination and submission found a privileged expression in the brutal vitality projected by massive types such as Albert Bassermann, Fritz Kortner, and Werner Krauss. Yet it was also explored in the slightly neurotic styles developed by the ascetic Conrad Veidt and the gaunt Rudolf Klein-Rogge. Emil Jannings perfected the peculiar vacillation between strength and weakness that, from the role of Henry VIII in *Anna Boleyn* to Professor Unrat in *Der blaue Engel,* made him equally convincing as a German actor at home and abroad. The performance of masculinity also extended to more contemporary types. Usually appearing in romantic comedies, Harry Liedtke, Willy Fritsch, and Gustav Fröhlich gained popularity as the ubiquitous young lovers, best friends, and average fellows who combined old-fashioned charm and bonhomie with the new body consciousness.

The development of genre cinema and the rise of film stars cannot be separated from the popular reception of other national cinemas. Foreign films returned to Germany with the lifting of the import ban in 1921; many were re-releases. By the mid-1920s, after the currency reform, more than half of all new releases were imports, evidence of a growing crisis in the industry after years of economic growth. The diatribes by many intellectuals against German films suggest that most audiences preferred the offerings from Hollywood, a claim that box-office receipts fail to confirm (Garncarz in Jung 1993). Foreign films dominated the market in numbers, but domestic productions generated most of the revenues. Moreover,

German actors regularly won in the annual popularity contests. In 1924, to mention only one year, the winners were Lya de Putti and Harry Piel. The top ten films from 1925 to 1932, according to audience polls, included a large number of relatively unknown films and a few famous hits such as *Die drei von der Tankstelle* (1930, *The Three from the Gas Station*) and *Der Kongress tanzt* (1931, *The Congress Dances*). The American films in these lists often featured European actors such as Garbo (in *Anna Karenina*) and Jannings (in *His Last Command*) or dealt with specific German topics, as did the Lewis Milestone adaptation of Remarque's anti-war novel *All Quiet on the Western Front* (1930). Among the classics, only *Metropolis*, *Heimkehr*, *Asphalt*, *Die weisse Hölle vom Piz Palü*, *Westfront 1918*, and *Der blaue Engel* reached mass audiences who otherwise preferred big-budget films with beautiful and famous stars and with dramatic or sentimental stories.

The influence of American culture on modern mass culture was visible in all areas of everyday life, from fashion styles and consumption patterns to the dramatic changes in social and sexual roles; but the pervasiveness of these new designs for living remained strongest in the cinema. Americanism became a shorthand for the mood of confidence and optimism – or, in negative terms, brashness and superficiality – characterising the new generation of white-collar workers and young city-dwellers. The polemical attacks and the equally passionate defences of the American way of life represented a way of addressing the Americanisation of German culture. America provided a cultural paradigm – of sensibilities, mentalities, atmospheres – that seemed at once worth emulating and opposing. Some critics saw Americanisation as a precondition for the democratisation of high culture, others as a sign of its corruption and decline (Horak 1993, Saunders 1994). Audiences valued Hollywood films for their pronounced physical humour and strong emphasis on action and suspense. Box-office hits from the time included works by Griffith, von Stroheim, and von Sternberg as well as almost every film with Jackie Coogan, Buster Keaton, Douglas Fairbanks, and Rin Tin Tin. The positive and negative reactions to Hollywood came together around the figure of Charlie Chaplin, whose *The Gold Rush* (1925), *Circus* (1928), and *City Lights* (1931) were critical and commercial successes and made him an instant celebrity in Germany during the late 1920s (Hake 1990). But where leftist intellectuals welcomed Chaplin as the embodiment of a truly democratic mass culture, conservatives saw his particular brand of slapstick humour as a poignant expression of modern alienation that could be overcome only through a return to German traditions and values.

The critical reception of Russian films during the 1920s followed the links established by the international communist movement and further strengthened by avant-garde practices such as constructivism and productivism. During the same period, many German films were exported to the Soviet Union (Bulgakowa 1995, Schöning 1995, Saunders 1997). From the first showing of Eisenstein's *Battleship Potemkin* (1926) to the succession of Pudovkin films such as *Mother* (1927), *The End of St Petersburg* (1928), and *Storm Over Asia* (1929), Russian films repeatedly experienced censorship problems and became the subject of political debates and demonstrations. Founded in 1925 with the goal of promoting Russian films in

Germany, Prometheus Film operated as part of various communist media initiatives that included Willi Münzenberg's influential publishing empire and the activist IAH (International Workers Relief Fund). Initially conceived as a distribution company for the Moscow-based Meschrabpom-Rus, Prometheus ended up producing films such as the famous Brecht–Dudow collaboration *Kuhle Wampe* (1932, *Whither Germany?*). For many left-liberal intellectuals, Eisenstein, Pudovkin, Vertov, and Dovshenko personified the future of cinema under communism, and even though some dogmatic Marxist thinkers took issue with their formalist tendencies, references to the so-called *Russenfilme* were ubiquitous in public debates on film and politics and played a central role in the conceptualisation of a revolutionary film art. By presenting the revolutionary masses as the new subject of history, and of narrative as well, the Russian films provided strategies for revolutionary action. Likewise, by privileging conceptual approaches to montage that uncovered the ideological investments behind bourgeois culture, these films offered an alternative to classical narrative cinema.

Among other things, the strong presence of foreign films was a product of the growing numbers of co-productions and border crossings within Film Europe (Thompson 1996). Spurred on by their dreams of film as an international language, European directors, designers, producers, and actors often worked across national boundaries and became specialists in the genres associated with their particular background. These developments contributed to the attractiveness of the UFA studios in Babelsberg as the centre of European film production. Given the strong links between early German and Scandinavian film, Danish actors and directors continued to work in Berlin – especially Urban Gad, Benjamin Christensen, and, of course, Carl Theodor Dreyer, who directed the equally sombre *Michael* (1924) and *Vampyr* (1932). Because of the close ties between the artistic avant-gardes in Weimar Germany and the Soviet Union, many Russians came to work in Berlin, including directors Dimitri Buchowetzki, Alexis Granowsky, and Fedor Ozep. Taking advantage of the German infatuation with things Russian, some directors specialised in historical epics that celebrated the simple peasant life and explored the depths of the 'Russian soul'. While the Russians developed a national style through their preference for tragic endings, appropriately called 'Russian endings', many Austrian and Hungarian directors cultivated a reputation for sentimentality by adapting turn-of-the-century settings to contemporary tastes. Through the many arrivals from Vienna – Lang, Oswald, May, and Pabst, not to mention the seemingly unending stream of actors – Central European traditions left an indelible mark on the romantic comedy and the musical comedy and added a much-needed touch of lightness, sophistication, and self-irony to Weimar art cinema.

It was precisely this spirit of European co-operation that, in combination with the early protectionist strategies, offered a valid alternative to the feared American-isation and guaranteed some degree of artistic autonomy for the European studios. In this model of Film Europe, to evoke the period's slogan, the UFA studios were frequently rented out to French and British companies. Young directors such as

Alfred Hitchcock, for instance, went to Berlin to study the acclaimed UFA style. UFA signed formal agreements with the French Etablissements Aubert in 1924, and with Gaumont-British in 1927; a German–Russian production and distribution company, the Derussa, was formed in 1926. The same year, the International Committee on Intellectual Co-operation of the League of Nations in Paris even passed a resolution urging film artists to avoid racist and nationalist stereotypes and to advance the international spirit of film. Of course, only a few years later, the situation in Europe looked quite bleak, given the world economic crisis and the resurgence of nationalism as a political force. The new sound technology made co-productions increasingly unprofitable, but it was above the new politics of cultural isolationism and national expansionism that, after 1933, would put an end to the ethos of collaboration.

The struggle for economic survival after the currency reform in 1924 was to a large degree a competition for audiences that affected everything from advertising, magazines, and fan clubs to programming practices, admission policies, and theatre architecture and design. Two closely related phenomena structured the gradual transformation of cinema as a public sphere: the unification of audiences under the guiding idea of a homogeneous middle-class society and the diversification of markets based on social, sexual, and regional differences. The cinema gained cultural respectability by emphasising quality, originality, and novelty; by imitating exhibition practices from the theatre and the variety; and by integrating the cinema into other contemporary lifestyles. To a large degree, popular tastes and preferences reflected the attitudes of white-collar workers, the fastest growing social group of the 1920s and the main representative of modern consumer culture. Their needs and desires found a privileged expression in cinema and its cult of surfaces, its celebration of movement and change, its unabashed sensationalism and senti-mentality, and its simultaneous claims on social mobility, cultural legitimacy, and aesthetic modernity.

These contradictory impulses were nowhere more evident than in the close attention to the conditions of moviegoing. The number of cinemas increased from approximately 2,300 in 1918 to 3,700 in 1920. By 1930, there were more than 5,000 movie-theatres in Germany. In terms of architectural styles, Berlin's cinemas covered the entire range, from the eclectic historicism of the Capitol and the UFA Palast am Zoo to the functionalist style of the Universum built in 1928 by Erich Mendelsohn. Opening nights often evolved into gala events that included intro-ductory lectures, short variety acts, and live music by large orchestras. Part of regular programming since the early 1920s, the UFA newsreels offered a mixture of political events, sports competitions, society scandals, cultural news, and international reportages. After 1930, these newsreels appeared in a sound version as the *UFA-Tonwoche*. Special attention was also paid to the pre-films, which included animated shorts, comic sketches, and cultural films. Even visual pleasure found its proper place in the programme through the celebration of the beautiful nude body in educational films such as the infamous *Wege zu Kraft und Schönheit* (1925, *Ways to Strength and Beauty*).

The transformation of cinema into a middle-class diversion radically changed the ways critics and theoreticians thought about individual films. From the beginning, film criticism had played a central role in educating audiences, especially in a culture with a long tradition of addressing questions of national identity through literature and literary criticism. Daily newspapers, illustrated magazines, and cultural journals took part in extensive debates on film and society, film and politics, and film as an art form. Trade journals such as *Lichtbild-Bühne* and *Der Kinematograph* continued to represent the interests of the industry with its various branches. Founded in 1919 as the first journal to be published on a daily basis, *Film-Kurier* tried more actively to reconcile economic and artistic perspectives. In its pages, the lively exchanges among Willy Haas, Hans Siemsen, and Rudolf Kurtz about the responsibilities of critics set high standards for journalistic writing but also pointed to the difficulties of maintaining the ideal of independent film criticism.

Critics often turned to the cinema to address other problems, from the future of literature and the relationship between art and technology to the promises and failures of classical modernity. Leading theatre critics Herbert Ihering, Alfred Kerr, and Alfred Polgar used film as a gauge for measuring the new approaches to acting and mise-en-scène and for redefining the role of contemporary theatre with regards to new audiences. In countless reviews and articles for the liberal *Frankfurter Zeitung*, Siegfried Kracauer explored the social and economic processes that contributed to the dramatic changes in popular culture, modern subjectivity, and, most importantly, urban experience. Informed by his sociological studies on white-collar workers, Kracauer's early essays on cinema were organised around a critical rereading of key concepts such as *Zerstreuung* (distraction) that acknowledged popular culture as necessary, legitimate, and inherently progressive. Béla Balázs examined film as the first democratic mass medium and explored its revolutionary potential through the notion of modern folklore. His study on *Der sichtbare Mensch* (1924, *The Visible Man*) focused on the relationship between the camera and the face to demonstrate the importance of filmic devices such as the close-up in revealing the universal language of the human body. His later *Der Geist des Films* (1930, *The Spirit of Film*) revised some of these ideas under the influence of the sound film. Finally, Rudolf Arnheim's *Film als Kunst* (1932, *Film as Art*) focused on the formal qualities that distinguished film from the other arts and analysed the new medium's approach to movement, time, space, and perspective through the inherent laws of visual perception. Influenced by Gestalt psychology, Arnheim's formalist study paid close attention to the difference between normal and filmic perception and, for that reason, rejected the new sound technology as a betrayal of film's original possibilities.

Film, politics, and the coming of sound

As the embodiment of art cinema, the expressionist film laid the ground for an extended struggle over the cinema's national and international commitments. These prestige productions became test cases for utilising the national – that is, certain notions of Germanness – as both an aspect of the commodity and a form of resistance to the process of commodification associated with Hollywood. The filmic references to German cultural traditions allowed for specific forms of viewer identification based on literary and musical education and the social articulations of taste that, more often than not, confirmed the leadership role of the educated middle class. Because of the intensive public debates on urbanism, Americanism, and modernism, it is often assumed that Weimar culture was a predominantly urban culture characterised by cosmopolitan attitudes in all areas of life. However, popular films from the period reveal to what degree regional culture, folk tradition, and rural lifestyles retained their powerful influence and in what way legends, myths, and fairytales contributed to a persistent anti-modernist tradition. These dispositions inspired countless sentimental stories of Heidelberg student life and of honour and glory in the military. But the nostalgic glances towards the imperial past and the romantic images of typical German landscapes also responded to more contemporary investments in the idea of nation and the ideology of nationalism.

Three originally unrelated events contributed to the troubling developments during the last years of the republic: the introduction of sound, the world economic crisis, and the rise of National Socialism. The enormous costs involved in the transition to sound and the legal battles over sound patents forced the film industry to streamline its operations. UFA, Terra, and Emelka, the largest studios at the time, consolidated their operations, redefined their artistic profile, and looked for much-needed infusions of investment capital. Under these conditions, closer contact with the state as the self-declared protector of German culture and industry seemed a welcome alternative to domination by the Hollywood majors. This economic restructuring coincided with Alfred Hugenberg's aggressive expansion of his vast media empire, and the growing influence of rightwing groups on media politics. A prominent member of the DNVP (German National People's Party) and an influential supporter of Hitler in the Harzburg Front of 1931, Hugenberg bought out the American interests in UFA in 1927 in order to align the studio more effectively with a nationalist agenda. Under the directorship of Ludwig Klitzsch, UFA's increasing conservatism in artistic matters led to the studio's active promotion of escapist fare, including spectacular musical comedies and sentimental patriotic dramas. The rising anti-Semitism became glaringly obvious with the dismissal of Pommer who, like many other producers and directors, was Jewish. He was replaced by Ernst Hugo Correll, who remained head of production until 1939; similar personnel decisions at UFA soon followed.

Because of the cinema's central position in Weimar culture and society, nationalistic groups during the early 1930s often used controversial films to bolster their arguments about the collapse of the democratic system and the double threat of Bolshevism and Americanism. Nazi groups boycotted *All Quiet on the Western Front*. Like its American counterpart, the Pabst anti-war film *Westfront 1918* had to deal with repeated censorship problems. Openly political films such as Grigori Rosal's *Falschmünzer* (1928, *Forgers*), which exposed the rightwing assault on academic freedom from an unabashedly leftist position, and *Cyankali* (1930, *Cyanide*), which was based on the Friedrich Wolf play against the restrictive abortion Clause 218, experienced similar opposition. These censorship cases revealed the deep crisis in democratic institutions and attested to the shifting balance of power in culture and society as a whole.

Confronted with the aggressive right-wing campaigns, left-liberal activists began to speak out against the politicisation of cinema and to call for demonstrations against nationalistic Prussian films such as *Das Flötenkonzert von Sanssouci* (1930, *The Flute Concerto of Sanssouci*). The progressive Volksverband für Filmkunst (People's Association for Film Art) was founded in 1928 by, among others, Piscator, Pabst, and Heinrich Mann. They organised political and cultural events and published *Film und Volk*, which, in 1930, merged with a theatre journal to become *Arbeiterbühne und Film*. It was only after long debates about the educational value of film that the established parties on the left took advantage of the new medium as a weapon in the revolutionary struggle (Lüdeke 1973, Kühn 1975, Berger 1977, Kinter 1985). The Social Democrats abandoned their traditional position on working-class culture for more media-based strategies and financed, among other things, Werner Hochbaum's *Brüder* (1929, *Brothers*), about the 1896 dock workers' strike in Hamburg. Insisting on the primacy of the economic base even in cultural matters, communists continued to promote revolutionary Russian films and attacked mainstream German films for their reactionary content. Their belief that art under capitalism reflected bourgeois ideology and that only socialism could give rise to a truly new cinema severely limited their film activities, as did their lack of financial and technological resources.

In leftist film-making, classical realist styles, including the cathartic effects advocated by Lukács, coexisted productively with avant-garde techniques promoted by the Russian *Proletkult* and developed further in Brecht's theory of epic theatre, with its emphasis on active audience participation and forms of critical detachment achieved through what has become known as the alienation effect (Mueller 1989). Prometheus tried to develop more realistic alternatives to the popular Zille films – named after the Berlin artist Heinrich Zille – that, in the style of Lamprecht's *Die Unehelichen* (1926, *Illegitimate Children*), offered sympathetic accounts of working-class life but rarely moved beyond a naturalist depiction of milieu. In *Mutter Krausens Fahrt ins Glück* (1929, *Mother Krause's Journey to Happiness*), Piel Jutzi ventured into the destitute tenements of Berlin to show the importance of class solidarity through conventionally melodramatic, but emotionally highly effective means. Using similar locations, *Kuhle Wampe* (1932), a collaboration of Slatan Dudow and Bertolt Brecht with music by Hanns Eisler, conveyed its political message through a combination of realist and epic devices, including Russian-style montage and non-psychological acting. The participants also used discussions and songs (for instance, the famous Solidarity Song) to examine the connection in capitalist societies between economic exploitation and political oppression. Enormously successful with Berlin audiences, *Kuhle Wampe* was banned several times and released only in a truncated version.

Initially, film companies showed little interest in the artistic possibilities and commercial applications of sound. It took the worldwide success of *The Jazz Singer* (1927) with Al Jolson – his *The Singing Fool* was the first sound film shown in Germany – to convince studio heads of the inevitability of technological change. Hans Vogt, Joseph Engl, and Joseph Massolle had already tested their Tri-Ergon-sound system in an early UFA film, *Das Mädchen mit den Schwefelhölzern* (1925, *The Matchbox Girl*). Because the results were so disastrous, UFA sold the Tri-Ergon patent to a Swiss concern in 1926, fully convinced, as were many critics, that the art of film had already reached its ideal form in the silents. Only two years later, pending patents wars and a confusing variety of sound systems prompted several companies to join forces under the name of Tobis (Sound Image Syndicate). Finally, the 'Paris Sound Film Peace' of 1929 established compatibility between American and European systems and divided the world into their respective zones of influence. In 1929, Tobis and the Klangfilm GmbH, financed by AEG and Siemens-Halske, entered into another agreement under the name Tobis-Klangfilm that, from then on, controlled European markets.

On 12 March 1929, Ruttmann's compilation film *Melodie der Welt* (*Melody of the World*) was released as the first long German sound film. Soon after, in December, came the first feature-length UFA sound film, *Melodie des Herzens* (*Melody of the Heart*), which was shot in a silent version and four foreign-language versions. Eventually, the new technology prevailed after improvements in the quality of sound and closer attention to the creative aspects of music and dialogue. The addition of the so-called *Tonkreuz*, a cross-shaped building equipped for sound recording, made the UFA studios in Babelsberg the most advanced of its kind in Europe. The installation of better sound equipment in motion-picture theatres also increased the attractiveness of the early sound film. Because of the high costs, the process of equipping cinemas with sound projection facilities was completed only in 1935. In 1928, of a total 183 feature films, eight were sound films; by 1931, only two of a total of 157 new releases did not have a sound track. In the process, countless smaller companies went bankrupt or were bought out by others. Contributing to the process of economic concentration, the large studios gained access to much-needed capital through new alliances with electrical concerns and media conglomerates. As production costs increased, the total number of films declined from 224 in 1928 to 132 in 1932; German imports to other countries also decreased dramatically. Film attendance fell from 328 million tickets sold in 1929 to 238 million in 1932, a result largely of the worsening economic and political situation. The representatives of the film industry responded to these troubling developments with the SPIO plan of 1932, which called for more state intervention and spoke out in favour of a centralised German film industry.

Despite the rise of nationalism, xenophobia, and anti-Semitism, the spirit of collaboration within Film Europe continued to influence film-making until 1933. The arrival of the sound film coincided in a second wave of emigration, with stars such as Marlene Dietrich, directors such as Wilhelm Dieterle, screenwriters such as Vicki Baum, and cameramen such as Karl Freund leaving for Hollywood. Because of their high level of technical expertise, the UFA studios were often rented out, especially for German–French co-productions that brought together actors and producers who worked successfully in both cinemas. Film studios tried to overcome language barriers by casting French and British stars in foreign versions of the same film. During a transitional period that lasted until 1935, almost one-third of all sound films were made with these foreign-language versions. For instance, Dupont's *Atlantic* (1929), promoted as 'the first 100 per cent sound film', was shot in three versions in the British Elstree studios. Carl Froelich's *Die Nacht gehört uns/La nuit est à nous* (1929, *The Night Belongs to Us*) became the first French–German sound production and the first sound film to use the new technology in more creative ways (for instance, by experimenting with off-screen sound). Eventually the practice of foreign-language versions was abandoned because of their exorbitant production costs.

Despite their international ambitions, foreign-language versions cultivated the identification of famous stars with national characteristics and played into the growing preoccupation with the body and, increasingly, language as the locus of national identity. The addition of dialogue put an end to the more expressive acting styles from the silent period and introduced many conventions of the stage, including idiosyncratic pronunciations such as the guttural 'r'. Whereas actors became closely identified with the question of national character, actresses continued to invite more playful explorations of identity across national boundaries. For example, Lilian Harvey appeared in the German version of *Der Kongress tanzt*, with her usual partner Willy Fritsch but was cast against Henri Garat in the French version. By contrast, the futuristic adventure film *F.P. 1 antwortet nicht* (1932, *F.P. 1 Doesn't Answer*) featured Hans Albers, Conrad Veidt, and Charles Boyer as the respective male leads in the German, English, and French versions.

The early sound film found its greatest inspiration in the musical traditions and their social uses that had been central to definitions of Germanness since the nineteenth century. Just as the added possibilities of dialogue reconnected the early sound film with the legacies of the bourgeois theatre as a 'moral institution', music aligned the project of nationalism with the alternately contemplative and heroic tones of the nation's rich musical culture. At the same time, the new alliances between film, music, and dance allowed for the translation of more contemporary American sounds and rhythms into the elevated mood and frenetic pace of late Weimar entertainment culture. Two forms predominated: the Viennese operetta with its obligatory waltzes and old-fashioned arias, and the music comedy with its optimistic hits songs and exuberant dance numbers (Uhlenbrok 1998, Hagener and Hans 1999). Evoking an imaginary nineteenth-century Vienna populated by charming noblemen, sweet girls, and dashing officers, *Liebeswalzer* (1930, *Love Waltz*) and *Walzerkrieg* (1933, *Waltz War*) played into the widespread yearning for the 'good old days' of the Austro-Hungarian Empire. Known for his extravagant stage revues, Eric Charell made *Der Kongress tanzt* the most expensive German film when he brought together the dream couple of the German film, Harvey and Fritsch, and used the most spectacular sets, beautiful costumes, and elaborate camera movements for a charming anecdote from the Congress of Vienna.

Whereas the past allowed for brief moments of nostalgia and sentimentality, the present required the kind of healthy pragmatism that distinguished successful depression comedies such as the smash hit *Die drei von der Tankstelle* as well as *Ein blonder Traum* (1932, *A Blond Dream*) and *Ich bei Tag und du bei Nacht* (1932, *I by Day and You by Night*). These films featured young actresses such as Hertha Thiele, Dolly Haas, and Renate Müller, who combined aspects of the classical *ingénue* and the modern city girl. In his contribution to early sound comedy, actor-turned-director Reinhold Schünzel used witty dialogues, ironic commentaries, and sexual innuendoes in ways reminiscent of the early Lubitsch. In *Die Privatsekretärin* (1931, *The Private Secretary*), problems such as unemployment and discrimination magically dissolve in the atmosphere of confidence and determination conveyed by the cheerful tunes. Most white-collar comedies from the 1930s use public settings like the office, the hotel, and the bar as a backdrop for demonstrations of individual folly, ingenuity, and resourcefulness. The underlying concern with appearances, especially in difficult personal situations, is most apparent in the many stories that involve cross-dressing, from *Ein steinreicher Mann* (1932, *A Stinking Rich Man*) with Curt Bois to *Der Page vom Dalmasse Hotel* (1933, *The Page from the Dalmasse Hotel*) with Dolly Haas. The shocking attitudes and unusual choices in these comedies often hide a more existential struggle for economic survival that is bound to shed light on the underlying dynamics of sex, money, and power.

The early sound film also opened up new opportunities for provocative subject matter. Based on the famous Heinrich Mann novel, Josef von Sternberg's *Der blaue Engel* (1930, *The Blue Angel*) famously showed the seduction and humiliation of a middle-aged German school teacher by a beautiful variety singer and, in so doing, laid the foundation for Dietrich's international career. Melodramatic forms relied heavily on the possibilities of sound to explore the emotional range of the auditory realm. Bergner continued her collaboration with Paul Czinner with *Ariane* (1931) and *Der träumende Mund* (1932, *Dreaming Lips*), two melancholy reflections on the sounds and images of loss. Similarly, Max Ophüls in the Schnitzler adaptation *Liebelei* (1933, *La Ronde*) explored the connections among desire, renunciation, and auditory pleasure to conjure up a distinctly masochistic aesthetic. Combining subtle psychological portraits with a sharp critique of Prussian authoritarianism, the all-female cast of Leontine Sagan's *Mädchen in Uniform* (1931, *Girls in Uniform*) gave rise to the first sympathetic depiction of lesbianism on the screen. Last but not least, the year 1933 produced the light-hearted cross-dressing comedy *Viktor und Viktoria* (*Viktor and Viktoria*) as well as the foreboding *Das Testament des Dr. Mabuse*, the melodramatic *Anna und Elisabeth* (Anna and Elisabeth), as well as the militaristic *Der Choral von Leuthen* (*The Choir of Leuthen*).

In the end, the cinema of the Weimar Republic may be described best through its productive tensions: between the discourses of popular culture, national politics, and film art; between middle-class diversions and proletarian media initiatives; between the emphasis on quality and the excesses of triviality; between the industry's demands of autonomy and its calls for protectionism; between the advancement of German traditions and the emulation of American styles; between the promotion of nationalist policies and the belief in European co-operations. Perhaps it was this lack of integration that gave cohesion to Weimar cinema in the form of overlapping and competing practices. Perhaps it was the fragmentation of audiences, artistic movements, and political debates that allowed for the coexistence of mass cultural as well as elitist, populist, and modernist elements and that distinguished the cinema as a place where the disintegration of society could at once be exposed and magically overcome. From the postwar manifestations of trauma and the brief period of confidence to the growing awareness of political and economic crisis, the cinema of the Weimar Republic continued to hold on to the utopian dream of film as a progressive, democratic mass medium and, in so doing, inspired not only contemporaries but many later generations of film-makers and critics.

1 Conradt Veidt and Lil Dagover in *Das Kabinett des Dr. Caligari*. Courtesy of BFI stills, Posters and Designs.

2 Gustav von Wangenheim and Henny Porten in *Kohlhiesels Töchter*. Courtesy of BFI stills, Posters and Designs.

3 Eugen Klöpfer in *Die Strasse*. Courtesy of BFI stills, Posters and Designs.

4 Alfred Abel and Rudolf Klein-Rogge in *Metropolis*. Courtesy of BFI stills, Posters and Designs.

5 Marlene Dietrich and Emil Jannings in *Der blaue Engel*. Courtesy of BFI stills, Posters and Designs.

6 Ernst Busch and Hertha Thiele in *Kuhle Wampe*. Courtesy of BFI stills, Posters and Designs.

7 *Viktor und Viktoria*. Courtesy of BFI stills, Posters and Designs.

3

THIRD REICH CINEMA
1933–45

From 1933 to 1945, the German film industry produced more than one thousand feature-length films and an even larger number of short films, newsreels, and documentaries. These numbers suggest two things: that the industry under the Nazis was a formidable economic force and that films were considered an important part of everyday life, propagating National Socialist ideas and providing entertainment along the lines defined by the regime. In order to understand this dynamic between entertainment and ideology, pleasure and power, one needs to approach filmic practices in a way that does not reduplicate this period's own obsession with boundaries. Labels such as 'Nazi cinema' or 'Nazi film' suggest a complete convergence of narrative cinema, cultural politics, and Nazi ideology that was never achieved, given the continuing popularity of foreign films and the ubiquity of American products; the conflicting ideas about film-making among members of the industry and the Propaganda Ministry; the changing attitudes towards propaganda and entertainment before and during the Second World War; and the difficulties of controlling the actual conditions of film exhibition in the Reich and its occupied countries.

In coming to power in 1933, the National Socialist German Workers Party (NSDAP) under its leader Adolf Hitler promised a spiritual revolution that would bring dramatic changes to all areas of German culture and society. His political rhetoric combined conservative, nationalist, racist, anti-communist, and, above all, anti-Semitic views with an extremist *völkisch* ideology that culminated in the glorification of the Aryan race, the celebration of *Volksgemeinschaft* (national community), the myth of *Blut und Boden* (blood and soil) and the rejection of liberal democracy for the hierarchical structures associated with the leadership principle. Central to the regeneration of the German spirit was the integration of traditional, modern, regional, folkloric, and popular mass culture within an 'authentic', but in fact highly eclectic model of German culture defined less through internal principles than through its ritualistic purging by all progressive, democratic, cosmopolitan, and intellectual influences.

Although the basic structure of cinema under National Socialism was firmly in place by 1934, the years until 1945 saw considerable changes in the application of political principles to filmic practices; the approach to movie audiences and

59

exhibition practices; and the definition of entertainment and propaganda. Three main phases can be distinguished: (1) 1933–37: institutional restructuring and consolidation, (2) 1937–42: further economic concentration and expansion as part of the war effort, and (3) 1942–45: monopolisation and mobilisation of all filmic resources for the final victory. On the institutional level, the subordination of all aspects of film-making to the interests of the state began with the restructuring of cultural production in 1933 and culminated in the nationalisation of the industry after 1938. Yet, as a popular entertainment, the cinema continued to function through the double myths of being both within and outside ideology. Such an important cultural and socio-psychological function raises a number of questions: Were all films made during the Third Reich Nazi films? Can we distinguish between propaganda films and so-called apolitical entertainment films? Are there moments of aesthetic resistance in particular genres or in the work of individual directors? Is it productive to describe most of the films as escapist in nature, and therefore political only in terms of institutional affiliations, or must we conceive of Nazi ideology as all-pervasive and all-powerful? Can the effectiveness of film as a form of mass manipulation be identified on the level of textual characteristics, or are the ideological effects realised only in the larger social and political context and under specific conditions of reception? Do the films exhibit aspects of what has been called fascist aesthetics, or do the continuities with Weimar cinema and Hollywood cinema predominate?

Two approaches have defined the scholarship on this period: propaganda studies, which take a thematic approach and usually include narrative and non-narrative forms, and more theoretically informed studies on the relationship between cinema and ideology that focus on genres, narratives, and fantasy effects. In the beginning, most film historians limited their inquiries to the propaganda films while ignoring the vast number of genre films (Hull 1973, Welch 1985, Leiser 1974). Drawing attention to this *terra incognita* of private pleasures and desires, some historians used extensive quantitative analyses and historical overviews to assess the significance of popular traditions (Albrecht 1969, Drewniak 1987). Other scholars focused on the economic and political manifestations of cultural hegemony and examined the complicated relationship between narrative and ideology through textual and contextual practices (Becker 1973, Petley 1979, Lowry 1991). More recently, a number of critical studies have been published that suggest how popular genres offered a solution to conflicts and contradictions in society, and how modern mass media radically redefined the relationship between art and politics in terms of fantasy production and public spectacle (Witte 1995, Rentschler 1996, Schulte-Sasse 1996, Reimer 2000, Hake 2002). This revisionist process has drawn attention to the stylistic and thematic continuities of German cinema, including in its relationship to Hollywood; the similarities between Third Reich cinema and other 1930s state-controlled cinemas in Italy and the Soviet Union; and the inherent connection between classical narrative and the textual articulation of ideological positions, whether called sexism, racism, or nationalism. The greater emphasis on the 'failures' of Third Reich cinema has allowed scholars to move the conceptual binaries of cinema versus politics, propaganda versus entertainment, and art versus ideology that, until recently, influenced critical assessments in not always productive terms.

The restructuring of the film industry

The Nazis took over the film industry swiftly and efficiently, establishing the institutional framework on 13 March 1933 with the creation of a new ministry, the Reichsministerium für Volksaufklärung und Propaganda (Reich Ministry for People's Enlightenment and Propaganda). Heading the effort to turn cinema into a continuation of politics with other means, Joseph Goebbels became the minister in charge of print media, radio, film, and, later, television; he controlled all aspects of political propaganda and mass communication. To industry representatives Goebbels announced that films should have a political tendency but that tendency and quality were not always the same. The resultant mixture of idealist phrases, economic promises, and political threats was an essential part of official film politics and stood behind the repeated calls during the 1930s for more *Gesinnung* (political attitude) and *Volkstümlichkeit* (popular taste) in the cinema.

The *Gleichschaltung* (forced integration) of the film industry in 1933 and 1934 completed the process of economic concentration and politicisation that had started in the late 1920s with the internal struggles at UFA. UFA, Tobis, Bavaria, and Terra quickly consolidated their positions as the largest film studios during the 1930s. Together they produced more than 80 per cent of all feature films. After 1933, writers, artists, actors, musicians, and so forth had to be organised in the Reichskulturkammer (Reich Culture Chamber), which controlled cultural production through its semi-autonomous chambers and a corporatist guild model that applied the National Socialist prescription for organising culture in a one-party state. The Reichsfilmkammer (Reich Film Chamber) was the first chamber to be created, an indication of the great importance attributed to film-making by the new regime. Only Germans, defined in terms of citizenship and racial origin, were eligible for membership in the Reich Film Chamber. This rule allowed the Propaganda Ministry to exclude all non-Aryans and politically unreliable persons from working in the industry and, in so doing, to purge German cinema of 'alien' influences; of course, exceptions were always granted. In 1935, the provisional revoking of screening licences for all films made before 1933 had a similar purging effect by rewriting film history from a National Socialist perspective. The names of Jewish directors were removed from the credits of older films, and political rallies organised against German films that still featured Jewish actors. The strategic thinking behind the enforcement of the new racial policies dissolved any remaining concerns about the future of film-making, and of society as a whole, into the antagonistic terms of anti-Semitism, with the Jews vilified as the ultimate other.

Most Jews working in the industry left Germany in 1933 and 1934 for other European countries, often with hopes of a speedy return. The forced integration of the industry had a devastating effect on individual lives; but it also destroyed a lively cinema culture that had emerged in the 1920s with significant contributions by Jewish actors, directors, and producers. Like the European border crossings during the 1920s, the exile experience after 1933 must be considered an integral part of German cinema, whether in the form of structuring absences or through the import of German – or, to be more precise, Central European – traditions into other national and cultural contexts, especially the Hollywood film of the 1930s and 1940s. However, it would be misguided to claim the later films by Lang, Siodmak, or Wilder for the canon of German film history or to identify exile film-makers with a position of subversive otherness within Hollywood. After all, the dream factory, whether in Hollywood or Babelsberg, had always thrived on incorporating and exploiting the spectacle of difference, including through the identification of famous stars with particular national stereotypes and ethnic cultures.

Pommer and Wilder were among the lucky few to leave for Hollywood as early as 1934, with studio contracts in hand. The largest number of exiles came to Hollywood in the late 1930s under less favourable conditions. The difficulties of exile were perhaps most pronounced in the case of actors, whom language problems often limited to bit parts and 'accent parts'. Apart from Marlene Dietrich, only Peter Lorre, and Conrad Veidt, had significant American careers. Known for their professionalism and technical expertise, cameramen such as Rudolf Maté and Eugen Schüfftan quickly found artistic recognition, as did composers Friedrich Hollaender and Erich Maria Korngold. Directors Fritz Lang, Billy Wilder, Curtis (Kurt) Bernhardt, Robert Siodmak, and Douglas Sirk (Detlef Sierck) became famous for infusing classical American genres with traditional European cultural sensibilities and for articulating political concerns coloured by the experience of exile. Some of these exile sensibilities found expression in the bleak visions and dark moods identified with film noir (Hilchenbach 1982, Belach and Prinzler 1983, Horak 1984 and 1996, Koepnick 2002).

The purging of the film-related professions and the subsequent exile waves were only the beginning of more fundamental changes that brought greater state control over most legal, financial, and administrative, and, of course, artistic aspects of film-making. The *Reichslichtspielgesetz* (Reich Film Law) of 1934 clearly spelled out the new principles of film censorship (Maiwald 1983). Anything considered critical of National Socialism, from aesthetic styles to moral sensibilities, could be prohibited, banned, and confiscated. A more far-reaching pre-censorship based on submitted scripts replaced the standard post-production censorship; now the *Reichsfilm-dramaturg* (Reich Film Dramaturge) was in charge of the approval process. The close involvement of the Ministry in the pre-production phase limited the economic risks for the studios while extending ministerial control to all stages of production. Not surprisingly, the total number of censored films remained insignificant, with the majority of cases occurring during the early 1940s. Among the twenty-seven censored films mentioned by Wetzel and Hagemann (1982), the majority featured an actor or director who had become *persona non grata*. A few films were banned despite, or because, of their National Socialist fervour. In other cases, the censors considered certain representations (for instance, of bombed cityscapes) too demoralising for wartime audiences.

An elaborate system of direct and indirect financing provided new incentives for struggling companies and proved just as effective as more direct forms of political control. Almost one-third of the feature films received distinctions, or ratings, of some sort, an indication of the Ministry's considerable efforts to promote specific genres and subjects. Financial support was available through the Filmkredit-bank (Film Credit Bank) which, by 1935, already provided financing to almost 70 per cent of the films in production; these loans were often not repaid. The system of distinctions, which included 'educational' and 'artistically (especially) valuable', came/with certificates of tax reduction or, in the highest category, with tax exemption. To these existing distinctions, the Filmprüfstelle (Film Office) added 'politically (especially) valuable' and the honorary designation 'film of the nation', which was awarded only four times: to *Ohm Krüger* (1941), *Heimkehr* (1941, *Homecoming*), *Der grosse König* (1942, *The Great King*), and *Die Entlassung* (1942, *The Dismissal*). All four films were so-called *Staatsauftragsfilme* (state-commissioned films), big-budget films with clear propagandistic intentions commissioned by the Propaganda Ministry to promote key concepts of Nazi ideology in narrative form. Their stories focused on Prussia's triumphs and defeats, the struggles of ethnic Germans abroad, and the heroic lives of great men. Many contributions confirmed race as the foundation of German character and turned to the past as a premonition of German manifest destiny. Because of their over-determined conditions of production, the state-commissioned films were essentially a genre to themselves, defined less through particular textual characteristics than through such contextual qualities as the transformation of opening nights into public spectacles and the many parallels between the events on the screen and concurrent political developments.

Goebbels, who supervised the implementation of these new policies, had a personal interest in film and, like Hitler, socialised extensively with people from the film world. Indeed, the film community – and, in other contexts, the literary and musical establishment – played a significant role in giving cultural legitimacy to the new regime. Courted by the power elite, many actors and directors lived in a world of luxury and privilege. For the most part, their encounters between the representatives of the Ministry took place in a collaborative spirit, and both sides profited equally from the undiminished popularity of German films with German audiences. Goebbels gave special permission to individuals deemed too valuable to be lost to the new membership laws. These exceptions concerned several Jewish actors and directors and banned authors such as Erich Kästner who, under the pseudonym Berthold Bürger, wrote the screenplay for *Münch-hausen* (1943). However, the brute force that could always punish insubordination also manifested itself in two tragic incidents: the 1942 suicide of actor Joachim Gottschalk, who had refused to divorce his Jewish wife, and the 1943 death of director Herbert Selpin in a Gestapo prison after disputes during the production of *Titanic*.

Supported by the new political and cultural elites, the cinema after 1933 emerged as the most important medium for forging a national community beyond class boundaries and for staging political fantasies beyond the public–private divide. The new contingency system sharply limited the numbers of imported films and curtailed the participation of non-Germans in domestic productions. But even the concerted efforts by German directors to imitate Hollywood styles did not diminish the appeal of foreign films, which remained a strong presence until the war and compensated for the dearth of quality films with artistic ambition and social relevance. In 1933, almost half of all films shown on European markets were of American origin. After only one year, their market share declined to 20 per cent. Nonetheless, more than six hundred foreign feature films would still be seen by German audiences during the 1933–45 period, with the majority released between 1933 and 1939 in subtitled or dubbed versions. Confirming the un-diminished influence of American popular culture in all areas of everyday life, audience favourites from the 1930s included the Nelson Eddy and Jeanette MacDonald operetta films, the musicals with Fred Astaire and Ginger Rogers, and, of course, everything with Tarzan and Mickey Mouse. Clark Gable, Shirley Temple, Greta Garbo, Joan Crawford, and Gary Cooper all had a large following. In 1936, Dietrich could still be seen in the Lubitsch production *Desire*, despite official polemics against émigrés appearing in foreign films. It was only in 1939, after the release of Anatole Litvak's *Confessions of a Nazi Spy* (1939), that American films were taken out of distribution entirely.

The Propaganda Ministry's close attention to the conditions of film exhibition and the psychology of mass reception reflected persistent anxieties about the actualisation of a film's intended meaning. Feature-length films always ran as part of a mandatory programme that consisted of newsreels and short cultural films. Because audiences often skipped these pre-films, movie-theatre owners were advised during the war years to close their doors to latecomers once the newsreel had started. However, the elusiveness of audience tastes remained a source of deep concern, even requiring secret reports from the movies by the Sicherheitsdienst der SS (Security Service). In an effort to reach larger segments of the population, the Propaganda Ministry instituted the *Filmvolkstag* (Film People's Day), on which audiences could attend special screenings for a nominal fee. The *Jugendfilmstunden* (Youth Film Hours), organised by the Hitler Youth since 1934, showed docu-mentaries and short feature films aimed specifically at children and adolescents. In the 1942/43 season, these Youth Film Hours saw more than eleven million attendances by young people.

From the beginning, the leading film studios had to deal with the decline of their export business and, more generally, the effect of cultural isolationism on a visual medium that had always thrived on its international connections. Although there was little competition for German studios in neighbouring countries such as Austria and Switzerland, film exports, including to the United States, immediately declined by almost 80 per cent. Nonetheless, in 1939, 85 of the 272 foreign films shown in the United States were still produced by German (or Austrian) companies.

They found their small audiences in cities and states with a strong German-speaking immigrant population. The activities of various anti-Nazi groups put an end to such practices and increased public awareness of the difficult situation in Europe, including through the anti-Nazi films produced with the involvement of exile actors and directors.

Apart from ruining the export business, the Reich's withdrawal from the international film scene prevented much-needed artistic exchanges. The lack of creative talent after the purge in 1933 posed a serious obstacle to the studios' competitiveness in foreign markets. Co-productions remained limited to Austria, Hungary, Czechoslovakia and, after 1939, to Italy and Japan. The Venice Film Festival was reduced to a showcase for expensive but undistinguished productions by the Axis powers. Contributing to the systematic eradication of all creative and critical impulses, film criticism after 1936 offered only factual information and appreciative commentary. The major trade journals, including the dailies *Lichtbild-Bühne and Film-Kurier*, deteriorated into mouthpieces of the Nazi culture industry. Under such conditions, the founding of the Deutsche Akademie für Filmkunst (German Academy for Film Art) in 1938 came too late to develop alternatives to the pervasive spirit of conventionality, provincialism, and mediocrity.

The years 1937 to 1942 saw the systematic elimination of all independent companies through various economic and political measures. Shrinking export revenues and growing production costs forced even large studios such as Tobis to accept secret loans from the Ministry. Film attendance increased steadily and significantly; during the record year 1938, for instance, almost 440 million tickets were sold. However, the average costs of making a film more than doubled from RM250,000 in 1933 to RM537,000 in 1937. In 1937, when the losses at UFA approached RM15 million, the Reich bought more than 70 per cent of their stocks through a middleman, Max Winkler of the Cautio Trust; similar deals with Terra followed suit. Now effectively under state ownership, Tobis, Terra, and Bavaria kept their names but were more actively enlisted in the new alliance between cinema and politics. After the invasion of the Sudentenland in 1938, the politicisation and militarisation of everyday life found expression in a sharper division between entertainment and propaganda, with expensive prestige productions now openly promoting nationalistic attitudes and fuelling anti-Semitic and anti-Slavic sentiments. The conquest of neighbouring countries opened up new export markets, set new attendance records, and eventually turned the film industry into the country's fourth-largest industry.

The gradual transformation of the audience into a manifestation of the national community extended these expansionist and exclusionary practices into the most mundane aspects of cinema culture, beginning with the rules of admission. After 1938, Jews were no longer admitted to cinemas; similar prohibitions applied to foreign labourers and POWs. These practices implicated movie audiences directly in the staging of highly politicised group experiences and made them part of the rituals and fantasies subsumed under the concept of *Volksgemeinschaft*. The political mobilisation of cinema as a place of collective experiences and an instrument of ideological positioning required the implementation of stricter standards concerning programming practices (for instance, obligatory screenings of war newsreels). All of these changes contributed to the transformation of the motion-picture theatre into a public sphere where the nation could reach an illusory sense of self through a radicalised notion of cinema as a *Gesamtkunstwerk*.

The annexation of Austria in 1938 destroyed another German-speaking cinema that had offered extensive artistic exchanges and shared many cultural traditions. From its inception, Austrian cinema had conveyed an alternative image of Germanness in the larger context of national fictions and iconographies. With its decadent charm, ironic sentimentality, and old-fashioned *Gemütlichkeit*, the myth of Vienna provided more light-hearted but also more ambiguous interpretations of the conventional genres. Before 1938, Viennese studios had specialised in sound comedies with the inexhaustible Hans Moser, melancholy love stories with Willi Forst, and countless musical comedies and operetta films inspired by the identification of Vienna with music. The new Wien-Film, a state-controlled company established in 1938 under Karl Hartl, continued to specialise in these fictional constructs of Austrianness, producing musical biographies such as the Mozart films *Eine kleine Nachtmusik* (1939, *A Little Night Music*) and *Wen die Götter lieben* (1942, *Whom the Gods Love*), as well as Forst's famous Vienna trilogy, *Operette* (1940, *Operetta*), *Wiener Blut* (1942, *Viennese Blood*), and *Wiener Mädel* (1945/59, *Viennese Girls*).

The overall situation was very different in France after the German invasion in 1939. Since the invention of cinematography, France and Germany had enjoyed a close relationship, from the sharing of technologies and the exchange of actors to the many co-productions that continued throughout the 1930s (Sturm and Wohlgemuth 1996). In 1940 the Germans took over film production in occupied France through a sister company of UFA, Continental-Films, which, among others, produced Henri-Georges Clouzot's *Le corbeau* (1943, *The Raven*). Goebbels's goal was to produce films that retained their French qualities and could be promoted as domestic productions in the occupied zone. Maintaining an appearance of diversity was all the more important as American imports had an increasingly difficult time reaching European markets. However, such calculations failed to extinguish the spirit of resistance, as could be seen in the systematic boycotting of German films in the Balkans and the Netherlands.

Finally, in 1942, the film industry became fully nationalised, with Cautio acting as a trust company and the newly formed UFA-Film GmbH, sometimes also referred to as UFI, operating as a holding company with several subsidiaries. UFA-Film, which used the old UFA-quality label, was headed by Fritz Hippler as the newly appointed *Reichsfilmintendant* (Reich Film Administrator) responsible for co-ordinating all aspects of film production and distribution with official policies. Eleven firms were now united in one state-owned trust, including the UFA-Filmkunst, Terra-Filmkunst, Tobis-Filmkunst, Bavaria-Filmkunst, Wien-Film, Prag-Film, and Continental-Film. The monopolisation of film production made possible a more effective division of labour in the cinema among the competing demands of propaganda, ideology, and entertainment. After several years of aggressive politicisation, the Ministry returned to the double strategy of producing a few big-budget propaganda films and a large number of conventional genre films with strong entertainment value. Under such conditions, the war ended up being highly profitable for the industry, raising the number of tickets sold from 624 million in 1939 to 1.117 billion in 1943. By the early 1940s, only the United States had more exhibition venues than the Third Reich with its approximately 8,600 theatres both in Germany and in the occupied countries and territories. Revelling in these successes, UFA celebrated its twenty-five-year anniversary in 1943 with the blockbuster production of *Münchhausen*, an all-star historical action adventure, shot in colour, which cost the studio an unprecedented RM6.5 million.

While the war effort continued in full force, frivolous subject matter returned to the cinema with a vengeance, as did more defeatist attitudes and melancholy styles. Any direct references to the present yielded to stories without a discernible time and place. Within such an illusionist structure, the eruptions of the real, whether in the form of particular words or images, proved a constant source of concern. For example, the inclusion of documentary material in war films such as *U-Boote westwärts!* (1941, *Submarines Westward!*) or *Stukas* (1941) corroborated the myth of individual heroism, but also drew attention to the difference between the war experience and its filmic representation. Likewise, in 1940, the commercial failure of the anti-Semitic historical drama *Die Rothschilds* (*The Rothschilds*), as well as some audiences' uneasiness about *Der ewige Jude* (*The Eternal Jew*), the infamous compilation film by Fritz Hippler, revealed the inherent dangers for film-makers in relying on all too simplistic assumptions about intended meanings and actual responses. Despite such problems, the Propaganda Ministry tried to supply war audiences with a constant stream of entertaining films, including many re-releases. Because of the massive destruction caused by allied bombing of cities, even many venerable state theatres were turned into movie-theatres. The Barrandov studios in Prague became the preferred place for war-weary film professionals. Until the very end, some film officials remained convinced of a German victory – if not on the battlefield of war, then in some imaginary cinema of the future.

Third Reich cinema as popular cinema

While the institutional framework established in 1933 remained the determining factor in the production of films, their immense mass appeal must neither be confused with the all-pervasive power of Nazi ideology nor regarded as evidence of a cultural sphere unaffected by politics. Box-office receipts point to a popular cinema positioned within ideology precisely through its commitment to pleasure and entertainment. The list of greatest successes was led by *Die goldene Stadt* (1942, *The Golden City*) with 12.5 million tickets sold, followed by *Der weisse Traum* (1943, *The White Dream*) and *Immensee* (1943), each with 10.1 million, *Die grosse Liebe* (1942, *The Great Love*) and *Wiener Blut*, each with 9.2 million, and *Wunschkonzert* (1940, *Request Concert*) with 8.8 million tickets. A variety of factors contributed to these phenomenal successes: their acceptance of genre as the most efficient form of addressing diverse audiences; their cultivation of the star system as a convenient structure for audience identification; their incorporation of other popular traditions such as folklore, operetta, literature, and broadcasting; and, most importantly, their reliance on the conventions and styles associated with the classical Hollywood film.

Not surprisingly, Third Reich cinema was from the beginning a cinema dominated by male and, above all, female stars. Famous stars established patterns of identification, imitation, and admiration beyond individual films. The collapsing of actor and role in the persona of the star provided an outlet for powerful emotions in a society oppressively concerned with sexual and racial difference and severely anxious over public and private identities. In contrast to character actors such as Gustav Gründgens, Heinrich George, and Werner Krauss, who endowed film with cultural significance, and unlike supporting actors like Grete Weiser and Theo Lingen, who added local wit and regional humour, the new leading stars became closely identified with the cinema's national and international ambitions. With their beauty, charm, and sex appeal, actresses conjured up a cosmopolitan atmosphere necessary for films' commercial success at home and abroad. Yet the transformation of the female body into a marker of national identity also introduced more problematic ideas about race and gender that proved essential to the socio-psychological function of mass entertainment during the Third Reich (Beyer 1991, Romani 1992).

Adored by their fans, photographed in the illustrated press, and written up in gossip columns, actresses embodied the other, unofficial side of post-1933 society associated with tolerance, sophistication, fashion, leisure, luxury, and eroticism. The Propaganda Ministry recognised the stars' public function by accommodating personal requests and paying sometimes exorbitant salaries. In 1937, for instance, Albers earned as much as RM562,000. By contrast, a skilled worker earned only RM2,500 a year. Secret lists circulated with the names of those actors to be employed at all times and those to be avoided as 'box-office poison'. Many famous actresses were modelled on Hollywood stars, with Zarah Leander promoted as a 'German Garbo', Harvey resembling Miriam Hopkins, and Marika Rökk frequently compared to Eleanor Powell and Ginger Rogers. While blond *ingénue* Kristina Söderbaum may have personified the ideal Aryan woman, the majority of actresses displayed physical features and character traits with little resemblance to official images of German womanhood. Through their exotic looks, refined tastes, and fashionable styles, they provided the extravagance and glamour that had been eliminated from official culture.

This identification with otherness was especially pronounced in actresses whose careers began after 1933. Many were foreigners (Söderbaum, Leander, Rökk) or made foreignness part of their erotic appeal. In contrast to the idea of female beauty prevalent in painting and sculpture, feature films promoted the slender, androgynous type embodied by Käthe von Nagy and Brigitte Helm. With the exception of strong mother figures, most female stereotypes were equally represented in the respective genres. Olga Tschechowa excelled in playing the worldly older woman.

Combining simplicity and inner strength, Austrian Paula Wessely brought emotional complexity to the woman's film. After Renate Müller's premature death in 1938, the young Ilse Werner became audience's favourite 'girl next door'. Often cast as a dangerous *femme fatale*, Brigitte Horney appeared regularly in melodramas but, like Tschechowa and Wessely, also lent her intense performances to several propaganda vehicles. Sibylle Schmitz, whose suicide inspired Fassbinder's *Die Sehnsucht der Veronika Voss* (1982, *Veronika Voss*), found a perfect showcase for her dark exotic beauty in highly stylised melodramatic settings.

With her classical features and theatrical training, Marianne Hoppe was predestined to cover the widest range as an actress, playing in light-hearted sophisticated comedies like *Capriolen* (1937, *Capers*) and melancholy marital dramas like *Romanze in Moll* (1943, *Romance in a Minor Key*), as well as in home front films such as *Auf Wiedersehn, Franziska!* (1941, *Goodbye, Franziska!*). While possessing some of androgynous charm that linked *ingénues* such as Harvey, Müller, and Nagy to their Weimar precursors, Hoppe became most closely identified with the difficulties experienced by modern women in reconciling the demands of career, marriage, and motherhood. Her screen persona combined a strong desire for independence, articulated in her playfulness and confidence, and a knowing recognition of the limitations put upon her by society. The casting of Hoppe as Effi Briest in the Fontane adaptation *Der Schritt vom Wege* (1939, *The Step off the Path*) took advantage of this tension and offered a subtle commentary on the emotionality of unfulfilled yearning and quiet subordination.

In contrast to female stars and their close identification with issues of gender, male actors were more directly implicated in the articulation of national identity. Romantic leads such as Willy Fritsch and Gustav Fröhlich became identified with the youthfulness of the new generation, whereas the more mature, heavy-set character actors from the theatre conveyed the kind of authority and strength associated with the past. Heinrich George brought his intense physicality to many historical settings. Werner Krauss and Emil Jannings specialised in rulers, industrialists, and inventors. All three regularly took leading roles in the propaganda vehicles. With the exception of the brash Hans Albers and the suave Willy Birgel, whose screen personas thrived on irresolvable ambiguities, most actors appeared either in romantic or dramatic parts. The available stereotypes included urbane charmers such as Hans Söhnker, quiet masculine types like Paul Hartmann, and, in more heroic roles, Carl Raddatz and Paul Klinger. The appeal of Heinz Rühmann hinged on his simultaneously humorous and pathetic compulsion to act out the petty-bourgeois desire for social acceptance with all of its psychological complications. As the personification of the little man – oppressed, repressed, but always in a good mood – Rühmann comically re-enacted the crises of masculinity in numerous comedies about the difficulties of everyday life. Yet his most famous films from the period, *Quax der Bruchpilot* (1941, *Quax the Crash Pilot*) and *Die Feuerzangenbowle* (1944, *The Red Wine Punch*), also brought out the underlying tension between male aggression and regression that sustained Rühmann's phenomenal career as the Reich's most popular comedian.

While there was no shortage of good actors, the lack of talented directors and screenwriters after the introduction of the Aryan clause remained a serious problem throughout the decade. Most directors were seasoned professionals who had started making films before 1933 and would continue after 1945. The prolific Carl Boese directed almost fifty films during the Third Reich, including many comedies set in the petty-bourgeois milieu. The credits of screenwriter and director Robert A. Stemmle are equally extensive. Carl Froelich worked with Henny Porten in the early 1920s, directed and produced throughout the 1930s, and, as a member of the Nazi party, was appointed president of the Reich Film Chamber in 1939. Froelich's best-known films include *Heimat* (1938, *Homeland*), a melodrama featuring George and Leander as estranged father and daughter, and *Die vier Gesellen* (1938, *The Four Comrades*), a romantic comedy about female friendship and the quest for self-fulfilment with the young Ingrid Bergman. Head of production at UFA since 1943, Wolfgang Liebeneiner's highly adaptable artistic sensibility allowed him to work with some of the greatest actors from the German stage. Liebeneiner specialised in light comedies before he applied his directorial skills to the infamous euthanasia film, *Ich klage an* (1941, *I Accuse*) and two biographical films about the 'Iron Chancellor', *Bismarck* (1940) and the aforementioned *Die Entlassung*.

Many directors established working relationships with famous actors or became specialists in certain genres that allowed them to capitalise on their cultural or ethnic backgrounds. Often in collaboration with the composer Robert Stolz, Hungarian Géza von Bolvary specialised in film operettas that nostalgically evoked Old Vienna in the mold of *Wiener Geschichten* (1940, *Viennese Stories*). Viktor Tourjansky made a name for himself with marital melodramas in the style of *Der Blaufuchs* (1938, *The Blue Fox*) and more dubious political parables such as *Der Gouverneur* (1939, *The Governor*). Beginning with *Liebespremiere* (1943, *Love Premiere*), Arthur Maria Rabenalt directed several films set in the world of show business, whereas Herbert Selpin preferred adventure dramas in the style of *Sergeant Berry* (1938) and *Titanic* (1943). Directors with pronounced political commitments were often strongly identified with the biographical or historical film. Hans Steinhoff, who emerged as a leading director with *Hitlerjunge Quex*, became a master at portraying great individuals, whether in the field of medicine (*Robert Koch*, 1939) or art (*Rembrandt*, 1942). From *Flüchtlinge* (1933, *Refugees*) to *Heimkehr*, Austrian Gustav Ucicky infused historical events with nationalistic sentiment, not least by extolling the virtues of male friendship and personal sacrifice. Popular formulas' precedence over political messages, especially when ideological positions were at stake, repeatedly threatened the career of Karl Ritter, an ardent National Socialist and anti-communist whose propagandistic zeal in *Verräter* (1936, *Traitors*), *Patrioten* (1937, *Patriots*), and *Pour le mérite* (1938) was not always appreciated by the Propaganda Ministry. Even with distinctions such as 'politically valuable', his high-profile films found outspoken critics among cultural polemicists such as Alfred Rosenberg, who regarded their nationalist, rather than National Socialist, rhetoric as an obstacle to a quality-based definition of political film-making.

In a national cinema defined primarily through popular genres and famous stars, was there any room for individual sensibilities and critical perspectives? Experiments were certainly not encouraged, but it would be reductive to explain the lack of innovative directors solely by the oppressive political conditions. Of course, it would be equally problematic to read all signs of creative film-making as a manifestation of aesthetic opposition or subversive meanings. To begin with, the early sound film brought back many dramatic conventions and staging techniques from the theatre and contributed to the growing preference for seamless narratives without authorial interventions. However, film-makers' emphatic rejection of modernist techniques such as montage and stream-of-consciousness was also driven by their aesthetic and ideological opposition to the two filmic styles that had distinguished German art cinema until that point: social realism and expressionism. Other traditions survived in modified forms. Using musical comedies as a conduit to the irreverent atmosphere of the late Weimar years, Reinhold Schünzel cultivated his visual and verbal witticisms in *Amphyitryon* (1935), a political parody set among the gods of Antiquity. Similarly, Willi Forst conjured up an atmosphere of cosmo-politan sophistication in the amusing comedy-of-errors *Allotria* (1935, *Capers*). During the same period, the rediscovery of melodramatic forms allowed newcomers such as Detlef Sierck to explore stylisation as a means of distanciation in *Schlussakkord* (1936, *Final Chord*), before perfecting this compelling mixture of formal and emotional excess in his famous films with Zarah Leander. While these exceptional contributions were sustained by larger developments within 1930s cinema inter-nationally, later examples of film authorship must be explained through the gradual erosion of institutional controls and formal conventions during the last years of the war. In this light, Helmut Käutner's melancholy study of Hamburg harbour milieu in *Grosse Freiheit Nr. 7* (1944, *Great Freedom Street No. 7*) and his poetic realist study of Berlin's canals and bridges in *Unter den Brücken* (1946, *Under the Bridges*) can alternatively be read as moral defeatism, individual resignation, or passive resistance – all qualities that made Käutner well suited for postwar cinema.

Only one other director besides Riefenstahl was able to develop a unique filmic vision in full accordance with Nazi ideology: Veit Harlan. The elements that dis-tinguished Harlan's most infamous films, *Jud Süss* and *Kolberg*, also predominated in his melodramas, but rarely in that extreme mixture of ideology, melodrama, and stylistic excess. Harlan preferred to work with the same actors, most notably his wife Kristina Söderbaum, and often relied on realist and naturalist authors in presenting his simple views about biology as destiny. Used for such deterministic scenarios, Hermann Sudermann inspired *Die Reise nach Tilsit* (1939, *The Journey to Tilsit*), Theodor Storm *Immensee* (1943), and Rudolf Binding *Opfergang* (1944, *Sacrifice*). Stylistically, Harlan aimed at a level of intensification and exaggeration that, from the use of ethereal music to the heavy colour symbolism, endowed even idyllic rural settings with an aura of artificiality, decadence and, ironically, degeneracy. His insistence on the sublimation of sexual desires and his morbid fascination with death revealed the true libidinal source behind the compulsive scenarios of fate, desire, and renunciation that made him the most recognisable auteur of the Third

Reich. Not surprisingly, the director of *Jud Süss* was singled out after the war to stand trial for crimes against humanity. The first trial in 1949/50 resulted in a not-guilty verdict; even subsequent law suits failed to stop Harlan from continuing his career throughout the 1950s.

A few exceptions notwithstanding, the denigration of film authorship and the validation of genre in the most affirmative sense meant the suppression of all artistic ambitions and critical intentions. With their familiar stock characters and dramatic complications, genres after 1933 tended to operate within clearly defined rules and structures. The introduction of variations into such a system of repetition and sameness produced aesthetic pleasure, while at the same time confirming the *status quo*. One of the main psychological functions of genre in general is to produce specific emotions (joy, fear, sadness) and process them through predetermined forms that offer imaginary solutions to social problems. During the Third Reich, the prohibition on addressing more serious problems put severe restrictions on this process. Film-makers were told to avoid detective films, courtroom dramas, and suspense thrillers that might draw attention to taboo subjects such as crime and violence. Literary sources allowed some directors to infuse familiar stories with new meanings. The popularity of musical forms confirmed the primacy of music in definitions of German national identity. At the same time, comedies provided a framework for expressing dissatisfaction with the available designs for living. All of these genres contributed to the normative discourse on identity shared by popular culture, official culture, and high culture. The narrativising of identity gave coherence to an eclectic system of beliefs, ideas, and attitudes about gender, family, community, and society. Yet the disruptions of identity also provided an imaginary space for engaging with a feared and vilified other defined in racial, national, and political terms.

With these conflicting investments, genres provided the most effective framework for accommodating various social groups and for catering precisely to the specialised interests and sensibilities that allegedly had been dissolved into the unifying concepts of nation and race. While the openly political films constituted the viewing subject in collective terms and addressed the audience as a unified body, the genre films participated in the illusory validation of differences: between social and individual norms, public and private behaviour, gender roles and class differences. This division between the collective experiences provided, for instance, by the state-commissioned films and the individual dreams and desires satisfied by the entertainment films acknowledged class and gender simultaneously as continuing sources of social conflict and individual crisis. Films addressed audiences through a model of identification – often associated with the ideology of populism or, to use the Nazi term, *Volkstümlichkeit* – that allowed them to participate, though only symbolically, in the creation of a unified, imaginary subject with specific ambitions and desires. That this subject position can be described as petty-bourgeois has a lot to do with the petty-bourgeois origins of the Nazi movement and its exploitation both of economic fears in the impoverished middle class and of fantasies of social ascent among members of the working class and lower middle class. Spectatorship completed the shift from a political ideology that recognised social differences, though only in order to eradicate them, to the filmic fictions that used national and racial difference as the foundation of their all-encompassing dreams of *Volk*. The concept of Germanness allowed audiences to participate in visions of national greatness while at the same time confronting their own disappointments and inadequacies. In validating the perspective of the 'little man', which itself is distinguished by ambivalence and ambiguity, films were able to incorporate often contradictory impulses under the overarching principle of common sense and to celebrate the virtues of compliance through the pleasures precisely of being average. These stabilising effects informed the filmic articulation of petit-bourgeois consciousness and sustained the attraction of genre cinema throughout the 1930s, but as a cinema in which popular, populist, and petty-bourgeois positions had finally been reunited through the integrative category of *Volk*.

Almost half of the feature length-films produced after 1933 were comedies: romantic comedies, sophisticated comedies, family comedies, rustic comedies, and, above all, musical comedies. Many carried on in the tradition of the drawing-room comedy, with infidelity, boredom, temptation, and the need for revenge as the driving force behind heated exchanges, compromising situations, and inevitable happy endings. Comedies inspired by regional peculiarities and urban milieus offered formulaic stories of personal rivalries, family feuds, neighbourhood intrigues, and so forth. Only the white-collar comedies, which continued in the tradition of the early 1930s, retained some awareness of social and economic problems through their focus on competent young women and, increasingly, insecure and resentful petty-bourgeois men.

The relationship to Hollywood found paradigmatic expression in the irreverent spirit and quick pacing of sophisticated comedies such as *Glückskinder* (1936, *Lucky Kids*), the successful Fritsch–Harvey vehicle modelled on Frank Capra's 1934 *It Happened One Night*. However, these comedies did not just imitate the American originals or translate American situations and characters into German contexts. Film-makers developed their version of a Germanised Americanism by incorporating local and regional traditions and validating social and cultural differences. Likewise they modified the Prussian model of Americanism by relying heavily on the Central European tastes and sensibilities that had influenced many comic registers during the 1920s and early 1930s. Whereas the spirited banter between the sexes in the New Deal comedies was based on the recognition of social and economic inequities, the men and women in the comparable German versions expressed their psychological resentments outside all social and political categories. Highly normative assumptions about love, romance, and sexuality informed the characters' short-lived revolts against bigotry and hypocrisy. Without the kind of visual commentaries developed to perfection by Lubitsch, the humour in these comedies remained language-based and exhausted itself in the confirmation of social prejudices and traditional gender roles. The anxieties over questions of gender and class found an emotional outlet only in brief moments of transgression.

Especially the many instances of social mimicry, false identity, and cross-dressing provided a temporary release from typical 'German' qualities such as discipline, modesty, and reliability. But by acknowledging the constructed nature of identity, the comedies also demonstrated the importance of compliance and conformity; therein lay their less obvious socio-psychological function.

The equally popular musical genres confirmed the importance of music in defining national identity while also promising an escape from the pressures of everyday life through a greater emphasis on pleasure, illusion, and fantasy. Film operettas, opera films, musical comedies, revue films, and films about great composers and musicians all took advantage of the studios' close ties to public broadcasting and the recording industry. Popular musical styles ranged from the operetta scores of Eduard Künneke and Robert Stolz to the more contemporary sound of Michael Jary and the hit songs by Peter Kreuder. Many films featured international recording stars such as Jan Kiepura; others were adaptations of famous operettas, such as Johann Strauss's *G'schichten aus dem Wienerwald* (1934, *Stories from the Viennese Woods*) and Ralph Benatzky's *Im Weissen Rössl* (1935, *At the White Horse Inn*). The strong Austro-Hungarian influence produced countless films barely held together by the sentimental melodies and nostalgic feelings associated with Old Vienna. *Wir machen Musik* (1942, *We Make Music*) and a few other musical comedies from the 1940s cultivated more contemporary styles, including the kind of modified jazz tunes officially denounced as 'degenerate music'.

A generic hybrid, the popular revue film offered an alternative to the Hollywood musical through its different approach to elaborate song-and-dance sequences that emphasised the achievements of the individual (Belach 1979). Confirming the prohibition on erotic imagery, even La Jana's semi-nude dances in *Es leuchten die Sterne* (1938, *The Stars Are Shining*) and *Stern von Rio* (1940, *Star of Rio*) inspired above all thoughts of classical sculpture and racial health. Hollywood influences were most pronounced in revue films that, like *Wir tanzen um die Welt* (1939, *We Dance around the World*), used a professional dancing troupe to create ornamental choreographies inspired by Busby Berkeley but also eerily reminiscent of what has been described as the fascist mass ornament, given their marked preference for military costumes and formations. The revue film's peculiar mixture of optimism and aggression was developed to perfection by the inexhaustible Marika Rökk, who was known for her Hungarian 'Puszta charm'. Frequently working under the direction of her husband, Georg Jacoby, Rökk appeared in *Hallo Janine* (1939), *Kora Terry* (1941), and *Die Frau meiner Träume* (1944, *The Woman of My Dreams*). The Rökk character frequently had to chose between the freedom of artistic expression and the security of love and marriage – a typical female dilemma that only underscored the symptomatic function of the modern career woman as the object of punitive and transgressive fantasies.

With renunciation firmly established as a central motif in the romantic comedy and the revue film, the melodrama was able to explore more ambiguous views on gender and sexuality. During the early 1930s, melodramatic modes found

74

expression in the elusive mixture of sentimentality, melancholy, and irony cultivated by Forst in classic Viennese films such as *Maskerade* (1934, *Masquerade*). The genre's more typical combination of heightened emotionality and formal stylisation reached an ideal embodiment in Zarah Leander, the statuesque Swedish-born singer and actress. An acute awareness of femininity as a performance informed her signature roles in Detlef Sierck's *Zu neuen Ufern* (1937, *To New Shores*) and *La Habanera* (1937), as well as her later films with Rolf Hansen, *Die grosse Liebe* (1942) and *Damals* (1943, *Then*). The basic narrative elements are always the same: guilt and redemption, love and renunciation, transgression and punishment. The visual representation of female desire and its constant companion, female suffering, relied extensively on extreme close-ups, dramatic lighting, claustrophobic settings, and exaggerated costumes. Unquestionably, the increased production of melodramas during the last years of the war must be explained through their intended socio-psychological functions, namely, to translate suffering into aesthetic terms and to make pleasurable the delay of gratification. Nonetheless, these emotional and stylistic excesses sometimes had a destabilising effect on wartime audiences. For even as they contributed to the preservation of the *status quo* by presenting women as victims, melodramas at least recognised those strengths borne of victimisation and turned them into instruments of critical introspection.

As the 'guardians of morality' and the 'protectors of life', women played a key role in the battle over images and identities in the genre films. However, the representation of women in the feature film rarely reflected the normative definition of femininity in Nazi ideology; instead they functioned as complementary designs. Maternal melodramas such as *Mutterliebe* (1939, *Mother Love*), with Käthe Dorsch as the woman who sacrifices everything for her children, remained the exception in a popular cinema that, despite the official cult of motherhood, treated female characters above all as objects of male desire. Before the war, working women of the kind depicted in the misogynistic *Frau am Steuer* (1939, *Woman at the Wheel*) regularly inspired mockery and ridicule. Labour shortages in the war economy and the difficulties of the home front contributed to the need for more sympathetic portrayals of working women like the competent female math teacher in *Unser Fräulein Doktor* (1940, *Our Miss PhD*). Concerns about low birth rates stood behind the idealisation of family life in romantic comedies like *Hurra, ich bin Papa!* (1939, *Hurrah, I Am a Dad!*), that offered more positive portrayals of unwed mothers. For the most part, genre cinema confirmed traditional definitions of gender and portrayed independent women as a disruptive and destructive force. Femininity remained identified with a threatening sexuality that had to be contained. At the same time, the expectations about appropriate female characteristics, attitudes, and forms of behaviour were constantly adjusted to the changing demands of the times, especially during the war years. Under these conditions, genre films developed their cautionary tales of modern femininity through contradictory positions that could never be resolved, not through the melodrama's imbalance between strong women and weak men and not through the rustic comedy's tacit understanding of male indolence and female competence (Bechdolf 1992, Traudisch 1993, Fox 2000).

In sharp contrast to the psychological interiors presented by the female-dominated comedies and melodramas, the male-dominated adventure film thrived on action, movement, adventure, discovery, and individual initiative. These action adventures often included elaborate stories about technological innovations and corporate power struggles. Remarkable athletic stunts and action scenes verging on slapstick distinguished the countless Harry Piel films in the style of *Der unmögliche Herr Pitt* (1938, *The Impossible Mr Pitt*). More dramatic films often featured Hans Albers who, with his blond hair, blue eyes, sharp profile, and tall muscular frame, came to personify the Aryan ideal of masculinity. Albers played modern adventurers in the futuristic thriller *Gold* (1934) and the seafaring drama *Unter heissem Himmel* (1936, *Under Hot Skies*) and conquered new territories in the Canadian Western *Wasser für Canitoga* (1939, *Water for Canitoga*). The genre's foreign locations and exotic settings did not only provide an imaginary landscape for the articulation of nationalist and racist principles; it also opened up another space, unmarked by social conventions and political pressures, that allowed for imaginary escapes from the ordinary and the familiar.

Closely connected to Nazi fantasies about *Volk* and *Heimat*, the *Heimatfilm* (homeland film) emerged as the most convenient narrative form for offering a romanticised, but completely depoliticised, view of country and nation. Quintessential German landscapes like the Bavarian Alps, the Rhine valley, and the Baltic Coast provided idyllic images of rural life where simple peasants lived in harmony with nature. The genre's regionalist orientation, especially in the folk dramas and rustic comedies produced in Bavaria, sometimes prevented co-optation by the more abstract concepts of racial theory and the ideology of 'blood and soil'. Featuring well-known folk actors, these comedies promoted their own brand of provincialism and xenophobia. The validation of traditional Bavarian culture, including as a counter-design to Prussianism, found expression in numerous Ganghofer adaptations, rustic farces with Karl Valentin and Liesl Karstadt, and humorous vignettes of traditional village life by the prolific actor/director Joe Stöckel. More dramatic treatments gave rise to rare instances of regional resistance and anti-capitalist struggle in the style of *Der ewige Quell* (1939, *The Eternal Spring*) and *Der ewige Klang* (1943, *The Eternal Sound*), whereas the association of *Heimat* with female strength and independence inspired yet another screen adaptation of *Die Geierwally* (1940, *The Vulture Wally*), this time with Heidemarie Hatheyer. Throughout the period, the genre's emphasis on regional culture offered audience an alternative to the highly politicised idea of nation that, in the historical films, culminated in the equation of Prussia with the Reich and that, in the state-commissioned films, reduced the abstract idea of *Volk* to that of race, rather than of ethnicity. Because of these elusive investments, the genre most frequently associated with Third Reich cinema also emerged as the one with the most problematic relationship to the more politicised fantasies of national community.

Third Reich cinema as political cinema

In the same way that Nazi ideology was based on an eclectic and largely derivative mixture of political theories and philosophical ideas, the cinema of the Third Reich was held together less through a monolithic aesthetic or ideological structure than through the Ministry's institutional power over pockets of difference. Propaganda films made up only 10 per cent of the entire production and remained limited to historical dramas, war films, genius films, and a few home front films. Most popular genre films carefully avoided references to the regime – only to serve it by promoting the sexist, nationalist, and racist ideologies essential to its existence and by sustaining the illusory division between an official culture of political spectacle and the seemingly apolitical sphere of private pleasures, individual choices, and modern diversions. Ministerial directives about the length of films and the adequate portrayal of nationalities and professions confirm to what degree the apparatus tried to control all aspects of film-making. However, the inordinate attention to detail only underscores the ultimate failure of these efforts and explains the need for constant readjustment. Conflicting interpretations of ministerial guidelines and suggestions, tensions between various branches in the state bureaucracy and film industry, and personal rivalries among studio managers and cultural officials simultaneously strengthened and undermined the integrative power of the political system.

The changing definitions of film propaganda can be traced back to the different positions taken by Hitler and Goebbels in the early 1930s. Hitler expressed very decisive ideas about propaganda and its relevance to the movement. Film and other modern media, he argued, could be instrumental in winning followers and propagating National Socialist ideas; hence the need of direct emotional appeal. For Hitler, propaganda meant the condensation of complicated issues into a few simple ideas and their further intensification through repetition, exaggeration, and visual symbolism. Goebbels favoured a more indirect approach to propaganda that concealed its intentions and placed greater emphasis on the style of presentation than on the actual subject matter. For him, the politics of representation was more important than the representation of politics. These differences found expression in the intense controversies over three early feature films about the National Socialist movement. On the one hand, the movement films shared a number of characteristics: the celebration of youthful idealism and martyrdom; the validation of community, discipline, and solidarity; and the close attention to public ritual and the symbolic power of flags and uniforms. National Socialism was presented in terms of essences, as the result of a process of self-discovery rather than an expression of political beliefs. By aligning politics with emotional experiences, the three films offered a model of identification for all later propaganda films. On the other hand, the relationship between fascism and modernism introduced significant differences. *Hitlerjunge Quex* (1933, *Hitler Youth Quex*) showed the conversion of a communist working-class youth to the ideals and the spirit of National Socialism in a style reminiscent of Weimar social realism. By contrast, *SA-Mann*

Brand (1933, *SA-Man Brand*) presented the early years of the movement so crudely and simplistically that it was shunned by critics and audiences alike. And *Hans Westmar* (1933), inspired by the story of Horst Wessel, was initially withdrawn from distribution because the Nazis feared the commercialisation of their symbols and rituals. After 1933, the representation of comparable situations in other times and places proved much more effective than any direct references to the Third Reich and henceforth determined the political function of filmic stories and images within the larger framework of National Socialist ideology.

To what degree the aestheticisation of politics gave rise to what some critics have called fascist aesthetics has been the central question behind the ongoing scholarly debates about the most famous film of the period, Leni Riefenstahl's *Triumph des Willens* (1935, *Triumph of the Will*). Shot during the 1934 Party Congress in Nuremberg, the film stages the encounter between the *Führer* and the *Volk* in tightly choreographed forms that mythologise social processes (Barsam 1975). This merging of myth and modernity takes place through symbols such as flags, clouds, and fire and formal elements such as repetition, symmetry, and counterpoint. The process is predicated on the transformation both of the historical city into a stage set and of the party event into a visual spectacle. Riefenstahl's apotheosis of the national community culminates in the human ornaments of frozen perfection that become part of the monumental architecture. But her vision also gives rise to a cult of the beautiful that finds expression in the many close-ups of ecstatic faces and steely bodies. This aesthetics of racial perfection, including the cult of male strength and power, found an even more stylised expression in Riefenstahl's documentary about the 1936 Olympic Games, *Olympia* (1938), with its two parts *Fest der Völker* (*Festival of Nations*) and *Fest der Schönheit* (*Festival of Beauty*). Since then, Riefenstahl's films have found defenders who praise their formal qualities and detractors for whom the obsession with beauty remains an essential part of 'fascinating fascism' (Hinton 1991, Downing 1992, Riefenstahl 1993).

Despite all fantasies of harmony and unity, professional groups and cultural institutions continued to fight over their adequate representation in the grand narratives of German nation; the same problems haunted the representation of political enemies. To give only one example: when generals complained about the treatment of the army in *Triumph des Willens*, Riefenstahl made a short documentary, *Tag der Freiheit* (1935, *Day of Freedom*), to appease them. During the war years, propagandistic intentions could not always keep up with changing military situations and political alliances. While Bolshevism had always invited negative stereotyping, especially in the conflation of Bolshevik with Jew, the Non-Aggression Pact in 1939 inspired a brief wave of sentimental films about Old Russia, including the Pushkin adaptation *Der Postmeister* (1940, *The Postmaster*). Even the anti-Russian film *Friesennot* (1935, *Frisian Plight*) was banned in 1939 but, after the German attack on the Soviet Union, reissued in 1941 as *Dorf im roten Sturm* (*Village in the Red Storm*).

Triumph des Willens illustrates the workings of fascist aesthetics, but its exceptional status also underscores the fact that Third Reich cinema never gave rise to a homogeneous body of work or consistent set of practices, even where official pronouncements suggest such coherence. The fundamental problem of controlling images and, more generally, meanings, can be seen in the Ministry's close attention to non-narrative forms with a greater investment in, or closeness to, questions of the real. Whether as party convention films, weekly newsreels or cultural films, these non-narrative forms played as significant a role in the redefinition of reality as those narrative forms more typically associated with fantasy and illusion. Considered the most effective tool of political propaganda, newsreels after 1933 became increasingly sophisticated in their rhetoric and style (for instance, through rapid editing and trick photography). Newsreels changed even more under the demands of total media warfare and the militarisation of public life. Already the invasion of the Rhineland in 1936 included cameramen and journalists. After 1939, all independent newsreels were consolidated in the *UFA-Tonwoche* which, in 1940, was renamed *Deutsche Wochenschau* (German Newsreel) to stress its patriotic orientation. Film footage from the front was provided by special military units, the *Propagandakompanien* (Propaganda Companies). Lasting up to one hour, the war newsreels relied heavily on incendiary commentary and dramatic music in order to create an aestheticised view of warfare free of death and suffering. Documentary footage and staged scenes were joined together to create a filmic reality ruled less by the ethical standards of news reporting than by the need to enlist the powers of the imagination in the pursuit of a final victory. In *Feldzug in Polen* (1940, *The Polish Campaign*) and *Sieg im Westen* (1941, *Victory in the West*), Svend Noldan relied heavily on maps, graphics, and animation to show the strength of the German army.

National Socialist ideology found privileged expression in the cultural films that were part of the supporting programme but differed from the newsreel because of their pronounced educational goals and artistic ambitions. Since the 1920s, screenings had typically included pre-films on topics ranging from geography and biology to ethnography and art history. After 1933, these themes, while always closely linked to the question of Germanness, were presented in more nationalistic tones. Compilation films such as *Blut und Boden* (1933, *Blood and Soil*) and *Der ewige Wald* (1936, *The Eternal Forest*) enlisted the familiar iconography of landscape, nature, and *Heimat* in anti-modern diatribes. Countless shorts presented the Reich's technological, architectural, and organisational accomplishments, from the building of the *Reichsautobahn* (federal expressway system), Albert Speer's grandiose building plans for Germania to the projects of the Reichsarbeitsdienst (Reich Labour Service) and the cultural programmes of the Kraft durch Freude (Strength Through Joy) organisation. Sometimes these non-narrative forms provided an opportunity for formal experimentation. Resisting the mixture of romance and heroism found in films such as *Wunder des Fliegens* (1935, *The Wonders of Flying*), with famous aviator Ernst Udet, a few documentary film-makers continued to present modern technologies in the cool New Objectivist style. Willy Zielke's *Das Stahltier* (*The Steel Animal*), commissioned for the centennial of the first German railroad line in 1934, as well as Ruttmann's *Deutsche Waffenschmieden*

(1939, *German Armaments Factories*) and *Deutsche Panzer* (1941, *German Tanks*), relied extensively on modernist techniques such as associative montage, rapid editing, unusual perspectives, and extreme close-ups to celebrate the convergence of modernism and modernity in the iconography of the beautiful machine. The influence of the Weimar cross-section film can be traced to Leo de Laforgue's *Symphonie einer Weltstadt* (*Symphony of a World City*), completed in 1942 and shown for the first time in 1950 as the last filmic record of Berlin before the bombings.

The division of labour between different mass media such as film, radio, and television played a crucial role in creating a seamless ideological continuum on the level of institutional structures and representational practices. Public broadcasting, which operated under total state control, offered the most effective form of political propaganda by bringing the voice of the *Führer* into almost every household. Aware of radio's untapped possibilities, the Nazis produced an inexpensive model, known as the *Volksempfänger* (people's receiver), that allowed them to forge an instant community of eight million listeners. The sense of accessibility, simultaneity, and omnipresence conveyed by the medium contributed to the era's prevailing fictions of communion and empowerment (for example in the famous Christmas broadcasts from the front). Yet at the same time, the conditions of reception created through broadcasting fragmented the public sphere and limited participation in political events to the auditory realm. Programming practices offered various surrogate forms of participation, from live broadcasts of classical concerts and variety shows to the popular request concert series depicted in *Wunschkonzert*.

Even in its early experimental stage, television promised to expand further the possibilities of mass manipulation (Reiss 1979, Zeutschner 1995). Telefunken presented the new technology at the Fifth German Radio Exhibition in 1928, and public television was experimentally introduced as early as 1935, though only on a limited basis and largely in public settings such as urban television lounges. The cost of a television set remained too high for most private citizens. The brief daily television broadcasts included newsreels, narrative shorts, cultural films, variety shows, popular music, and comic sketches; many older films were shown in abbreviated form. Even after 1939, when viewers in the Berlin area could receive regular programmes, television remained a technologically and aesthetically flawed experience.

The main contribution of feature films to the re-emergence of German nationalism lay in the displacement of present concerns into past events and the rewriting of collective history as individual melodrama. Most propaganda films were also historical films, with the meaning of history significantly changed in the process of ideologisation. To begin with, the many films about the trauma of the First World War and the despised Weimar Republic relied on traditional notions of cause and effect that found expression in the polemical rhetoric of humiliation and retribution. With the Third Reich firmly installed as the telos of history, the emotional effect of these narratives was not one of historicity but of urgent contemporaneity. To the degree that modes of address in the propaganda film made protagonists and spectators identical, the latter were invariably implicated in the historical narrative as executors of its unfulfilled promises. The revenge for past suffering was a narrative construction that did not only help to legitimise new racial policies and ongoing military actions. Through the notion of *Volk*, the films also provided an identity beyond the problems of the present and provided the necessary sense of unity that justified all possible transgressions in the future.

Many films about the First World War used simple identification patterns to establish such historical parallels, and they depicted instances of German oppression with a clear view towards then-contemporary political conflicts. Accordingly, *Flüchtlinge* (1933, *Refugees*) recounts the fate of Volga Germans persecuted by the Bolsheviks during the postwar period. *Menschen ohne Vaterland* (1937, *People without Fatherland*) has German civilians fighting in the Baltics, whereas *Patrioten* (1937, *Patriots*) articulates the drama of national identity through the figure of a German pilot captured by the French. *Pour le mérite* (1938) reaches narrative denouement in the rearmament of Germany after a long period of self-denial, whereas Rabenalt's famous . . . *reitet für Deutschland* (1941, *Riding for Germany*) has an injured war veteran regain his strength after embracing the idea of nationalism. A few films responded indirectly to political events and military developments. *Menschen im Sturm* (1941, *People in the Storm*) used the suffering of Germans under the Serbs to justify the attack on Yugoslavia. And one of the more infamous contributions to the genre, *Heimkehr* (1941, *Homecoming*), dramatised the discrimination of ethnic Germans in Volhynia in a way that retroactively 'made sense' of the invasion of Poland in 1939.

The effectiveness of these propaganda films relied on the combination of repression and aggression that seduced private desires into the political arena; their appeal always extended beyond psychology and included the realm of the aesthetic. From the casting of stars to the conception of characters, the narratives were driven by very specific ideas about race, nation, and identity that assumed an essential bond between the individual and the nation. With identity dramatised along these lines, the propaganda films of the late 1930s and early 1940s often intervened directly in the organisation of public and private experiences. The resultant fictionalisation of politics eased anxieties about social and political change by reducing them to emotional constellations, while at the same time making the cinema the founding site of new definitions of politics based in the imaginary. The narratives of identity formation provided a transgressive space where emotions were validated through their inscription into new political scenarios, including the meta-narratives of race. Narrative denouement, the deliverance from alienation, could be achieved, if not on the screen, then in the reality of war and genocide. All filmic elements contributed to the dissolution of psychological and social conflicts into the unifying idea of national community and the mapping of identity across the body of the racialised other. The reintroduction of these fiction effects into the rituals of everyday life completed a cycle of symbolic representations sustained by the discourses of melodrama, history, biography, mythology, and folklore. Without such mediations, the propaganda film revealed its political intentions all too clearly and, despite its effective use of racial and national stereotypes, often failed to translate political ideology into fictional terms.

The historical film provided sufficient distance from the present to emerge as the preferred propagandistic vehicle in the articulation of racist and nationalist ideas (Happel 1984, Schulte-Sasse 1996). The conflation of history and narrative blurred all distinctions between public and private, individual and collective, past and present. Everybody could become part of the nation's struggle for survival and, through identification with the historical leader, find a place in the interstices of the imaginary and the real. Perhaps most importantly, the new historical films provided a vehicle for dissolving history into the ostensibly eternal categories of nation and race. In so doing, history allowed for an imaginary return to the pre-industrial world of peasantry and agriculture; a validation of the community of *Volk* and the rootedness of *Heimat*; and an idealised view of German nation based on its beautiful landscapes, simple peoples, and great traditions.

Historical accounts of war and revolution and the mapping of expansionist fantasies on to the mise-en-scène of an imaginary Europe gave form to the founding myths of a new Germanness. Most often, history was enlisted in the self-representations of the regime through established patterns of causality and continuity. In such a teleological construction, the Third Reich appeared as the culmination of German history. Advocating the leadership principle, *Bismarck* (1940) retold the founding of the Wilhelmine empire from the perspective of the strong leader, whereas *Die Entlassung* (1942, *The Dismissal*) linked the political crisis after Bismarck's dismissal to the rise of liberal parliamentarianism. *Carl Peters* (1941) explained the struggle for German colonies in Africa through the continuous threat of British imperialism, while *Ohm Krüger* (1941) used the Boer Wars to justify the Reich's military actions against Great Britain. Parallels between past and present also surfaced in the representation of other national histories. Thus *Der Fuchs von Glenarvon* (1940, *The Fox of Glenarvon*) and *Mein Leben für Irland* (1941, *My Life for Ireland*), two anti-British films about the Irish uprising of 1921, treated these liberation movements as historical models for the struggle of the National Socialist movement during the 1920s.

As a sub-genre of the historical film, the Prussian film stood out through its unabashed glorification of the absolutist state and its autocratic ruler. Associated with authoritarianism, the myth of Prussia most satisfied National Socialist fantasies about a militarisation of public life. In the figure of the Aryan, Prussian virtues like discipline, order, duty, and obedience found their most radical expression. Prussian history showed the conditions under which war, to paraphrase Clausewitz, could become a continuation of politics through other means. The Prussian films focused on two historical periods: the period of Frederick II the Great, which brought the Seven Years War (1756–63) and the rise of Prussia as a major European power, and the War of Liberation (1813–15), through which Prussia freed itself from Napoleonic rule and created the conditions for the emergence of German nationalism. The Fridericus films, whose popularity during the 1920s and 1930s took advantage of the uncanny resemblance of Otto Gebühr to the Prussian king, became closely identified with a number of ideological positions central to the new regime: the need for a political system based on absolute power; the importance of internal unity as a defence against foreign influences; and the acceptance of patriarchy as a model for the family and the state. The comradeship among the soldiers in the Prussian films was predicated both on the equation of love and death and on the repression of heterosexual desire in the building of a fully militarised society. The underlying tension between discipline and punishment, on the one hand, and suppressed desire and deferred satisfaction, on the other, was resolved in the almost godlike representations of Frederick the Great. Showing his transformation from the rebellious son into the lonely soldier king, *Der Choral von Leuthen*, *Der alte und der junge König* (1935, *The Old and the Young King*), and *Der grosse König* sketched an ideal-typical trajectory for the formation of the national comrade. Harlan's *Kolberg* (1944), which was shot with more extras than soldiers in the actual siege in 1807, almost reversed the relationship between history and narrative by paying more attention to the technical demands of image production than to the material needs of contemporary audiences. The film premiered in the beleaguered Atlantic fortress of La Rochelle and a bomb-weary Berlin: a telling indication of the ways in which fantasy and reality had finally become indistinguishable.

The representation of the leader figure as rebel and tyrant was of particular relevance to the propagandistic uses of history. Whether focusing on political leaders, great scientists, and famous artists, the so-called genius film confirmed male subjectivity as the foundation of German identity. In accordance with National Socialist myths about its revolutionary origins, the 'great men' expressed their innovative and revolutionary impulses through patriotic feelings and nationalist ideas. Likewise, the genre showed a marked preference for individuals – the physician *Robert Koch* (1939), the inventor [Rudolf] *Diesel* (1942), and the fifteenth-century Swiss scientist *Paracelsus* (1943) – whose quest for truth put them in conflict with the prejudices of their times. The creative individual's triumph over adversity was also thematised through the idealism of the young playwright *Friedrich Schiller* (1940), whose call for a national theatre caused the Nazis to claim him as a precursor of National Socialism; the stubbornness of 'Prussian Michelangelo' *Andreas Schlüter* (1942), whose programme for a national architecture prefigured the contribution of Speer; and the personal struggles of *Friedemann Bach* (1941), whose artistic and political rebellion against a dominant father resonated deeply with the oedipal self-representation of the Nazis as a movement of the sons.

The need for articulating nation and race within fully developed narratives found its clearest expression in the anti-Semitic films made between 1939 and 1940. Their main function was to prepare the populace for the 'final solution of the Jewish question'. The surprisingly small number of anti-Semitic films produced during the Third Reich suggest that ideological positions were as much articulated through structuring absences than through filmic representations. The mixed reception of these films increased the need for mediated approaches that could sustain anti-Semitism as a unifying public discourse and, later, discriminatory and exclusionary practice. Ministerial directives to film reviewers prohibited any references to anti-Semitic representations. For the most part, stereotypes were presented as part of a larger system of defining others in ethnic and national terms. Because of the potentially disruptive effects of negative stereotyping, questions of racial difference were often displaced on to the problem of sexual difference, with the (sexualised) body of the woman standing in for the disturbance of race that needed to be contained. As a result, anti-Semitic sentiments surfaced in the unflattering portrayal of intellectuals and small businessmen and influenced the general approach to character development in screenwriting and casting decisions. The same mechanisms influenced the ways in which modernist styles were mocked and cosmopolitan attitudes denounced. Ethnicity and nationality provided a system of differences that, in the less successful films, reduced all characters to these external determinants. The defamatory conflation of Jew/Russian/Bolshevik in *GPU* (1942) resulted in such exaggerated stereotypes that it destabilised the entire system of representations. In the infamous *Jud Süss* (1940), Harlan proved much more effective by embedding anti-Semitic representations within the structure of classical bourgeois tragedy. Based on the story of Joseph Süss-Oppenheimer at the eighteenth-century court of the Duke of Württemberg, the film offered historical justification for the persecution of Jews by, among other things, combining a critique of the political and aesthetic excesses of the Baroque feudal system with a race-based definition of the nation state built on 'typical' German traits such as modesty, honour, and duty. By adding the rape and subsequent suicide of a young German woman, the director exploited widespread myths about Jewish sexuality to articulate the question of race along gendered lines and to conjure up the threat of racial impurity and miscegenation. Thus Harlan's film combined two central aspects of anti-Semitism, namely the projection on to the Jews of those individual qualities that must be regarded as threatening to society and the identification of the Jews with exceptional abilities that are bound to incite social envy and resentment (Hollstein 1983).

An exception in many ways, *Der ewige Jude* (1940, *The Eternal Jew*) relied on the format of the compilation film to combine documentary images of ceremonial prayer and ritual slaughtering with excerpts from Weimar feature films betraying 'Semitic tendencies'. Made under the supervision of Reich Film Administrator Hippler, this vicious *Hetzfilm* (hate film) about the 'world Jewish conspiracy' attempted to demonstrate the 'self-explanatory' nature of these images and to uncover the more elusive aspects of the 'Jewish character' through an incendiary mixture of allusions, insinuations, and comparisons, including through the metaphor of swarming rats. The centrality of filmic images both to the construction of Jewishness and to the self-representation of the regime became painfully evident in a later pseudo-documentary about Theresienstadt made expressly to deceive a concerned international community. Directed by one of the inmates, the Jewish actor Kurt Gerron, *Der Führer schenkt den Juden eine Stadt* (1945, *The Führer Grants the Jews a City*) presented the concentration camp as a model community, a place of healthy work and wholesome entertainment – a troubling comment also on the powerful role of modern mass media in national and international relations.

Until the end of the regime, the cinema remained a work of compromise, serving the contradictory functions of entertainment and propaganda, satisfying different interests and tastes, and conveying both the populist arguments and politicised attitudes considered essential to its appeal. No matter whether genres continued in the tradition of Weimar cinema and imitated American models or whether styles specifically marked as German fed into the National Socialist propaganda machine, ideology remained an integral part of representational practices, from the way subjects were constructed in social and political reality to the way they partook in the remaking of national identity through filmic images and narratives. While the Propaganda Ministry determined the terms of productions and the forms of reception, the enduring popularity of the films since the postwar years has made them an integral part of German cinema. Especially the so-called *Überläuferfilme* (literally, deserter films), films started before 1945 but only completed or released after 1945, bring into relief the continuities and ruptures that defined the cinema of the Third Reich from the beginning to the end and still make it the perfect test case for more general reflections on cinema, nation, and ideology.

4

POSTWAR CINEMA
1945–61

Until very recently, most writings on postwar cinema followed the logic of those on Third Reich cinema by arguing an interrelation between ideological contamination and aesthetic deprivation. Behind the seemingly harmless, trivial subject matter, went the argument, most of the films made after 1945 remained conservative, if not reactionary, in their social values and political beliefs. Along similar lines, postwar audiences were regularly described as driven by a psychological need to forget the traumas of the past and ignore the problems of the present. Characterised in these negative terms, postwar cinema offered its detractors little more than the displaced fears, desires, and resentments that sustained the project of economic and social reconstruction but prevented a truly new beginning for German cinema and society after 1945 (Schmieding 1961, Hembus 1981).

These alleged failures of postwar cinema allowed the emerging Young German Cinema of the 1960s to announce its own zero hour with the 1962 Oberhausen Manifesto. Its signatories polemically declared: 'Papa's movies are dead'. Their blanket dismissal of an entire period of film-making had a profound effect on scholarship. Under the influence of the New Waves and the theory of auteurism, scholars have either dismissed popular cinema between 1945 and 1962 as unworthy of critical attention or limited themselves to socio-psychological readings in the larger context of postwar history. As a result of the Cold War, the many movements across East–West borders and the stylistic and thematic continuities in what still must be described as one German cinema have been ignored in favour of two separate accounts of the cinema of the Federal Republic of Germany (FRG) and the German Democratic Republic (GDR). Since unification, several comparative studies have opened up new perspectives on the creative dialogues between the two cinemas and their different approaches to important social issues such as women's rights and workers' rights (Strauss 1996, Moldenhauer and Zimmermann 2000, Trumpener 2001).

The prevailing tendencies in West German and Anglo-American scholarship have given rise to two critical paradigms in the assessment of postwar cinema. Many popular accounts have placed the films made after 1945 within the formal and thematic traditions of UFA and justified these remarkable continuities through apologetic, nostalgic or even ironic re-readings (Seidl 1987, Jary 1993, Bertram

1998). Scholarly approaches committed to ideology critique have examined the close connection between conventional genre cinema and the reconstruction of the film industry under the conditions of late capitalism (Kreimeier 1973). Others have relied on socio-psychological categories and used feature films as a privileged access to the unconscious mechanisms identified with *Vergangenheitsbewältigung*, the difficult process of coming to terms with the Nazi past (Becker and Schöll, 1995, Greffarth 1995).

The restorative tendencies of the 1980s already brought greater awareness of the institutional struggles and ideological contradictions that informed the difficult process of economic and cultural reconstruction (Schobert and Hoffmann 1989). But above all, it was German reunification that, since the 1990s, has drawn attention to the continuities of popular cinema before and after 1945 and forced scholars to look more closely at the correspondences between filmic practices in East and West Germany from the 1950s to the 1980s. In the resultant debates on national identity, more complicated connections and similarities beyond the politicised East–West divide have come into view: between the few big-budget prestige productions and the mass of undistinguished adaptations, serials, and remakes; between an unabashedly popular cinema of petty-bourgeois tastes and sensibilities and a highly politicised film culture of bans, boycotts, and controversies; and between an intense interest in international film movements and an equally strong commitment to national traditions, including the cinema's close ties to music and literature. Following such an expanded definition of national cinema, scholars have begun to examine postwar cinema's contribution to the process of economic and political reconstruction, as well as to more long-term changes in the cultural landscape after 1945 (Westermann 1990, Fehrenbach 1995).

The reconstruction of the film industry

Like the forced co-ordination in 1933, the reconstruction of the film industry after 1945 must be described in terms of historical ruptures and continuities. The first and foremost goal of the Allies after German capitulation was the dismantling of the hierarchically organised, monopolistic structure of production facilities, distribution companies, and motion-picture theatres overseen by the Propaganda Ministry. The difficult assignment taken on by the UFA Liquidation Committee (ULC) after the passing of the so-called Lex Ufi in 1949 was not completed until 1953. Bavaria was turned over to private ownership as late as 1956. During these years, the military governments tried to strike a workable compromise among the demands of political re-education, economic recovery, and cultural renewal. Initially, the Allies fought over UFA studio's technological equipment and film archives as valuable war booty but soon more urgent political considerations prevailed in their different approaches to the legacies of National Socialism. The Information Control Division (ICD) of the US Army initially treated the rebuilding of cinema as a project of political re-education. Mandatory screenings of *Die Todesmühlen* (1945, *Death Mills*), about the Nazi death camps, confronted

Germans with the truth about the Holocaust. American newsreels such as *Welt im Film* reported extensively on Nazi atrocities and, later, the Nuremberg war tribunals, but did so with less and less emphasis on German collective guilt; similar tendencies characterised the Soviet-made *Der Augenzeuge*. Turning to feature films, the Allies supported their political interests far more effectively through the imports, often from the 1930s, that soon established competing spheres of influence: through old Hollywood films in the Western sectors and the classics of Stalinist cinema in the Eastern sector.

In the first years after the war, new film projects required licensing in their respective zones, and film professionals had to undergo de-Nazification (for example, through questionnaires). The Allied Commission reviewed all German films produced between 1933 and 1945 and established a list of films banned from public exhibition – primarily state-commissioned films – that remains largely binding to this day (Kelson 1996). In the beginning, the Allies agreed on the importance of feature films in stabilising the political situation after 1945; hence their willingness to re-release many films from the Nazi period as part of their plans to rebuild German cinema in accordance with their political objectives, economic structures, and cultural traditions. The Western Allies treated films as an integral part of modern mass culture and its institutionalised division between entertainment and information. The reorganisation of public broadcasting followed the model of the BBC in the greater commitment to local, regional, and national culture and the insistence on radio as an important forum of public debate in a liberal democracy. Yet in the rebuilding of the film industry, the Hollywood model prevailed. Throughout the 1950s, the Americans introduced many of their own industry practices, beginning with the practice of block booking and blind booking.

Founded on 17 May 1946, the Deutsche Film AG (DEFA) became the first German film studio to resume production in Berlin-Babelsberg after receiving a licence from the Soviets for its first project, *Die Mörder sind unter uns* (1946, *The Murderers Are among Us*). Director Wolfgang Staudte belonged to the Filmaktiv, a group of exiled writers and directors that included Friedrich Wolf, Kurt Maetzig, and Gerhard Lamprecht. In their efforts to rebuild German cinema in the spirit of democratic antifascism, they were actively supported by cultural officers such as Sergei Tulpanov of the Soviet Military Administration in Germany (SMAD). The foremost goal of DEFA was, on the one hand, to move beyond the filmic traditions of UFA and the political burdens of the Third Reich and, on the other, to reclaim 'the positive cultural legacy of the Germans' for a future socialist society. Committed to humanistic principles, the DEFA founders in 1946 set out to make films that countered the forces of nationalism and militarism and promoted the ideas of international co-operation.

The beginning of the Cold War complicated the rebuilding of the German film industry in the West and introduced new tensions over political and economic decisions among the Information Control Division (ICD) of the American occupation forces, the Motion Picture Export Association (MPEA), which represented the Hollywood majors, and, last but not least, the new German-owned production and distribution companies (Hauser 1989). The initial spirit of openness quickly gave way to the ideological divisions that culminated in the Berlin Blockade in 1948 and the founding of the two German states, the Federal Republic of Germany and the German Democratic Republic, in 1949. These developments had a profound impact on the rebuilding of the industry according to market principles in the West, especially after the currency reform in 1948. But they also contributed to DEFA's transformation into a state-owned company with close ties to the Socialist Unity Party (SED) and a more direct involvement in the ideological 'freezes' and 'thaws' of the 1950s. However, in the transitional period between the first and second phase of the German division (i.e., between 1949 and 1962), the daily business of film production and the mundane rituals of moviegoing especially in the divided city of Berlin still allowed for many border crossings in the literal and figurative sense.

While East German cinema got an early start with DEFA, the rebuilding of the film industry in West Germany required the creation of new institutional and organisational structures. This process began in 1949 with the founding of the SPIO, the main professional organisation of the German film industry. The SPIO instituted the Freiwillige Selbstkontrolle (FSK, Voluntary Self-regulation) as an agency of self-censorship modelled after the MPPDA and with a very similar codex of taboo subjects – nudity, vulgarity, blasphemy, and so forth. After 1951, the Filmbewertungsstelle (FBS, Film Evaluation Office) established a system of economic support – and political censorship – based on many of the same quality distinctions (for example, 'artistically valuable') used during the Third Reich. The Federal government introduced new laws and created specific agencies for controlling the cinema in accordance with the political forces that, during the 1950s, came together in the fight against communism. While guaranteeing the freedom of speech, the Federal Film Law allowed for the banning of all films that promoted nationalist, racist and communist ideas or posed a serious threat to national security. Working under the auspices of the Ministry of Finance, the new Interministerial Film Commission oversaw the import of films from Eastern Bloc countries. Of the more than a thousand films examined during the 1950s, ninety were banned because of their communist tendencies.

As the first companies to be licensed by the Western Allies in the late 1940s, distribution companies quickly established market dominance by showing old Hollywood films, including many B pictures, as well as a large number of UFA films reclassified as harmless entertainment. Ilse Kubaschewski's powerful Gloria-Verleih, known as the main purveyor of *Schnulzen* (weepies), played a key role in providing postwar audiences with the desired mixture of melodramatic, romantic, and sentimental stories. Surpassing smaller companies such as Herzog- and Schorcht-Verleih, Constantin under Wandfried Bartels established itself as the second most powerful distributor, and eventually also producer, in the late 1950s by specialising in inexpensive but commercially successful film serials.

In the early years, film production confronted a number of problems: bombed-out and plundered production facilities; lack of basic materials and resources; and technical and creative personnel unfamiliar with contemporary styles and techniques. In the American zone, production resumed in the Bavaria studios in Munich-Geiselgasteig; it was also in Munich that Harald Braun founded the Neue Deutsche Filmgesellschaft (NDF). In the British zone, Rolf Thiele and Hans Abich established a small centre of film-making in Göttingen with Filmaufbau AG, a studio that became known for its controversial subject matter. Gyula Trebitsch and Walter Koppel gained a similar reputation in Hamburg through their work for Real-Film. In the western sectors of Berlin, a number of smaller companies took advantage of the concentration of talent in the former capital. They included Kurt Ulrich's Berolina-Film, which launched the successful *Heimatfilm* wave of the 1950s, and Horst Wendland's Rialto-Film, which started the popular Edgar Wallace and Karl May series in the early 1960s. The most successful Berlin-based company was Artur Brauner 's CCC studio, whose mixture of literary adaptations, social dramas, and lifestyle comedies embodied best the postwar compromise between cultural ambition and economic growth (Dillmann-Kühn 1990). Brauner achieved this precarious balance by promoting European co-productions with international stars such as Maria Schell, Lilli Palmer, and Curd Jürgens. The head of CCC also played a key role in bringing back exile directors such as Lang and Siodmak and in producing a number of 'Jewish films', beginning with *Morituri* (1948), about the fate of Polish Jews during the Second World War.

With the financial help of the American Marshall Plan and under the conservative government of Chancellor Konrad Adenauer, the Federal Republic in the 1950s embarked on an ambitious project known as the Economic Miracle. These years of economic and political normalisation were characterised by an almost desperate activism, a compulsive pragmatism, and a pronounced unwillingness on the part of political and cultural institutions, and in the public sphere as a whole, to deal with the Third Reich and the Holocaust. The ethos of the Economic Miracle gave rise to an affluent middle-class society in which an American-style materialism coexisted with the conservative Christian values advanced by the leading political party, the Christian Democrats (CDU). In the same way that the narrow-mindedness of this emerging *Wohlstandsgesellschaft* (affluent society) functioned as a protection against past trauma, the insistence on social conventions helped to ward off uncomfortable questions about collective guilt and responsibility. Growing prosperity brought a return to the conservative family values shared by the educated bourgeoisie and the nouveau riche, whereas the increased stresses caused by social mobility found compensation in the promise of self-realisation through consumerism.

The first films made after 1945 still acknowledged the power of politics through the images of destroyed cities, occupying armies, and other postwar phenomena such as the black-market economy. Eventually, these images disappeared from filmic representation and public consciousness. They were replaced by a depoliticised popular cinema whose visual and narrative strategies depended on the systematic suppression of politics in the discourse of humanism and the inevitable return of ideology in the form of a rabid anti-communism. This process began with the so-called *Trümmerfilme* (rubble films) that thematised the nation's political defeat and wartime destruction through their unusual stories, characters, and locations and, in so doing, performed an important function in postwar culture and society (Shandley 2001). Enlisting expressionist styles and melodramatic effects in the rebirth of individual and nation, *Die Mörder sind unter uns* not only introduced the main elements of the rubble film but also defined the position of depoliticised humanism that, often with an existentialist bent, characterised most later representations of the Third Reich and its postwar legacies. The film's ending captured the new public morality in its famous closing lines: 'We don't have the right to judge but we have the duty to bring charges and demand atonement in the name of those millions murdered innocently.'

Unlike foreign rubble films such as Roberto Rosselini's neorealist *Germania anno zero* (1947, *Germany in the Zero Hour*) and Billy Wilder's *A Foreign Affair* (1949), German productions rarely took advantage of the extraordinary cityscapes and their often bizarre spatial and visual effects. Only Lamprecht's *Irgendwo in Berlin* (1947, *Somewhere in Berlin*), another DEFA production, relied on documentary footage and on-location shooting to imagine a future committed to socialist humanism. The majority of films remained committed to the German tradition of translating interiority into exteriority and of articulating social problems through psychological problems. Typically, in these films, a man returns home from the war and, confronted with the ubiquitous signs of destruction, is forced to make sense of his personal tragedy and, by extension, that of the German nation. In this context, the ruins visualised the desired erasure of the past and the promise of a new beginning captured in the myth of Zero Hour. Accordingly, the cityscape in ruins provided above all a mise-en-scène for the allegorical staging of agony, doubt, hope, and renewal.

In most cases, the rubble films offered individual solutions that extricated the protagonists from the burdens of history. *Zwischen gestern und morgen* (1947, *Between Yesterday and Tomorrow*) and . . . *und über uns der Himmel* (1947, *And above Us the Sky*) relied on archetypal family conflicts to work through the traumas of nation. Through the choice of a car as the narrator, *In jenen Tagen* (1947, *In Those Days*) avoided the question of agency altogether and presented its seven owners as innocent victims of circumstance. Offering a welcome break from such treatments, R. A. Stemmle's *Berliner Ballade* (1948, *Berlin Ballad*) enlisted the proverbial 'Otto Normalverbraucher' (i.e., the average German) in a satirical commentary on typical postwar problems (housing crisis, food shortages) and equally typical postwar debates (for instance, in the new political parties). To what degree satire and farce often served to justify a position of non-involvement can also be seen in Käutner's post-lapsarian fantasy in *Der Apfel ist ab* (1948, *The Apple Is Picked*).

All rubble films partook in *Vergangenheitsbewältigung* and its various strategies of self-explanation and self-exculpation. Despite the bitter pronunciations on the inhumanity of the world, the essential goodness of humankind was always reaffirmed in the end. By shifting the focus from social to individual perspectives,

91

the stories served psychological functions not dissimilar to the process of secondary revision; hence the frequent use of flashbacks and voice-over narration. The pleasurable staging of victimisation protected postwar audiences against feelings of guilt; yet the moralising tone also generated hope and confidence for the future. Through the emphasis on human suffering, the main protagonists could be portrayed as innocent, and history presented as fate. The bracketing of the political and the containment of history culminated in the exculpation of ordinary Germans as victims of anonymous forces. The real victims and perpetrators, the Jews and the Nazis, remained unnamed. Yet even behind the range of dispositions offered by melancholia, cynicism, pragmatism, and a defiant optimism, all rubble films remained haunted by the experience of war and defeat and the loss of nation and homeland. In the end, the intrusion of contemporary problems in the form of new themes and styles proved rather short-lived; the rubble film disappeared from the screen after 1948. Soon film-makers in the West returned to the generic formulas and strategies of incorporation perfected during the Third Reich, but this time less in the form of a levelling than in a harmonising of differences.

Sustained by such continuities, the work of Helmut Käutner, as well as several other well-known directors, can be described as symptomatic of the often difficult relationship between film and politics in postwar cinema as a whole (Jacobsen and Prinzler 1992). Having been associated with 'inner emigration', Käutner after 1945 continued to translate political conflicts into the heightened terms of (unfulfilled) romantic love, first in *Die letzte Brücke* (1954, *The Last Bridge*), about Bosnian partisans during the Second World War, and then in *Himmel ohne Sterne* (1956, *Sky without Stars*), one of the earliest films to acknowledge the existence of the zonal border. The director's neutral stance on the German division earned him sharp criticism from conservatives, but also guaranteed him regular screenings by the anti-communist 'Committee for an Inseparable Germany'. During the 1950s, Käutner developed a reputation for commercially viable and technically flawless films; some critics attacked his work for being conciliatory and defeatist. His adaptation of Zuckmayer's *Des Teufels General* (1955, *The Devil's General*) offered enthusiastic postwar audiences a positive image of Germanness based on the cult of heroic masculinity. By contrast, the much more innovative *Ludwig II., Glanz und Elend eines Königs* (1954, *Ludwig II*) explored the decadent cult of beauty and madness around the master builder of Neuschwanstein through filmic sensibilities that had no place in the conformist culture of the 1950s.

In the same way that Käutner's oeuvre draws attention to the problematic legacies of the 1940s, Wolfgang Staudte's career after 1945 bears witness to the many movements between East and West in a society increasingly polarised by the Cold War (Orbanz 1977). Staudte frequently experienced censorship problems, first in his work for DEFA, and later with several films made in the Federal Republic. Already during the production of *Die Mörder sind unter uns*, the Soviets demanded that the director should change the original ending because it presumably advocated violence as a means of political justice; after all, the film's original title was 'The Man I Am Going to Kill'. His next film about working-class life in the

Berlin of the 1930s and 1940s, *Rotation* (1949), focused on an apolitical 'little man' torn between the desire for personal happiness and the necessity of political action. Here, too, Staudte had to change several scenes because their pacifist message was deemed inappropriate during a period of militarisation in the GDR's anti-fascist alliance with the Soviet Union. *Der Untertan* (1951, *The Subject*), based on the famous Heinrich Mann novel, traces the prehistory of National Socialism back to the authoritarian structures of Wilhelmine Germany; this film was banned in the Federal Republic. During the 1950s, Staudte was attacked for formalist tendencies in the East and denounced as a communist in the West. Although the director refused to sign a statement of political loyalty for a West German producer, he ended up spending the latter part of the decade as an 'apolitical moralist' marginalised within the culture of the Economic Miracle. Even after the critical success of *Rosen für den Staatsanwalt* (1959, *Roses for the State Attorney*), a political satire about the postwar career of a high-ranking Nazi officer, this last 'all-German' film director no longer found a place among the kind of film professional personified by Kurt Hoffmann.

Responsible for more than twenty films during the period in question, the prolific and versatile Hoffmann provided good middle-brow quality entertainment for the entire family (Tornow 1990). He found his ideal actress in the young Lieselotte Pulver, whose perkiness carried such hits as the Hungarian summer romance *Ich denke oft an Piroschka* (1955, *I Often Think of Piroschka*). In the typical Hoffmann film, fantasy offers a convenient way of assuming various identities, of testing new attitudes, but always within the confines of private desires and with a clear view towards a harmonious integration of differences. When not indulging his preference for bygone eras, rural settings, or vacation times, Hoffmann took on more ambitious literary projects. Yet in the same way that sentimentality diffused the humour in his comedies, it softened the ironic or satirical elements in his adaptations of Thomas Mann's *Bekenntnisse des Hochstaplers Felix Krull* (1957, *The Confessions of Felix Krull*) and Friedrich Dürrenmatt's *Die Ehe des Herrn Mississippi* (1961, *The Marriage of Mr Mississippi*). Considered his most important work, *Wir Wunderkinder* (1958, *We Prodigies*) reconstructs the German past through the different biographies of two school friends, a decent 'little man' and an opportunistic social climber. But even here, Hoffmann's insistence on the modesty of desires and the virtue of contentment ends up only validating the petty-bourgeois mentality that, in fact, fuelled and sustained postwar society in the West. Not surprisingly, this film became a welcome target for Wolfgang Neuss when he made *Wir Kellerkinder* (1960, *We Slum Kids*), a biting parody about the entire discourse of *Vergangenheitsbewältigung*.

In terms of aesthetic and ideological commitments, no director could be more removed from Hoffmann than Slatan Dudow. His films for the DEFA studio continued in the Weimar tradition of social realist film-making, with the early Russian films and Brecht's theory of epic theatre as major reference points. Known for his close attention to social characterisation, the Bulgarian director continued to develop his modernist sensibilities through a heavy reliance on montage and music as means of defamiliarisation and critical analysis (for example, in collaboration with Hanns Eisler). His name is often linked to the so-called *Aufbaufilme* (reconstruction films) and their often highly didactic stories about the difficulties of building a socialist society. In *Unser täglich Brot* (1949, *Our Daily Bread*), for instance, Dudow shows how a group of workers take ownership of a bombed-out factory in East Berlin. In the process, they overcome their petty-bourgeois prejudices and learn socialist virtues such as responsibility, solidarity, and commitment to the collective. *Frauenschicksale* (1952, *Women's Fates*) uses several women searching for love and marriage in a divided Berlin to demonstrate the superiority of socialism even in personal matters. Again the happy ending confirms the collective as the true narrative agent. In the late 1950s, Dudow also turned his attention to the past when he directed *Stärker als die Nacht* (1954, *Stronger than the Night*), one of the few DEFA films about the communist resistance during the Third Reich and an important early contribution to the history of the German working-class movement.

DEFA director Kurt Maetzig is generally regarded as the leading proponent of the so-called *Chronikfilm* (chronicle film). Infusing conventional narratives with socialist ideas, the chronicle films played a pivotal role in the formation of early GDR identity. Melodramatic elements supported the central political arguments already in the director's first and most famous film, *Ehe im Schatten* (1947, *Marriage in the Shadow*); its tragic story of a German-Jewish couple during the Third Reich was inspired by the fate of actor Joachim Gottschalk. Focusing on one working-class family, *Die Buntkarierten* (1949, *The Chequered Sheets*) follows three generations of women from the 1920s to the 1940s to chronicle their political awakening after difficult personal experiences. Similar elements can be found in *Roman einer jungen Ehe* (1952, *Story of a Young Couple*) where the marital problems of two actors serve to illustrate the ideological struggles in a divided postwar Berlin. In accordance with the early antifascist phase at DEFA, these three films hold their apolitical or opportunistic protagonists partly responsible for the rise of fascism and, by extension, anti-communism. The same sense of moral responsibility informs *Der Rat der Götter* (1950, *Council of the Gods*) in which Maetzig recounts the scandalous history of the IG-Farben concern during the Third Reich through the competing perspectives of workers, scientists, and managers.

In the late 1950s, Maetzig abandoned such reflections on individual guilt and responsibility for more straightforward propagandistic intentions. Shot in the obligatory socialist realist style, his later national epics concentrated on the revolutionary working class and its heroic achievements. Set in the largely rural Mecklenburg province, the two-part chronicle, *Schlösser und Katen* (1957, *Castles and Huts*), introduced a large cast of characters to show the difficulties of agricultural collectivisation in what might be called the DEFA version of the *Heimatfilm*. The state-commissioned, two-part *Ernst Thälmann – Sohn seiner Klasse* (1954, *E.T., Son of his Class*) and *Führer seiner Klasse* (1955, *E.T., Leader of his Class*), with Günther Simon in the title role, presented an idealised biography of the famous Communist party leader to legitimise the existence of the German

Democratic Republic; the formal debts to the earlier genius films are undeniable. An incredible success, the Thälmann films were seen by millions, often as part of official party events.

The only other DEFA director whose work was closely tied to the building of the socialist state is Konrad Wolf; he spent the Nazi years in the Soviet Union. His divided identities as a communist and a German Jew made him particularly susceptible to the contradictions within postwar German society. A formal innovator, political artist, and influential public figure, Wolf is generally regarded as the most important director associated with DEFA. Especially in hindsight, his films from the 1950s to the 1970s must be considered central to the rewriting of German history (Silberman 1990). Wolf's chronicle films presented the GDR as part of the continuities and discontinuities of German history, and often from the perspective of a female protagonist. Thus *Lissy* (1957) examines the rise of National Socialism through the story of a young woman from Berlin's working class who is forced to confront the consequences of her political apathy. The formally remarkable *Sonnensucher* (1958/72, *Sun Seekers*), about life and work in a uranium mine in Wismut, portrays a motley group of simple workers, ruthless adventurers, unruly women, and idealistic party cadres with a surprising sensitivity towards individual differences.

Wolf's tendency towards stylisation is most apparent in two films that directly address German anti-Semitism and the Holocaust. During a decade dominated by the liberal rhetoric of human injustice and suffering, the director affirmed his commitment to anti-fascism precisely by insisting on the specificity of the Jewish question. In the first German film about the Holocaust, the German–Bulgarian co-production *Sterne* (1959, *Stars*), Wolf focused on the encounter between a Jewish woman on her way to Auschwitz and a German officer who, in an ending eliminated from the film's West German version, responds to this emotional experience by joining the Bulgarian partisans. Then, adapting a play by his father Friedrich Wolf, *Professor Mamlock* (1962), the director used the figure of a respected physician from Weimar Berlin's upper middle class to demonstrate the shortcomings of traditional bourgeois notions of class in understanding the historical roots of anti-Semitism.

Rewriting history, forging new identities

Käutner, Staudte, Dudow, Hoffmann, and Wolf participated in the corresponding processes of nation-building that, in the FRG and the GDR, hinged on a critical assessment of the Third Reich and the Holocaust. This representational project involved two equally important steps: the construction of a historical trajectory that gave political legitimacy to the new regimes in East and West; and the interpretation of these social and economic systems as a radical break with the legacies of National Socialism. Bourgeois individualism, economic liberalism, and social conservatism defined the new identity of the Federal Republic; the primacy of the collective and the necessity of struggle and self-sacrifice that of the German

Democratic Republic. The West subsumed the question of anti-Semitism under the category of crimes against humanity. The East incorporated the Jewish question into the grand narratives of anti-fascism. In both cases, the creation of a postwar identity involved a complicated process of inclusion and exclusion, acceptance and denial.

The inevitable consequences of this process can be measured in the filmic reflections on the history of anti-Semitism and the contributions by the few exile film-makers who returned to Germany. In the DEFA film *Affäre Blum* (1948, *The Blum Affair*), Erich Engel reconstructed a famous murder trial against a Magdeburg Jewish businessman to trace the rise of anti-Semitism in the Weimar Republic. *Morituri* (1948), Artur Brauner and Eugen York's rarely seen film about the inmates in a concentration camp in Poland, drew on personal experiences by the CCC producer. Likewise, Fritz Kortner's portrayal in *Der Ruf* (1949, *The Appointment*) of an exiled university professor who returns to Germany only to confront anti-Semitic attitudes among his colleagues and students resonated with the actor's own experience of exile. When confronting the traumas of the past, several exiled directors turned to the psychological motif of doubling to describe the relationship between victim and perpetrator or to examine the psychological mechanisms behind hypocrisy, indifference, and cowardice. Thus in *Der Verlorene* (1951, *The Lost Man*), Peter Lorre used the familiar Dr Jekyll/Mr Hyde motif to evoke the disturbing image of a nation ravaged by guilt. And in the noirish thriller *Nachts wenn der Teufel kam* (1957, *At Night when the Devil Came*) and the mildly satirical *Mein Schulfreund* (1960, *My Friend from School*), Robert Siodmak focused on the representatives of law and order who, before and after 1945, protected their positions through all means necessary. Indicative of the international resonance of the German dilemma, even Rossellini returned to make *Angst/Paura* (1954, *Fear*), an expressionist melodrama about a happy marriage almost destroyed by a dark secret from the past – a more than telling allegory of the Federal Republic.

The early West German films about the Third Reich initially evoked the past to support the project of political stabilisation and economic recovery. Yet, increasingly, film-makers enlisted historical figures and events to give legitimacy to the new government in the antagonistic terms of the Cold War. Thus the category of the 'purely human' gave rise to a number of fictional oppositions introduced to distinguish the Federal Republic from both the Nazi past and the East German regime. The withdrawal from ideology was achieved through the insistence on individual rather than public morality and a preference for ethical rather than political categories of historical explanation. With the Nazis depicted as either classic villains with a neurotic lust for power or as mere executioners of an anonymous power structure, melodramatic forms proved most effective in demonising the Third Reich as an aberration of German history. Only a sharp distinction between the regime and the nation, between the political leadership and the ordinary people, could after all exculpate the Germans as the victims of history: reason enough for contemporary film-makers and audiences to abandon earlier notions of collective guilt for the celebration of individual heroism.

These socio-psychological needs stood behind the enormous success of two films that emphasised the resistance within the military leadership, *Des Teufels General*, about famous aviator Ernst Udet, and *Canaris* (1954), about the head of the counter-intelligence agency. Both films identified the opposition to the Nazi regime with two military men whose actions in the films are guided by an old-fashioned sense of duty and honour. Perhaps even more important, the film-makers relied heavily on the famous UFA style in their chamber play approach to mise-en-scène and their star treatment of actors Curd Jürgens and O. E. Hasse, respectively, as icons of German masculinity. Two other films about the failed assassination attempt on Hitler by the resistance movement around Count Stauffenberg, Pabst's *Es geschah am 20. Juli* (1955, *It Happened on the 20th of July*), and Falk Harnack's *Der 20. Juli* (1956, *The 20th of July*), took a more restrained approach by combining pseudo-documentary scenes with theatrical dialogues and interiors; both films failed at the box office.

In the beginning, West German audiences had to turn to war films made in Hollywood, especially Henry Hathaway's *The Desert Fox* (1951) and Anatole Litvak's *Decision Before Dawn* (1951), to indulge their desire for images of male heroism unburdened by political ideologies. But beginning in 1955, with the creation of the Bundeswehr and the country's entry into NATO, warfare and military life returned as an important subject matter in genres ranging from historical dramas to military comedies. Paul May's trilogy *08/15* (1954–55), based on the best-seller by Hans Hellmut Kirst, set the tone by romanticising military life in the barracks and at the front, all the while paying lip service to standard pacifist themes. In *Hunde, wollt ihr ewig leben* (1959, *Dogs, Do You Want to Live Forever*), about the historical battle in the encircled city of Stalingrad, and *Nacht fiel über Gotenhafen* (1959, *Night Fell over Gotenhafen*), about the court-martial of a German navy officer, Frank Wisbar (or Wysbar) focused exclusively on the military code of honour, the value of discipline and obedience, and the occasional break-downs in the chain of command; references to National Socialism remained conspicuously absent. In the light of these revisionist tendencies, the submarine warfare depicted in *U47 – Kapitänleutnant Prien* (1958, *U47 – Lieutenant Commander Prien*) proved ideally suited to separate the excitement of battle from the political forces behind German territorial aggression. In *Der Arzt von Stalingrad* (1958, *The Doctor of Stalingrad*), the brutal treatment of German soldiers in a Soviet POW camp offered even an opportunity for the inclusion of anti-Russian stereotypes and anti-Soviet remarks. In such an atmosphere of remilitarisation, *Kinder, Mütter und ein General* (1955, *Children, Mothers and a General*), a well-intended anti-war parable told from the female perspective, failed to find an audience – unlike the pacifist war drama *Die Brücke* (1959, *The Bridge*).

The Cold War influenced the two German film industries on all levels: the narrative representation of German history, including the years of reconstruction; the official positions on the German division and its ideological underpinnings; and the highly politicised circumstances under which some films were made, released, shown, and reviewed. In the Federal Republic, the emphatic rejection of all ideologies in the name of humanist liberalism established anti-communism as the unifying force that at once legitimated the retreat from politics in cultural life and made possible its return in the form of a paranoid, manichean world view. The institutional structures for de-Nazification established by the Allies became very useful in the fight against alleged communists: they either took the form of secret investigations (for example, against producers Koppel and Trebitsch) or resulted in the denial of federal subsidies (for example, to directors working in East and West). The Federal government's policy on DEFA films changed from a general ban in the early 1950s to a more selective, if not arbitrary, approach that continued throughout the 1960s. Despite the political polemics about the threat of communism, few West German films ever thematised the impact of the Cold War on personal relationships, social structures, and definitions of national identity. With the exception of the sentimental love story of *Himmel ohne Sterne* and Will Tremper's sensationalist adaptation of a story from *Stern* magazine, *Flucht nach Berlin* (1961, *Escape to Berlin*), West German film-makers avoided all direct references to the border with East Germany. By contrast, DEFA provided ready-made arguments for the German division in its series of cheaply made espionage films that depicted the decadent, corrupt capitalist West as a serious threat to the new socialist state.

Beyond such political polemics, the continuities and discontinuities of German cinema in East and West continued to find a privileged expression in the abiding preference for literary adaptations. In the West, the naturalist dramas of Hauptmann, who inspired two Maria Schell vehicles, Siodmak's *Die Ratten* (1955, *The Rats*) and Staudte's *Rose Bernd* (1957), offered a notion of milieu that could easily be applied to contemporary problems (for example, the refugee problem). At DEFA, the critical engagement with the legacies of nineteenth-century realism propelled Artur Pohl to rewrite the *nouveau riche* narrative of Fontane's *Frau Jenny Treibel* in the class-conscious terms of *Corinna Schmidt* (1951). Competing claims on the illustrious Mann family stood behind the first failed attempt at a German–German co-production; that project was later completed in the West as a conventional two-part star vehicle, *Buddenbrooks* (1959, *The Buddenbrooks*). With *Der Untertan*, the DEFA studio reclaimed Heinrich Mann for a Lukácsian tradition of critical realism. Two years later, the Filmaufbau in Göttingen turned to Thomas Mann to rewrite the happy marriage between German culture and American money depicted in *Königliche Hoheit* (1953, *His Royal Highness*) as a programmatic statement about the Federal Republic.

At DEFA, the classics of German literature allowed film-makers both to claim the traditions of humanism for socialism and, on several occasions, to articulate marginalised sensibilities through new interpretations of well-known texts. Thus *Wozzeck* (1947), based on the Büchner play, allowed its director to visualise experiences of individual oppression through starkly expressionist styles. The adaptation of *Das Fräulein von Scuderi* (1955, *Mademoiselle de Scuderi*), a story by E. T. A. Hoffmann, explored the attractions of the uncanny with little regard for the ongoing debates about the problematic legacies of German romanticism.

98

Taking the more common approach, later adaptations of Schiller's *Kabale und Liebe* (1959, *Cabal and Love*) and Lessing's *Minna von Barnhelm* (1962) complied fully with the cultural ambitions of the regime by appropriating the values of bourgeois emancipation for the new socialist ethics and morality. Similar intentions stood behind big-budget DEFA opera films such as *Die lustigen Weiber von Windsor* (1950, *The Merry Wives of Windsor*) and *Zar und Zimmermann* (1956, *Tsar and Carpenter*) that tried to reconcile petty-bourgeois tastes and high-culture pretensions by adding some populist flourishes.

The politicisation of cinema in the East

Bringing together the old and new intellectual elites, DEFA was founded in the spirit of democratic antifascism: to aid in the project of reconstruction, to disseminate the ideals of humanism, and to fight the dangers of nationalism and militarism. Thematically, most prestige productions from the 1940s and 1950s responded to two interrelated sets of issues, the cultural practices most relevant to the building of a socialist society and the equally important project of defining the meaning of anti-fascism. Both gave rise to rarely told stories from the working class that showed the conditions of industrial labour and tenement living and that affirmed the importance of political struggle. New approaches to characterisation and audience identification (for example, through collective agency) conveyed the studio's obligation to the socialist state and to Marxist ideology. Introduced in the context of socio-psychological analysis (for instance, of German guilt), the concept of anti-fascism and its relevance to GDR identity underwent significant changes during the 1950s and slowly deteriorated to an obligatory gesture in the master-narratives of cultural and political isolationalism (Kannapin 1997).

Even through the self-declared 'all-German' studio defined film production in political rather than economic terms, it still had to deal with disappointing attendance figures; often DEFA films were simply not as popular as foreign films. Throughout the 1950s, the studio suffered from a low annual productivity rate, with individual projects slowed down by long pre-production discussions, numerous script revisions, and last-minute re-shooting of scenes. In several cases, the studio withdrew films from distribution before or right after their public release. Adding to these problems, the Babelsberg studio had to mediate between the conflicting demands of party and state agencies and respond to their changing definitions of film-making under socialism. Official positions on culture and entertainment wavered between attempts at liberalisation and demonstrations of hard-line dogmatism. Initially, communications between the DEFA and the SED were facilitated by the Central Cultural Commission. It ceded power to the DEFA Commission in 1950 and the State Committee for Film Questions in 1952. After 1954, DEFA-related questions were handled by the Ministry of Culture. The infamous Hauptverwaltung Film (HV Film), which consisted of studio representations, party members, and cultural functionaries, was responsible for the approval of all new film projects. During this period of institutional restructuring,

DEFA in 1953 was turned into a state-owned company that brought together the various branches of the industry in one hierarchical structure. Separate units were created for feature film production, newsreels, documentaries, scientific films, and children's films, as well as for animation and dubbing. Film distribution from then on was handled through Progress-Verleih and, in export matters, through the DEFA-Aussenhandel.

The first phase in the precarious relationship between cinema and politics lasted approximately until 1953. The 1947 First German Film Authors Conference, which had called for a German cinema united beyond zonal boundaries, remained a powerful influence and, among other things, contributed to the uncritical acceptance of the familiar UFA styles. As a result, the early reconstruction films addressed the most pressing problems in the GDR – the collectivisation in agriculture in *Freies Land* (1946, *Free Land*), the restructuring of the mining industry in *Morgenrot* (1948, *The 'Dawn' Mine*) – through established generic patterns. Even the first film about the early working-class movement, Artur Pohl's *Die Unbesiegbaren* (1953, *The Invincible Ones*), took a psychological approach to character development. Yet soon after the founding of the GDR, functionaries began to demand a more extensive contribution from the DEFA studio to the first five-year plan and, more generally, the building of socialist society. There was pressure on filmmakers to support the struggle against American cultural imperialism and resist the influence of cosmopolitanism and what was now denounced as bourgeois psychologism. With these arguments, the formalism debate of the early 1950s forcefully put an end to aesthetic experimentation. Modernist elements survived only in the form of expressionist or neo-realist styles and an almost noirish sensibility in some of the later espionage films.

The official debates about the nature of realism produced the doctrine of socialist realism, which was modelled after the Stalinist epics of the 1930s and informed by the theoretical writings of Lukács. With reality in the cinema defined no longer as a reflection of what existed but as a representation of what should be, narrative films were supposed to support social change through typical stories and characters; effective mechanisms of identification; ample opportunities for idolisation and heroisation; and through what later critics denounced as overly schematic dramatic conflicts and formulaic narrative and visual devices. The doctrine of socialist realism gave rise to a national cinema sustained by, and accountable to, the socialist collective; responsive to the questions and debates most relevant to GDR society; and committed to the fight against monopoly capitalism and imperialist aggression. As a result of the dogmatic turn, Harnack's *Das Beil von Wandsbek* (1951, *The Axe of Wandsbek*) was withdrawn from theatres because of its complex treatment of Nazi supporters and fellow travellers.

Soon thereafter, the so-called New Course in 1953 ushered in a brief period of greater freedom. The death of Stalin, public mistrust of the party leadership, and dissatisfaction among workers contributed to the deep crisis of legitimisation that culminated in the strikes on 17 June. Reversing earlier pronouncements on the socialist realist style that produced the famous Thälmann epics, the Central

Committee now called for more films about everyday problems such as love, marriage, and family life. The moment seemed to have arrived for exploring a wider range of aesthetic sensibilities, recognising different filmic traditions, and even articulating dissenting political views. The new films from Poland, including Andrzej Wajda's *Kanal* (1956) and *Ashes and Diamonds* (1958), inspired younger DEFA directors – such as Kurt Jung-Alsen in *Betrogen bis zum jüngsten Tag* (1957, *Betrayed until Judgement Day*) – to reconsider their own accounts of the Second World War, for instance through a greater emphasis on the disillusionment of the war generation. In rewriting the Third Reich from an individual perspective, film-makers also learned to validate the contribution of children and women as the subjects of a different history and historiography. Wolf's *Sie nannten ihn Amigo* (1959, *They Called Him Amigo*), about a working-class boy sent to a concentration camp, and Frank Beyer's first film, *Zwei Mütter* (1957, *Two Mothers*), about a French child caught between two mothers, were part of that larger project.

The growing awareness of the problems of youth – and its implicit challenge to traditional notions of class struggle – showed the limits of the official discourse of unity and integration. Maetzig's *Vergesst mir meine Traudel nicht* (1957, *Don't Forget My Traudel*), with Eva-Maria Hagen in the title role, still used the experiences of a rebellious young woman to propagate the new ethos of social responsibility. But already the Berlin films by Gerhard Klein and Wolfgang Kohlhaase, *Alarm im Zirkus* (1954, *Alarm in the Circus*), *Eine Berliner Romanze* (1956, *A Berlin Romance*), and *Berlin – Ecke Schönhauser* (1957, *Berlin Near Schönhauser Street*), offered a more open engagement with American youth culture and its pivotal role in the rituals of protest shared by urban youth in East and West Berlin. Engaging with the quotidian on a thematic and aesthetic level, the films proved as provocative in their contemporary subject matter as in their neorealist style. Not surprisingly, both *Eine Berliner Romanze* and *Berlin – Ecke Schönhauser* encountered difficulties prior to their official release.

Following the paradoxical logic behind the sequence of 'freezes' and 'thaws', the slowing down in the transformation of socialist society and the partial relaxing of official positions on culture eventually made necessary a reideologisation of cinema. In 1956, the Hungarian uprising and Khrushchev's denunciation of Stalin increased the political instability in many Eastern Bloc countries. These events prompted the SED leadership to re-examine their cultural policies and to look more closely at the new films in production. In an attempt to return to the dogma of socialist realism, the 1958 Film Conference organised by the Ministry of Culture polemically evoked the spectre of revisionism to justify their punitive campaigns against those film-makers still committed to critical realism. Even highly respected directors such as Wolf and Maetzig were forced into humiliating exercises of self-criticism. At the centre of many arguments stood the representation of the alienated individual in a non-capitalist society. Opposed to the thematisation of alienation through innovative narrative and visual techniques, the party leadership insisted on approaches that showed the ideal conditions in the workers' and peasants' state. They also demanded more films about the historical struggles of the revolutionary working-class that applied the heroic perspectives explored in *Thomas Müntzer* (1956), about the religious leader of the reformation, and *Tilman Riemenschneider* (1958), about the great medieval wood sculptor, to the twentieth century. Whereas the past emerged as the perfect projection screen for retrograde fantasies of Germanness, the relevance of the future for the project of socialism remained a subject of intense debates, as evidenced by the difficulties surrounding Maetzig's *Der schweigende Stern* (1960, *The Silent Star*), a German–Polish co-production based on a science fiction novel by Stanislav Lem (Soldovieri 1998).

Throughout the 1950s, DEFA's low productivity rate, inefficient use of resources, and lack of competent directors and screenwriters forced studio heads to rely heavily on artistic personnel commuting from West Berlin. At times, they constituted 70 per cent of all full-time employees. Those with a considerable UFA past included veteran directors such as Rabenalt and prolific screenwriters such as Georg C. Klaren, who later became the first chief dramaturge at DEFA. Even silent star Henny Porten appeared in two historical dramas made in Babelsberg, including *Das Fräulein von Scuderi*. Among the better-known actors with screen credits in East and West were Werner Peters, the quintessential 'authoritarian subject', and Wolfgang Kieling, who, like Peters, specialised in 'evil Germans', including in Hitchcock's 1966 Cold War thriller *Torn Curtain*. In response to the party's increasingly isolationist stance, DEFA made a concerted effort to terminate the employment of individuals who still commuted from the West. Yet the hope that the absence of such 'alien' elements would give the studio a more unified artistic profile remained unfulfilled.

Since DEFA failed to produce enough feature films for the domestic market, motion-picture theatres depended heavily on imports, especially from the Federal Republic. Almost seventy such films were released in the GDR during the 1950s (Gersch in Schobert and Hoffmann 1989, 100–9). Interestingly, audiences in East and West enjoyed many of the same screen favourites and hit films. Musical comedies and romantic comedies proved extremely popular in the East; the *Heimatfilm* not at all. In many ways, the West German imports fulfilled an entertainment function comparable to the Hollywood films in much of Western Europe; more ambitious artistic contributions were usually provided by French and Italian films. New releases from other East European countries, including innovative Polish and Czech films and Soviet prestige productions such as Mikhail Kalatosov's *The Cranes are Flying* (1957), could always be seen in the capital. However, foreign films critical of the Federal Republic or, such as *The Salt of the Earth* (1955), of the United States often failed at the box office despite aggressive marketing. In the smaller cities, audiences generally preferred the conventional genre films produced by Bavaria, Rialto, and CCC. Even in West Berlin, the inexpensive border cinemas attracted scores of East Berlin youth with their sensationalist fare. By the late 1950s, these uncontrollable movements in the former capital and the exposure to Western television in many border regions was considered a serious problem by the leadership. To counteract such tendencies, DEFA made a concerted effort to promote the commissioned films (*Auftragsfilme*) and their presentation of important social topics as an essential part of national anniversaries, public celebrations, and party seminars. But these measures did not prevent audiences from flocking to the melodramas of Harlan, Rabenalt, and others.

Even during the most heated debates on the meaning of socialist realism, the DEFA studio continued to develop its own version of genre cinema. In the late 1940s and early 1950s, many of these films dealt with contemporary problems in a rather schematic manner. Often called *Gegenwartsfilme* (contemporary dramas), they showed the present and its problems as part of a historical continuum. In the more acclaimed contributions, the goals of entertainment usually absorbed the didactic intentions. To give a few examples, *Razzia* (1947, *Raid*) used the exciting black-market setting for a cautionary tale about crime and money, and the melo-dramatic *Strassenbekanntschaft* (1948, *Street Acquaintance*) by the almost forgotten Peter Pewas showed the dangers of free sexuality in order to inform audiences about sexually transmitted diseases. Conventional narrative structures and forms of identification prevailed in the countless stories of everyday life under socialism, especially those set in the workplace. *Modell Bianka* (1951, *Model Bianca*) celebrated the socialist work ethic in the clothing companies through the formulas of romantic comedy, whereas *Sommerliebe* (1955, *Summer Love*) relied on the same narrative devices to show young workers in love at their favourite vacation resorts on the Baltic Coast.

During the 1950s, the DEFA studio experimented with a wide range of genres and styles, from expressionistic melodramas such as *Leuchtfeuer* (1954, *Light Fire*) and realistic milieu studies such as *Alter Kahn und junge Liebe* (1956, *Old Barge and Young Love*) to colourful revue films such as *Silvesterpunsch* (1960, *New Year's Eve Punch*). As in the West, references to the UFA tradition were ubiquitous. The postwar preference for melodramas produced *Genesung* (1956, *Recuperation*) about a veteran physician who practises medicine without a licence, a conflict familiar from similar West German medical dramas. Like the society dramas made before 1945, *Ehesache Lorenz* (1959, *Lorenz versus Lorenz*) explored the problems of a dual-career couple by placing the neglected husband in the throes of an adulterous affair. Last but not least, more extreme forms of socialist kitsch prevailed in the cheaply produced dramas and comedies that idealised workers' heroic efforts to reach their annual quotas in the nationalised industries and romanticised farmers' earnest attempts to deal with petty jealousies on the collectivised farms.

The DEFA studio achieved its greatest successes with fairy-tale films that were enthusiastically received throughout Eastern Europe (König et al. 1996). The production of children's films increased DEFA's export business and led to fruitful collaborations with other East European film studios during the 1960s and with GDR Television in the 1970s. The various genres subsumed under the category of 'children's film' included historical and contemporary adaptations of popular folk-tales and literary fairy-tales. The creative contribution of set designers and effects specialists such as Ernst Kunstmann proved essential to the genre's overall success, especially given its strong investment in alternative notions of reality. Despite their obvious educational purposes, the children's film also served as a vehicle for artistic experimentation. More specifically, the fairy-tale films provided a utopian space for examining the social and economic conditions that prevented the fulfilment of human needs and desires. In that sense, *Das kalte Herz* (1950, *The Cold Heart*), the first DEFA colour film, offered an alternative to the unproductive money economy in the ethos of Protestantism and, by extension, socialism. Celebrating the true wealth found in friendship, *Die Geschichte vom kleinen Muck* (1953, *The Story of Little Muck*), another Wilhelm Hauff adaptation, promoted a similar anti-capitalist message. And in *Das singende klingende Bäumchen* (1957, *The Singing Ringing Tree*), the re-education of a beautiful but spoiled princess played by youth idol Christel Bodenstein allowed GDR audiences to understand the importance of work and labour as a truly humanising force.

The depoliticisation of cinema in the West

A number of oppositions or, rather, triangulations defined postwar cinema on both sides of the border: German high culture, American mass culture, and socialist working-class culture; conventional genre films, cultural prestige productions, and political propaganda films; and, to move to aesthetic categories, the inherent tension among narrative traditions, realist tendencies, and modernist elements. Political categories permeated every aspect of cinema culture in the GDR, from the debates about socialist realism to the calls for more films about everyday life. By contrast, the ostensible absence of all things political characterised the self-representation of cinema in the FRG, from the promotion of new genres and stars to the official decisions about film imports and subsidies. For that reason, the filmic fantasies produced in the West have most frequently been examined as a reflection of, and reaction to, the new ethos of hard work and social mobility; the return to conservative family values and a repressive sexual morality; and society's enthusiastic embrace of modern mass media and consumer goods. However, the simulation of these psychological constellations in the filmic imagination provided a convenient framework not only for the reaffirmation of traditional gender roles and familial hierarchies but also for the subterranean articulation of more complicated issues related to class, ethnicity, and nationality.

In the Western zones, the cinema after 1945 emerged as the driving force behind the ongoing self-transformation of postwar culture and society. To accommodate growing audiences, the number of cinemas increased from a thousand in 1945 to three thousand by the end of the decade. In 1956, an attendance record was reached, with the average West German going to the movies 15.6 times a year. From then on, numbers declined steadily from 817 million tickets sold in 1956 to 443 million tickets sold in 1962. Popular tastes during these years tended towards conventional fare; the four-sector city of Berlin, with its more cosmopolitan tastes, remained an exception. The rubble films – and for different reasons, the anti-war films – failed at the box office because they were considered 'too depressing'. Audiences preferred so-called *Zeitfilme* or *Problemfilme* (contemporary dramas), which addressed social problems from an individual perspective and in accordance with established dramatic conventions. Questionnaires from the period suggest that audiences wanted familiar stories, characters, and settings. Producers accommodated their demands by emphasising the continuities within genre cinema. In 1950 even a mediocre Leander vehicle such as *Gabriela* proved more successful than the British noir classic *The Third Man*. Confirming the audience's preference for domestic productions, the standard ratio of two-thirds German films to one-third foreign films changed gradually during the 1950s, with Hollywood providing half of all imports. Foreign films only gained wider acceptance once dubbing became the predominant practice. This form of *Eindeutschung* (Germanisation) helped to reconcile national and international perspectives, especially when it came to censoring the content of foreign films considered anti-German in orientation (for example, in the dubbed versions of *Casablanca* and *Notorious*).

These audience preferences culminated around the star phenomenon. The old UFA stars satisfied widespread nostalgia for a period instantly rewritten as the 'golden years' by offering the familiar emotional registers: obnoxious cheerfulness in the case of supporting actors such as Grete Weiser, Hans Moser, and Theo Lingen and more melancholy dispositions in the case of stars such as Albers, Birgel, and Leander. Directors such as Josef von Baky, Viktor Tourjansky, and of course Veit Harlan continued to indulge in melodramatic excesses. Perhaps most importantly, the famous UFA style maintained its influence over postwar practices through the expert work of cinematographers such as Friedl Behn-Grund and Konstantin Irmen-Tschet, set designers such as Otto Hunte and Hermann Warm, screenwriters such as Bobby E. Lüthge, and composers such as Werner Richard Heymann. From their use of light and space to framing and editing, from their conception of characters to the nuances of dialogue, these consummate film professionals established the conditions that, more than any new and daring topics, guaranteed the illusion of an unbroken tradition in terms of aesthetic preferences, cultural sensibilities, and social mentalities. This desire for historical continuity extended even to the late Weimar period, which provided countless stories suitable for adaptations, serials, and remakes. Erich Kästner children's classics *Das doppelte Lottchen* (1950, *Double Little Lotte*) and *Emil und die Detektive* (1954, *Emil and the Detectives*) were the most successful products of this emerging revisionist wave.

The wider implications behind such continuities became most apparent in genres that, like the genius film, had been enlisted in the discourses of German nationalism during the Third Reich. Satisfying the audience's regressive desire for the mythological father, new biographical films in the style of *Sauerbruch – das war mein Leben* (1954, *Sauerbruch – This Was My Life*) or *Made in Germany* (1957), about the physician Ernst von Abbe, rediscovered the German man as a healer, as someone capable of saving, rather than destroying lives – a not insignificant achievement in the aftermath of the Holocaust. In linking past and present, these biographical films also established a model of individual accomplishment that found a real-life equivalent in a new generation of 'great Germans': entrepreneurial figures such as Max Grundig, Rudolf August Oetker, and Josef Neckermann, the heroes of the Economic Miracle. The conservative thrust of the entire genre culminated around *Stresemann* (1957), a biographical film that essentially rewrote the problems of the young Weimar democracy in terms of Adenauer's politics of stability and continuity.

The historical dramas satisfied the nostalgia for strong leader figures and for visions of empire unburdened by questions of guilt; some of the most escapist contributions even allowed for individual fantasies of resistance. The Biedermeier period emerged as the preferred setting for folkloric tales about noble robbers and rebels in the style of *Das Wirtshaus im Spessart* (1958, *The Spessart Inn*) and *Der Schinderhannes* (1959). Even the Wilhelmine period could be reclaimed as the 'good old times' through the mild critique of authoritarianism and militarism found in Rühmann star vehicles such as *Der Hauptmann von Köpenick* (1956, *The Captain of Köpenick*), *Der eiserne Gustav* (1958, *Iron Gustav*), and, in a slightly different context, *Der brave Soldat Schweijk* (1960, *The Good Soldier Schweijk*). The Austro-Hungarian Empire provided a colourful, animated backdrop for many classic film operettas, whereas Prussian history inspired more serious lessons on duty, honour, and sacrifice. Aided by beautiful costumes and spectacular settings, the identification of dynastic power with youth gave rise to positive images of empire. Often female figures occupied centre stage in the rediscovery of nationalism, from the heroine of *Königin Luise* (1956, *Queen Luise*), beloved for her dignified behaviour during the Napoleonic Wars, to Elisabeth of Bavaria who, in the incarnation of Romy Schneider, gained cult-like status after the phenomenal success of the Austrian-made *Sissi* trilogy (1955–57). The overidentification of star and role in the case of *Sissi* was sustained by the postwar archetype of the good daughter who restored the reputation of Germans at home and abroad, but it also had much to do with the clever marketing of commodity tie-ins such as Romy fashion dolls.

The fantasy of the fairy-tale princess embodied by Schneider, like the independent young women portrayed by Knef, remained the exception among female stars beloved and admired for their maternal, wifely or sisterly qualities. In fact, the 1950s are known primarily for promoting the kind of hard-working wives and mothers portrayed by the immensely popular Luise Ulrich in *Vergiss die Liebe nicht* (1953, *Don't Forget Love*) and *Eine Frau von heute* (1954, *A Woman of Today*) and the attractive married career women depicted by Heidemarie Hatheyer as a physician in *Liebe ohne Illusion* (1955, *Love without Illusion*). One of the most popular actresses of the 1950s, Ruth Leuwerik, personified the postwar ideal of the competent but non-threatening modern woman, whether as the mayor of a small town in *Die ideale Frau* (1959, *The Ideal Woman*) or as the UFA star Renate Müller in *Liebling der Götter* (1960, *Darling of the Gods*). Her pragmatic approach to life, combined with traditional female qualities like modesty and reserve, made Leuwerik a favourite among female audiences. By contrast, Maria Schell's penchant for melodrama allowed her fans to indulge in an excessive emotionality and, perhaps less obviously, a submissive eroticism; like Knef, she enjoyed a brief international career.

Leuwerik and Schell were often cast opposite Dieter Borsche and O. W. Fischer, the two leading male actors of the decade; these famous couplings helped to address growing concerns about the imbalance of power between the sexes. Whereas the rigid Borsche personified an old-fashioned masculinity unsettled by new demands for flexibility, the charming Fischer displayed a narcissistic nervousness suggestive of more contemporary sensibilities. Borsche frequently appeared in medical dramas that used the virtue and integrity attributed to the medical profession to counterbalance the pervasive materialism of postwar society. The wave of so-called *Arztfilme* had started out shrouded in the religious symbolism that gave credence to Harald Braun's critically acclaimed *Nachtwache* (1949, *Night Watch*), a symbolically charged parable about death, faith, and the power of healing. However, religion soon gave way to the gendered aesthetics of sacrifice and guilt. Thus the dramas of life and death in two later Borsche films, *Dr. Holl* (1951, *Dr Holl*) and *Die grosse Versuchung* (1952, *The Great Temptation*), ended up confirming not Christian values, as the Catholic and Protestant Churches hoped, but the importance of male authority in the public and the private sphere.

The return to traditional gender roles during the 1950s began with the *Heimatfilm* and the successful pairing of young Sonja Ziemann with the much older Rudolf Prack. It continued in the stereotypical casting of Curd Jürgens as the brooding hero, Nadja Tiller as the seductress, Lieselotte Pulver as the ingenue, Lilli Palmer as the lady, and Paul Hubschmid as the ladies' man. Off-screen, film magazines such as *Film-Revue*, *Film und Frau*, and *Star-Revue* fuelled the rituals of fandom and the cult of celebrity. Stars and starlets provided an interested public with the necessary scandals (affairs, divorces, suicides), but the glamour of the old film world of the 1930s was missing from the annual society galas and charity events organised by the industry. It was left to a younger generation of actors and actresses to remind 1950s audiences of the explosive mixture of sexual liberation and social rebellion last seen in the films of the 1920s. Appearing in the popular youth films, sultry blond Karin Baal in *Die junge Sünderin* (1960, *The Young Sinner*) and sunny boy Hardy Krüger in *Zwei unter Millionen* (1961, *Two Among Millions*), projected an aggressive desire for self-advancement that not only revealed its petty-bourgeois or working-class origins but also acknowledged the relationship between sex, money, and power. Their rebellious spirit often led these new screen idols into the world of petty crime depicted for the first time in *Die Halbstarken* (1956, *Young Hooligans*), the cult film that established Horst Buchholz as the German James Dean. By contrast, the androgynous child women made fashionable by Sabine Sinjen in the cautionary tale of *Die Frühreifen* (1957, *Precocious Youth*) re-enacted the corruption of youthful innocence in safe middle-class surroundings.

The films about contemporary problems, the *Zeitfilme*, were surprisingly open about the crisis of the traditional family and the corrosive effect of female emancipation and youth rebellion. Beginning with the rubble films, contemporary dramas focused on urban lifestyles to articulate the tensions within postwar society in the heightened registers of emerging sexuality. From the female delinquents in *Mädchen hinter Gittern* (1949, *Girl Behind Bars*) and the criminal adventures of

Nachts auf den Strassen (1952, *At Night on the Road*) to the illicit world of drug addiction, prostitution, and homosexuality evoked by Harlan's *Liebe kann wie Gift sein* (1958, *Love Can Be Like Poison*) and *Anders als du und ich* (1957, *Different From You and Me*), the formulas always remained the same. On the surface, these films diagnosed the crisis of postwar society by focusing on the dysfunctional middle-class family and its neglected young sons and daughters. However, the voyeuristic fixation on individual transgressions prevented any critical insights into the complicated relationship between the personal and the political. Whereas the rubble films and chronicle films still articulated the antagonisms in German history and society through classic family conflicts (that is, fathers versus sons, husbands versus wives), the contemporary dramas translated all social relationships into purely emotional terms: desire, greed, pride, anger, and resentment. These dramatic and melodramatic treatments were distinguished from earlier approaches only through the protagonists' aggressive pursuit of self-interest against all social and economic constraints placed on the individual in postwar society.

Rejecting lurid sensationalism for more authentic forms of self-expression, the critical youth films derived their antagonistic qualities from the polemical opposition between German high culture and American popular culture. Their stories, characters, and settings introduced a rebellious young generation defined primarily by specific consumer objects – blue jeans, leather jackets, motor scooters – and jointed together by particular idioms, tastes, attitudes, and recreational activities. After *Die Halbstarken* with its young criminals, the team of Georg Tressler and Will Tremper expanded their study of sexual attitudes and social values to the young workers from *Endstation Liebe* (1958, *Last Stop Love*). With their black-and-white cinematography and preference for on-location shooting, the early youth films betrayed the strong influence of Hollywood classics such as *On the Waterfront* (1954) and *Rebel without a Cause* (1955). Yet what the films with James Dean or Marlon Brando celebrated as a desire for new experiences, for intensity as a value in itself, translated into the sensationalist, but also highly didactic German versions as a dangerous threat to bourgeois moral values and conventions. Consequently, the disruptive potential of youth had to be contained and transformed into a corrective in the social contract among the generations. Whereas the youth films from the East aimed at the characters' reintegration into the socialist collective, those from the West resolved their dramatic conflicts through a return to traditional gender roles and the redemptive experience of true love.

Three film scandals from the decade confirm the centrality of gender and sexuality to the unstable power relations that propelled the melodramatic imagination but also coloured the public perception of rebellious youth. The first case involved Willi Forst's *Die Sünderin* (1950, *The Woman Sinner*). Because it dealt with female nudity and extramarital sex, Catholic bishops called for a nationwide boycott. Yet behind the public outrage about the proverbial whore as saint, whose only desire, after all, was to be married, lurked a much more fundamental fear about the disappearance of all distinctions between the respectable middle-class woman and the emancipated woman with her own needs and ambitions. Tapping into such fears, *Das Mädchen Rosemarie* (1958, *A Woman Named Rosemarie*), with Nadja Tiller in the title role, used the unresolved murder case of the prostitute Rosemarie Nitribitt to show the link between woman's economic independence and sexual liberation. The hostile reactions to the film drew attention to the system of double standards unifying the simultaneously prudish and lascivious society of the Economic Miracle. In such an atmosphere, the nude female body also provided a projection screen for the new/old phantasmagoria of race that stood behind the surprise success of *Liane, das Mädchen aus dem Urwald* (1956, *Liane, the Girl from the Jungle*), a German version of the Tarzan story with blond newcomer Marion Michael.

The power of social convention and the need for individual conformity found foremost expression in the *Gesellschaftsfilm* (society drama) that, like the Weimar chamber play film, used intimate settings and internal conflicts to show the difficulty of reconciling private and public identities; hence the genre's appeal to older audiences. Confirming the diagnosis of an amnesiac postwar culture, these melo-dramatic stories frequently revolved around double or false identities and concerned dangerous secrets or resentments from the past. The required adjustment of these conflicting identities to new social and economic pressures usually took place in an upper-middle-class milieu reminiscent of the nineteenth-century literary salon. Entertained by the obligatory token artists and intellectuals, the old and new social elites came together in these luxurious settings to practise the rituals of postwar public life, including its rules of inclusion and exclusion. Unable to move beyond these artificial worlds, society dramas such as *Ein Herz spielt falsch* (1953, *A Cheating Heart*), *Teufel in Seide* (1955, *A Devil in Silk*), and *Herz ohne Gnade* (1958, *A Heart without Compassion*) disappeared from the screen in the late 1950s – only to be revived in the context of television, the preferred new form of entertainment for young families, working women, and senior citizens.

Consequently, it was left to the *Heimatfilm* to provide the kind of cross-cultural and cross-generation encounters necessary for rejuvenating genre cinema and formulating a postwar identity for the Federal Republic. The apolitical notion of homeland provided an alternative both to the compromised history of German nationalism and to the contested status of the two Germanys during the Cold War. Beginning with Hans Deppe's *Schwarzwaldmädel* (1950, *Black Forest Girl*) and *Grün ist die Heide* (1951, *Green Is the Heather*), two famous Ziemann–Prack vehicles, the *Heimatfilme* emerged as the commercially most successful product of postwar cinema and regularly attracted more than five million viewers. Many scholars have explained the genre's enormous popular appeal through its essentially conservative nature: the validation of the patriarchal family; the return to a normative morality; and the retreat to the harmonious living conditions found in typical landscapes such as the Bavarian Alps, the Rhine region, the Black Forest, and the Lüneburg Heath (Höfig 1973).

However, the *Heimatfilm* showed an acute awareness of contemporary problems in its preoccupation with incomplete, dysfunctional, and unconventional families; its emphasis on the trauma of displacement and the experience of loss; and its attention to the difficult question of legacies, whether in the form of a sudden inheritance or a particular way of life. Through the conflicts among the generations and through the stereotypical figure of the stranger, the genre provided a fictional framework for coming to terms with the loss of nation and for turning the Federal Republic into a new homeland. Significantly, many of the strangers arriving in the genre's idyllic villages and beautiful landscapes were refugees from East Prussia and Pomerania. The efforts to reunite displaced families or create new ones found paradigmatic expression in *Suchkind 312* (1955, *Looking for Child 312*), about a family separated during the war, but also extended to the unusual circumstances depicted in *Toxi* (1952) where an Afro-German child appears on the doorstep of the average German middle-class family. The unifying impulse behind these restorative narratives was the desire for a harmonious reconciliation of traditional social structures with contemporary economic and political realities. But even the emphasis on authentic experience often failed to distract from the signs of dramatic change brought about by mass displacement, social mobility, and economic growth. With these contradictory investments, the *Heimatfilm* provided a simultaneously regressive and progressive fantasy of belonging that enlisted the well-known iconography of *Heimat* in the creation of a new collective identity based on more contemporary visions of modernisation, industrialisation, and commercialisation.

The highly symbolic acts of reconciliation in the *Heimatfilm* often took place during folk festivals, religious holidays, and communal celebrations and involved musical forms ranging from the folk songs in *Am Brunnen vor dem Tore* (1952, *At the Well outside the Gate*) to the operatic arias in *Wenn der weisse Flieder wieder blüht* (1953, *When White Lilac Blooms Again*). Remakes like *Der Meineidbauer* (1956, *The Perjured Farmer*) and *Das Mädchen vom Moorhof* (1958, *The Girl from the Moorhof*) still articulated melodramatic conflicts in the gendered terms that invariably end up penalising the sexual woman. Yet the contemporary setting of *Die Landärztin* (1958, *The Female Country Doctor*) also allowed for the integration of a modern career woman into the traditional village community. Austrian successes such as *Der Förster vom Silberwald* (1954, *The Forester of the Silver Forest*) seemed to suggest that the homeland existed outside all national boundaries, but films such as *Die Fischerin vom Bodensee* (1956, *The Fisher Woman from Lake Constance*) confirmed the importance of nation in preserving regional cultures. Liebeneiner's two-part homage to Austria's most famous singing family, *Die Trapp-Familie* (1956, *The Trapp Family*) and *Die Trapp-Familie in Amerika* (1958, *The Trapp Family in America*), succeeded in reconciling both perspectives, the desire for preserving national traditions and the need to satisfy the demands of the marketplace (von Moltke 1996).

Frequently the *Heimatfilm* overlapped with the quintessential consumerist genre of the 1950s, the travel or vacation film. Basically an extension of the tourist industry, the travel film served as a promotional vehicle for new recreational activities and consumerist attitudes. While the Americans in these films returned to the Old Country to experience their own *Heidelberger Romanze* (1951,

Heidelberg Romance), the Germans ventured forth to conquer Europe, but this time as paying tourists. With programmatic titles such as *Ferien vom Ich* (1953, *Vacation from the Self*), the travel films showed their overworked audiences how to take a break from the pressures of economic growth and prosperity. Viewers revisited favourite destinations such as Italy, France, and Hungary and discovered new ones such as the idyllic Schleswig-Holstein of the popular *Die Mädels vom Immenhof* series (1955, *The Immenhof Girls*). While many travel narratives still involved the romantic search both for the authentic self and for the exoticised other, film-makers increasingly relied on the rituals of mass consumption to achieve the desired recuperative effects. Moreover, these imaginary journeys to foreign locations helped to prepare German audiences for dealing with different cultures and nationalities, including the growing numbers of Italian, Spanish, and Greek *Gastarbeiter* (guest workers).

The ever-popular combination of film, song, and dance achieved similar harmonising effects by incorporating new musical styles such as jazz and rock 'n' roll. Even old-fashioned film operettas in the tradition of *Die Czardasfürstin* (1951, *The Czardas Countess*) and *Im Weissen Rössl* (1952, *At the White Horse Inn*) and spectacular revue films in the style of *Nachts im grünen Kakadu* (1957, *Nights at the Green Cockatoo*) and *La Paloma* (1959) showed a remarkable resilience in adapting to contemporary tastes and sensibilities. Especially in the international music and dance numbers, postwar society encountered a desirable reflection of its own contradictory culture of material excess and bourgeois solidity. From night clubs and variety shows to resort hotels and country inns, the social milieu depicted in the revue films (and, to a lesser degree, the travel films as well) seemed deceptively open towards other cultures and nationalities. Under such conditions, music provided a convenient formula for appeasing widespread concerns about the effects of Americanisation, as demonstrated by the fraternisation comedy *Hallo Fräulein* (1949, *Hello, Miss!*) and its happy compromise between American big band music and German folk song. Hybrid forms such as the *Schlagerfilm* (hit song film) achieved similar effects through the revitalisation of indigenous popular traditions under the influence of American styles. Taking advantage of the industry's ties to the recording industry, films such as *Liebe, Tanz und 1000 Schlager* (1955, *Love, Dance, and One Thousand Hits*) featured such popular singers as Caterina Valente and Peter Alexander, or launched new talents such as Cornelia Froboess and Peter Kraus, the youthful stars of *Wenn die Conny mit dem Peter* (1958, *When Conny and Peter*). Modelled on the Elvis Presley films but also affected by the bohemian culture of coffee houses and jazz clubs, the *Schlagerfilme* addressed a younger, fashionable audience not interested in melodramatic society dramas or sentimental *Heimatfilme*.

A similarly productive tension between cultural tradition and innovation, social convention and experimentation, sustained a number of comedies that dealt specifically with the problems of everyday life in the society of the Economic Miracle. The cult of mass consumption, mass transportation, and mass tourism found a most telling expression in the petty-bourgeois comedies with Heinz

Erhardt. Beginning with *Drillinge an Bord* (1959, *Triplets on Board*), this popular comedian perfected his screen persona of the middle-aged, overweight bachelor or single parent who responds to the challenges of daily life in the Federal Republic with a mixture of gullibility, slyness, and eccentricity. From his driving lessons in *Natürlich die Autofahrer* (1959, *Of Course, the Motorists*) to his vacation choices in *Der letzte Fussgänger* (1960, *The Last Pedestrian*), Erhardt explored various idiosyncratic survival strategies that, since the rediscovery of the 1950s during the 1980s, have made him an ironic figure of conformist nonconformity.

From the beginning, cinema in the Federal Republic had to deal with two sets of problems: the institutional legacies of the Third Reich and the Allied Occupation, on the one side, and the continuing lack of interest in new aesthetic and critical perspectives among film-makers and their audiences, on the other. While successful with moviegoers on both sides of the border, West German productions proved unsuited for the export business, with the exception of Austria and Switzerland. Lacking the financial and technical resources of Hollywood, but also lacking the artistic ambitions of their Italian and French colleagues, most film-makers continued to work exclusively for the domestic market and its entertainment needs. But given the ageing of the cinema's core audience and the growing competition from television and other mass diversions, this market was shrinking rapidly by the late 1950s. To provide economic support, the federal government early on had introduced a number of subsidy programmes for the ailing film industry. These were financed in part by the so-called *Filmgroschen*, a levy on every box-office ticket sold. Between 1950 and 1955, the *Bundesbürgschaften* (Federally Guaranteed Bonds) ended up subsidising almost half of the annual production by absorbing the financial losses suffered by film companies. However, in favouring big-budget productions and discouraging difficult subject matter, these government bonds sometimes functioned like censorship. The all-powerful distributors often used federal guarantees to finance an entire line-up of films. Later subsidy programmes created additional tax loopholes especially attractive to individual investors who financed unprofitable projects as a way of lowering their tax burden. Even the introduction of the federally funded *Deutsche Filmpreis* (German Film Prize), which came with a generous monetary award, did not improve the artistic quality of films. Few German films were ever shown at international festivals, and the films chosen for export were generally regarded as low-brow entertainment by more discerning audiences in Austria, Switzerland, Italy, and France.

The first changes in the public awareness of film as an art form came with the film club movement, which was organised in the Verband der deutschen Filmclubs (Association of German Film Clubs). Modelled after similar organisations in France and Britain, local clubs reviewed the classics of world cinema – silents included – and learned about new film movements. Informed by an apolitical notion of film art, discussions in these film clubs remained for the most part limited to aesthetic questions. Greater awareness of the relationship between cinema and society prevailed among the media organisations of the Catholic and Protestant Churches. Both denominations paid close attention to films in order better to understand modern mass culture and to develop strategies for restoring Christian values to contemporary society. Despite their occasional diatribes against immoral films, publications such as the Catholic *Film-Dienst* and the *Evangelischer Filmbeobachter* were invaluable sources of information for the growing number of movie buffs and cinephiles.

The revival of film criticism and scholarship occurred much more slowly. Gunter Groll remained one of the few journalists to practise an informed film criticism; Walter Hagemann and his Institut für Publizistik (Institute for Journalism) proved instrumental in reclaiming a place for film studies within communication studies. The new art theatres joint forces in the Gilde deutscher Filmkunsttheater (Guild of German Film Art Theatres) to promote aesthetically innovative films and raise awareness of the artistic possibilities of the medium. In 1957, Enno Patalas and Wilfried Berghahn started the journal *Filmkritik* as an alternative to the aesthetic concerns of the daily *feuilleton*. Committed to ideology critique, these young critics proposed to practise film criticism as social criticism: that is to say, as a form of intervening into the oppressive conditions of postwar society. The writing in *Filmkritik* betrayed the strong influence of Kracauer, including his history of Weimar cinema and his theory of filmic realism. Supported by these initiatives, a lively film culture emerged gradually at small film festivals such as the one in Mannheim, which was limited to the cultural film, and the famous Oberhausen Short Film Festival, which provided a forum for experimental films. These initiatives saw themselves in opposition to the annual Berlin Film Festival, which was conceived in 1951 with the explicit goal of turning the divided city into a symbol of the Cold War and a showcase of Western consumerism (Fehrenbach 1995, 234–53).

Adding to these economic and artistic problems, the arrival of television brought an intense competition over audiences that further accelerated the decline of cinema culture during the late 1950s. The creation of the NDWR, a precursor of the North and West German radio stations, had established the institutional structures in 1948 for organising television like public broadcasting. The ARD (Arbeitsgemeinschaft der öffentlich-rechtlichen Rundfunkanstalten der Bundesrepublik Deutschland), an association of regional broadcasting channels, started airing the First Channel in 1954; a Second Channel, the ZDF (Zweites Deutsches Fernsehen), began to broadcast in 1963. Initially, film and television officials emphasised the differences between the media, with television regarded as a live medium committed, like radio, to providing information. The arrival of the *Fernsehspiel* (television play), including such prestige productions as the six-part war drama *Soweit die Füsse tragen* (1958, *As Far as the Feet Will Carry*), complicated this convenient division of labour. Film companies began to rent out their studios to television productions or function as co-producers of television plays. With the televising of old UFA classics, the new medium emerged as a serious competitor in the production and distribution of mass-produced fantasies. These practices deprived the motion-picture theatres of their most faithful audience, the older Germans raised on conventional genre films. Young people had already embraced

American popular culture (for example, music, sports, fashion) with a vengeance. Consequently, postwar culture segmented more and more into high culture, folk culture, mass culture, and various artistic and intellectual subcultures. While large segments of the middle class retreated to domesticity and family life, younger people took advantage of a wide range of recreational activities, including partying, dancing, cruising, and travelling. In such an atmosphere, going to the movies was perceived as irrelevant and outdated, and that despite the new slogan of the SPIO: 'Enjoy a few relaxing hours. Go to the movies!'

The often cited 'death of the movies' came when the market share of German films fell to less than 30 per cent in the early 1960s, down from 40 per cent in the mid-1950s. A series of bankruptcies accompanied this seemingly inevitable decline, including that of the Allianz distribution company in 1956 and of the distribution branch of the dismantled UFA concern in 1961. Some production companies responded by shooting films in Cinemascope and Technicolor and by taking on more sensationalist subject matter. Other producers promoted European co-productions as a cure-all, hoping that big-name international stars would guarantee some commercial success. And yet other companies took advantage of new multimedia possibilities by making films based on best-sellers by Johannes Mario Simmel or by adapting serial novels published in the television guide *Hör Zu* or the daily tabloid *Bild-Zeitung*. But even the most innovative or most calculated marketing strategies could not disguise the fact that the formulas of genre cinema had reached an impasse. In a highly symbolic gesture that acknowledged the profound crisis of German cinema, the Berlin Film Festival in 1961 refused to hand out any Federal Film Prizes to the releases from that year.

8 Lilian Harvey and Willy Fritsch in *Glückskinder*. Courtesy of BFI stills, Posters and Designs.

9 Zarah Leander and Paul Hörbiger in *Die grosse Liebe*. Courtesy of BFI stills, Posters and Designs.

10 Carl Raddatz and Kristina Söderbaum in *Immensee*. Courtesy of BFI stills, Posters and Designs.

11 Hans Albers and Hilde Hildebrand in *Grosse Freiheit Nr. 7*. Courtesy of BFI stills, Posters and Designs.

12 Hildegard Knef and Ernst Wilhelm Borchert in *Die Mörder sind unter uns.* Courtesy
of BFI stills, Posters and Designs.

13 Dieter Borsche and Renate Mannhardt in *Die grosse Versuchung.* Courtesy of BFI
stills, Posters and Designs.

14 Horst Buchholz in *Die Halbstarken*. Courtesy of BFI stills, Posters and Designs.

5

EAST GERMAN CINEMA
1961–89

The asymmetrical relationship that defined postwar cinema ended with two equally significant events: the building of the Berlin Wall on 13 August 1961 and the signing of the Oberhausen Manifesto by a group of West German film-makers on 28 February 1962 (see Chapter 6). The Wall enabled the German Democratic Republic to stabilise its political, social, and cultural identity in relation to the Federal Republic and the ideology of western capitalism. The insistence on a specific GDR identity allowed the SED regime to embrace traditional notions of Germanness while resisting the reform initiatives started in other East European countries. Introduced in 1963 under Walter Ulbricht, the New Economic System promised to decentralise production and make the state-owned companies more compatible (and competitive) with other market economies. The liberalisation of the criminal justice system and greater attention to the nation's youth during a decade of international protest movements and counter-cultural practices brought some improvements in the quality of life. Under such conditions, even some DEFA film-makers hoped – in vain – that the real and imaginary boundaries drawn by the Wall would create more favourable conditions for artistic expression.

The years between the building and collapse of the Wall gave rise to a distinct GDR culture that, even in the realm of popular culture, remained indebted to German high culture and the ideas of the enlightenment, and that, even under the programme of a new socialist culture, brought a reassessment of established local and regional traditions. The resultant mixture of cultural ambition and political compliance, social critique and aesthetic convention, defined DEFA cinema from the 1960s to the 1990s and made it an essential part of socialism, German style. The building of the Wall completed the bifurcation of postwar cinema into two national cinemas, with the one an industry driven by competitive market principles, the other a state-owned company involved in the building of a socialist society. The shared generic traditions and filmic styles and the competing ideological frameworks that had characterised postwar cinema as both separate and united gave way to the political divisions reflected in the FRG's hollow rhetoric of unification and the GDR's official doctrine of 'two Germanys'. Nonetheless, both cinemas continued to respond to the same political developments, social phenomena, and cultural sensibilities, and that despite the lack of a sustained critical engagement with each other's films.

DEFA, like UFA, has become part of film history. More than seven hundred feature films were produced during almost fifty years of DEFA, and a large number are now considered classics of German cinema. Since reunification, the studio's leading actors and directors have begun new careers in film and television. Yet the retrospectives, publications, and public debates of the last decade point to much lingering bitterness about the sacrifices, battles, and lost opportunities linked to the larger project of DEFA and, by extension, of socialist film culture (Hochmuth 1993, Poss 1997). Like Third Reich cinema, GDR cinema raises fundamental questions about the changing constellations among film, politics, and ideology in a state-controlled industry; the contribution of cinema to the construction of national identity; and the interchanges between cinema and other popular diversions and public spheres. And like their West German counterparts, East German films from the 1960s and 1970s draw attention to the continuities of German cinema, including the various attempts to develop further a national tradition of art cinema and make connections to international film movements (Meurer 2000, Trumpener 2001). Since 1989, East German and Anglo-American scholars have begun to address some of these issues through comprehensive overviews of DEFA's feature film and documentary production, case studies of individual genres and directors, and more critical perspectives on the history and historiography of GDR cinema (Schenk 1994, Jordan and Schenk 1996).

The New Waves and the Eleventh Plenary

The DEFA films after 1962 make sense only in the larger context of GDR culture and the cinema's privileged position in debates over national identity and socialist ideology. Largely absent from international markets, DEFA films addressed their audience specifically as a GDR audience who shared important values and beliefs and who, especially during the 1970s and 1980s, employed similar strategies of disengaging from official rhetoric and retreating into private life. As a result, the process of building a national cinema remained fraught with conflicts and contradictions in which film functioned at once as an instrument of political education and as a corroding influence on public morality and the socialist work ethic. Similarly, the identity of the socialist national state remained closely tied to German culture, especially literature and the legacy of the classics, but it also depended more and more on the existence of an indigenous popular culture accepted by the younger generation.

Film occupied a special place in this balancing act between affirmation and subversion. The more the party leadership relied on intellectual and artistic elites in maintaining the *status quo*, the more cultural practices functioned as an extension of, and substitute for, political debates. Under greater constraints than literature but under fewer pressures than television, films had to answer to the often contradictory demands of art, education, information, and entertainment. As a cultural and, by extension, political force and as an integral part of socialist society, the DEFA studio was subjected to considerable ideological pressures from the

Hauptverwaltung Film (HV Film) within the Ministry of Culture. At the same time, film-makers enjoyed optimal working conditions that included the luxury of time and money, vast studio resources, a high degree of professionalism, and, perhaps most problematically, the social and cultural significance accorded to their work by the party leadership. Some directors have spoken nostalgically about the atmosphere of artistic collaboration and critical debate, while others have pointed to the stifling effect of an insidious culture of consensus building, forceful persuasion, and brutal silencing (Poss 1997). The so-called Künstlerische Arbeitsgruppen (KAGs), which formed under names such as 'Johannisthal', 'Babelsberg', 'Berlin', and 'Roter Kreis', provided an alternative to the cult of individual creativity by approaching film-making as a collaborative process and collective experience. While enjoying some autonomy during the 1960s, these production groups formed around the integrative figure of a *Dramaturg* (dramaturge) – one of the many reasons why DEFA films resist conventional notions of film authorship.

This emphasis on consensus makes it also difficult to speak of film-making either as a typical struggle between artistic freedom and political oppression or as yet another historical example of opportunist, conformist, and subversive artists working under an oppressive regime. The close relationship between the studio and the SED as well as that between the studio's director and its most respected writers, actors, and directors was sustained by an ongoing dialogue that confirmed their work's contribution to the larger project of socialism. Under these conditions, censorship took place both through official bans and punitive measures and the more pernicious kind of self-censorship carried out in the name of political idealism and obligation to the party. After all, the most controversial film-makers were also the ones most fiercely committed to communism; and it was precisely their elevated position in GDR society that repeatedly required symbolic acts of self-criticism.

However, the question of ideological and aesthetic hegemony cannot be reduced to the conditions of production in a state-controlled industry. Exceptional events such as the Eleventh Plenary and the waves of emigration during the 1970s and 1980s have focused too much attention on individual films and film-makers, and distracted attention from popular cinema as a social and cultural experience with national and international dimensions (Glass 1999). From such a perspective, cinema in the GDR also included the reception of foreign films, especially the popular Hollywood films and the innovative films from Eastern Europe; the role of film criticism in establishing and challenging interpretative guidelines; the public debates about specific films among working collectives, party associations, and other less regimented communities; and the rituals of fandom inspired by a small number of cult films and famous stars. Adding to these diverse influences, the emergence of the New Waves in East and West was not just part of a politicisation of cinema attributable to the work of a few radical directors and their radicalised audiences. In fact, these movements responded also to the crisis of classical genre cinema and the diminished appeal of film as the dominant form of popular entertainment. The convergence of politics and aesthetics in the various avant-garde movements of the 1960s must therefore be considered a product of the intensified competition among modern mass media, including television, and the resultant division of audiences. This diversification – and, in the case of cinema, beginning marginalisation – made possible a greater emphasis on the creative and critical possibilities of films that, among other things, found expression in more experimental approaches to the medium. By the end of the decade, these formal challenges to established patterns of perception would only further separate a younger mass audience from more educated art-house viewers and make domestic productions at once more powerful and less influential – a contradiction responsible for the subsequent crises of film-making during the 1970s and acknowledged in many DEFA films' self-depreciating references to their lack of popular appeal.

During the 1960s, East German cinema occupied an unusual position between the New Waves in France, Italy, Great Britain, and the Federal Republic, on the one hand, and the New Waves in Poland, Hungary, Czechoslovakia, and the Soviet Union, on the other. Like their Western colleagues, film-makers studied the neo-realist films by Roberto Rossellini, Vittorio de Sica, and, later, Michelangelo Antonioni and Pier Paolo Pasolini, and they were familiar with the main representatives of the Nouvelle Vague, above all Alain Resnais and François Truffaut. They also took note of the British Free Cinema's renewed commitment to the documentary tradition and its foundation in social activism. The influence of these movements is most apparent in the growing awareness of film as a construction of, and an intervention into, social reality. This critical sensibility often took the form of a detached, cool modernist style characterised by graphic black-and-white cinematography, fragmented narrative structures, and an analytical, self-reflective approach to the filmic medium. As part of these patterns of influence, Konrad Wolf's adaptation of Christa Wolf's famous novel *Der geteilte Himmel* (1964, *The Divided Heaven*) acknowledges the strong influence of Resnais's *Hiroshima mon amour* (1959) and confirms the director's close familiarity with the West European literary and filmic avant-gardes (Byg 1991). Traditionally a strong presence in the GDR, Soviet films, especially those made after the XX Party Congress in 1956, explored alternatives to the official realist styles; here the work of Mikhail Romm, Mikhail Kalatosov, and, most controversially, Andrei Tarkovsky proved especially influential. Again, to mention only one example, Kalatosov's *The Cranes Are Flying* (1957) has been cited as an inspiration for the expressionist imagery in Frank Beyer's *Fünf Patronenhülsen* (1960, *Five Cartridges*). Perhaps even more relevant to the double articulation of aesthetic and political modernism as both a critique of conventional genre cinema and official cultural politics were the films by a younger generation of Polish and Czech film-makers, including Andrzej Wajda and Milos Forman, whose decentred perspectives on socialism Soviet-style opened up possibilities for DEFA film-makers in thinking about their own work.

But most importantly, the film-makers of the 1960s received creative impulses from developments in contemporary literature. Literature had always played a central role in defining GDR culture, beginning with the First Bitterfeld Conference in 1959, which had insisted that the critique of productivism should include closer attention to the problems of everyday life. Instrumental, then, in introducing modernist elements into the dominant realist paradigm, writers moved tentatively towards literary modernism at the Second Bitterfeld Conference in 1964. Sharing a strong commitment to literature with both the political leadership and the cultural establishment, DEFA encouraged close working relationships between screen-writers and directors, thereby fostering Wolfgang Kohlhaase's work with Gerhard Klein and, later, Konrad Wolf; Helga Schütz's collaboration with Egon Günther; and Ulrich Plenzdorf's screenplays for Hermann Zschoche, Frank Beyer, and Heiner Carow, among others. Some of the most productive contributions during the 1960s came from younger writers such as Christa Wolf and Günter Kunert, who introduced avant-garde elements into their literary writings in an effort to revive what they saw as an increasingly ossified culture of official socialism. In so doing, these writers contributed to a particular quality in GDR cinema and culture that, in the tradition of Bertolt Brecht, involved utilising aesthetic practices for social and political analysis.

Thus positioned between aesthetic and political modernism, DEFA film-makers applied these new sensibilities to what, to this day, remains their most important contribution to German cinema: the anti-fascist films. In one of the most provoca-tive reflections on the aesthetics of fascism, Gerhard Klein in *Der Fall Gleiwitz* (1961, *The Gleiwitz Incident*) reconstructed the SS's staged attack on a radio station on the German–Polish border, which had served to justify the German invasion of Poland in 1939. Shot in a cool, documentary style with strong experimental tendencies, the film at the time faced accusations of objectivism because of its deliberate detachment from the physiognomy of power and the rituals of violence. Even more remarkable, the two-part *Die gefrorenen Blitze* (1967, *The Frozen Flashes*) by Janoc Veiczi presented the Third Reich's secret military experiments with rocket technology through a daring combination of narrative and pseudo-documentary elements, including archival footage and still photography. Analytical and detached in tone, his representation of the German war effort avoided the usual firework of drama and suspense. Veiczi had applied the same formalist principles to an earlier political thriller, titled *For Eyes Only* (1962). Its story about a GDR agent working under cover at the CIA profited from the myths surrounding Markus Wolf, then the head of East German counter-intelligence.

The modernist style provided film-makers with an analytical framework for challenging established views on the origins of fascism, the legacies of anti-fascism, and the impact of recent political events on the self-understanding of the GDR as both the 'real' and the 'other' Germany. Thus Joachim Kunert's *Die Abenteuer des Werner Holt* (1965, *The Adventures of Werner Holt*), reconstructed the wartime disillusionment of several young middle-class men through a fragmented narrative structure that includes flashbacks and stream-of-consciousness. Other directors introduced personal perspectives to examine the relationship between storytelling and history. On the one hand, Wolf's autobiographical *Ich war neunzehn* (1968, *I Was Nineteen*), about his experiences as a German-born soldier in the Soviet Army, presented the divided identities associated with nation and *Heimat* and explored their implications for the anti-fascist master-narrative. On the other hand,

Carow in *Die Russen kommen* (1968/87, *The Russians Are Coming*), which was banned, used a young boy's tragic death in the last days of the war to draw attention to the subjective dimension of political events, including a character's spontaneous or unconscious reactions to threatening situations. While Carow's highly subjective approach avoided the social typisation usually found in Maetzig and Dudow, it lacked the additional dimension of personal experience that distinguished Wolf's contribution to the discourse of anti-fascism. Moreover, the differences between Wolf and Carow, one of the few promising directors to emerge during the 1970s, revealed the ideological divide that had opened up between the founding generation and the first generation born in the GDR.

The spirit of experimentation and critical examination during the early 1960s even extended to the basic philosophical principles that had defined GDR identity from the reconstruction in the late 1940s through the 'freezes' and 'thaws' of the 1950s. Accordingly, some of the more influential films, including Günther Rücker's *Die besten Jahre* (1965, *The Best Years*), began to reconsider fundamental ideological positions about the socialist work ethic, the primacy of the collective, and the belief in technological and social progress. In *Der Frühling braucht Zeit* (1965, *Spring Needs Time*), Günther Stahnke presented the disagreements between an apolitical engineer and an ambitious manager over technical problems at a power plant through highly stylised elements evocative of the modern uncanny; these elements only sharpened the underlying critique of the New Economic System and its fixation on production quotas. The interest in modernist sensibilities as a potentially subversive force also extended to the representation of love and marriage and the oppressive effect of social institutions on personal relations. Here Günther's *Lots Weib* (1965, *Lot's Wife*), about a woman who forces a divorce from her status-conscious husband by committing petty theft, offered a compelling argument for a woman's right to personal happiness, and it did so precisely through its almost clinical detachment from the dramatic events.

All of these developments culminated in the Eleventh Plenary of the Central Committee of the SED in December of 1965. Planned as a forum on economic policies, the Plenary banned an entire year's production of twelve films that had just been released or were still in production. Studio director Jochen Mückenberger was dismissed, and many careers interrupted or destroyed. In the discussions, the Plenary focused on *Denk bloss nicht, dass ich heule* (*Just Don't Think that I Am Crying*) and *Das Kaninchen bin ich* (*I am the Rabbit*); hence the frequent reference in the scholarship to the so-called *Kaninchenfilme* (rabbit films). The main charges against these films can be summarised as 'scepticism', 'nihilism', 'relativism', and 'subjectivism'. The directors' failure or unwillingness to develop a dialectical conception of reality, the argument went, had resulted in stories, images, and, perhaps most importantly, dispositions and attitudes that were irrelevant, if not detrimental, to the self-definition of GDR society. Some scholars have ascribed far more complex reasons for this banning of films – among them, the party's desire to distract from the failures of the New Economic System and to put an end to the dangerous process of liberalisation. There is no doubt that the events surrounding the Plenary were less a demonstration of political power than a manifestation of crisis in leadership. Nonetheless, the Eleventh Plenary destroyed any remaining illusions about the beneficial effects of the Wall and forced film-makers to retreat to uncontroversial topics and conventional treatments (Mückenberger 1990, Dalichow in Hoff and Wiedemann 1992, 16–43).

The famous *Regalfilme* (shelved films), as the *Kaninchenfilme* are also called, included a rather diverse group defined less by some political agenda than by their shared historical fate. In Maetzig's *Das Kaninchen bin ich*, the love story between a young woman and the married judge who had earlier convicted her dissident brother gives rise to a sharp critique of the political justice system and the opportunism of the party elites. *Karla* by Zschoche uses a young idealistic female teacher to question authoritarian teaching methods. The film's diagnosis of a disconnection between the first and the second generation of GDR citizens concludes with a plea for reconciliation that still assumes some basic agreement about the utopian project of socialism. Similar tendencies can be found in three other *Regalfilme* that focus on younger protagonists: a high-school student who rails against the hypocrisy of adult society in Frank Vogel's *Denk bloss nicht, dass ich heule*; a young boy with a magical flashlight equipped to identify liars in Günther's *Wenn du gross bist, lieber Adam* (*When You Are Grown Up, Dear Adam*); and the rebellious adolescents in *Berlin um die Ecke* (*Berlin around the Corner*), another Berlin film by the well-known team of Klein and Kohlhaase. In a marked departure from their earlier Berlin films, both refused to reduce the central conflict to the problems of an urban youth seduced by American mass culture. Instead, the film-makers focused on the growing sense of alienation between those who lived through reconstruction and those who, born after 1945, no longer shared many unquestioned assumptions and beliefs. In the formally most radical film among the *Regalfilme*, *Jahrgang 45* (*Born in 1945*), Jürgen Böttcher focused on the problems of a young couple from Berlin's Prenzlauer Berg neighbourhood to diagnose the complete breakdown of narrative continuity, critical dialogue and the ideological system.

The aesthetic and political after-effects of the Eleventh Plenary were noticeable immediately, including in the filmic representation of the German division. . . . *und deine Liebe auch* (1962, . . . *And Your Love, Too*) and the critically acclaimed *Der geteilte Himmel* in 1964 had been the first films to thematise the effects of this division on personal relationships, one through a love triangle set in the divided capital, the other through a couple's painful personal and political separation. Such psychological treatments soon gave way to the hyperbole of espionage thrillers such as *Reserviert für den Tod* (1963, *Reserved for Death*) and the didacticism of *Geschichten jener Nacht* (1967, *Stories of That Night*), an omnibus film with several episodes about exemplary citizens who made the right choice in the night of 12/13 August 1961. Many of these films articulated the power imbalance between East and West Germany in gendered terms, with the ambitious young men leaving for better economic and professional opportunities in the West and with the more idealistic women confirming their commitment to the socialist collective.

The Eleventh Plenary had a devastating effect on filmic practices. The bans diminished the role of cinema as a repository of the grand narratives of socialism and curtailed its possibilities in offering alternative stories and interpretations. It became clear after 1965 that even the most basic assumptions about GDR history, society, and culture and, more specifically, the relationship between social reality and filmic representation, could be subject to controversy. After all, critics and functionaries might ask, did DEFA films still allow for any positive engagement with Marxist theory and practice? Were film-makers offering an analysis of the existing social conditions or expressing their desire for radical change? Were the modernist forms a result of, or a reaction against, the loss of social consensus? Such questions not only revealed the deep ideological schism between film-makers and party leadership. The diagnosis of a crisis also responded, and contributed, to the further segmentation of film audiences into a large and predominantly young audience interested primarily in conventional entertainment; a smaller middle-class audience firmly committed to DEFA's original political mission; and an even smaller group of artists, intellectuals, and cinephiles fascinated by and supportive of the international New Waves. As a consequence, the conformist political elites and the nonconformist artistic and intellectual groups continued to clash over the appropriate contribution of the DEFA studio to definitions of national identity. Meanwhile, the majority of East German audiences satisfied their entertainment needs through Hollywood films, and, increasingly, through television.

The events surrounding the Eleventh Plenary profoundly affected the career of the only new director to emerge during the 1960s, Frank Beyer. Working within the confines of classical narrative cinema and taking advantage of its emotional powers, Beyer repeatedly pushed the limits of verisimilitude to create new filmic realities through dream sequences, fairy-tale elements, visual symbolism, and so forth (Schenk 1995a). Anti-fascism remained a central concern in his work, but more and more in the form of a historical (rather than biographical) investigation and a critical reflection on the relevance of history to the present. Accordingly, the setting of the Spanish Civil War in *Fünf Patronenhülsen* allowed him to reflect on the possibility of resistance and the importance of solidarity. In *Königskinder* (1962, *Royal Children*), Beyer introduced the romantic motif of unrequited love to examine the different personal and political choices of three Berlin working-class children from the 1920s to the 1940s. In *Karbid und Sauerampfer* (1963, *Carbide and Sorrel*), Beyer relied on picaresque elements to uncover the ideological divisions of the Cold War through the adventures of a Don Quixote figure, played by Erwin Geschonnek, who transports barrels of carbide through the devastated landscapes of postwar Germany. The director also thematised the relationship between victims and victimisers in a highly acclaimed adaptation of the Bruno Apitz novel *Nackt unter Wölfen* (1963, *Naked among Wolves*), the first postwar film set in a concentration camp. Finally, Beyer's most famous film, *Spur der Steine* (1966/89, *Trace of Stones*), which was banned immediately after its release, focused on the organisational problems at a large construction site and, by extension, the difficulties of reconciling political principles with the realities of life and work under socialism. The film's modernist investigation of subjectivity, reality, and storytelling has secured its status as one of the classics of DEFA cinema.

The Eleventh Plenary stifled the artistic and political momentum at DEFA, but the resulting prohibitions were unable to stop the dissemination of lifestyle modernism into more conventional forms. This influence was most noticeable in designs and fashions indebted to pop culture and inspired by the counterculture of the 1970s. But the new sensibility also expressed itself in the looks, movements, and mannerisms of many younger actors. This more pervasive, but also less provocative modernisation of cinema focused on the various manifestations of the new in everyday life, from consumer trends and musical tastes to summer vacations and romantic arrangements. The resultant shift from public to private life opened up the self-representations of GDR society to lifestyle choices separate from, if not opposed to, the official emphasis on the socialist collective. Defending the need of citizens to take a break from the ubiquitous production quotas, *Das verhexte Fischerdorf* (1962, *The Hexed Fishing Village*), depicted the collective at love and play on the Baltic Coast. Traditional gender roles and the institution of marriage saw a revival in hybrid forms such as the vacation-revue films *Reise ins Ehebett* (1966, *Journey into the Conjugal Bed*) and *Hochzeitsnacht im Regen* (1967, *Wedding Night in the Rain*). Even the persistence of petty-bourgeois attitudes found humorous acknowledgement in the popular Rolf Herricht comedies *Geliebte weisse Maus* (1964, *Beloved White Mouse*) and *Der Reserveheld* (1965, *The Hero in the Army Reserve*) that addressed problems of everyday life through the familiar figure of the 'little man'. And the cult film *Heisser Sommer* (1967, *A Hot Summer*), which featured popular singers Chris Doerk and Frank Schöbel, demonstrated how young comrades could remain committed to socialist ideals while enjoying American-style pop tunes, fashions, and diversions. To what degree these contemporary comedies offered little more than conciliatory fantasies can be seen in the more controversial *Die Glatzkopfbande* (1963, *The Skin Head Gang*), which presented the dark side of a counterculture drawn to rock 'n' roll, motorcycles, and gratuitous violence.

These examples confirm that DEFA was capable of producing entertaining genre films with contemporary relevance. At least in the form of lifestyle choices, the modernist sensibilities of the 1960s had become an integral part of the public sphere. However, even the better contributions limited their reflections on GDR society to familiar milieus and ordinary situations. To compensate for the palpable sense of confinement after 1962, DEFA briefly experimented with crime capers such as *Der Dieb von San Marengo* (1963, *The Thief of San Marengo*) that, like similar French, Italian, and West German productions, offered colourful glimpses into the kind of luxurious settings, cosmopolitan attitudes, enticing situations, and eccentric personalities associated with the Côte d'Azur. The same compensatory function can be attributed to the costume films that, despite the studio's reputation for historical accuracy, more often than not failed to provide audiences with some much-needed action, adventure, and visual spectacle. Using the robber romances of Kurt Hoffmann and the French cloak-and-dagger films with Gérard Philipe as an inspiration, some directors gave new relevance to these historical settings by adding some anti-feudal arguments and revolutionary confrontations. But even the casting of audience favourite Manfred Krug in a folksy adaptation of Kleist's *Der zerbrochene Krug, Jungfer, sie gefällt mir* (1962, *Young Maiden, You Strike My Fancy*), and a populist version of the events surrounding the Congress of Vienna in *Hauptmann Florian von der Mühle* (1968, *Captain Florian von der Mühle*), the first DEFA film shot in the 70 mm format, could not hide the shortcomings of an old-fashioned genre caught between low-culture pleasures and high-culture pretensions. Perhaps it was precisely the anachronistic nature of the period film that made the quaint *Die Heiden von Kummerow* (1967, *The Heathens of Kummerow*) so well-suited as the first East–West co-production.

The conflicting demands of popular entertainment and social relevance found a perfect compromise in the *Indianerfilme* (Indian films) with Yugoslavian actor Goiko Mitic. The film's appearance after the Eleventh Plenary confirms their socio-psychological function as an escape from political problems and a displacement of social fantasies on to the threatened culture of the American Indians. The Indian films appealed to audiences through their dreams of open space, free movement, and individual and collective heroism – qualities missing from most DEFA films with a contemporary setting. In redefining the typical conflicts of the traditional Western, these productions profited from the long-standing German fascination with the Wild West, especially among boys and young men reared on Karl May novels. Clearly influenced by the success of retro-Westerns such as *The Magnificent Seven* (1960) and so-called spaghetti westerns such as *A Fistful of Dollars* (1964), the DEFA films tried to offer an alternative to the West German *Winnetou* series by emphasising the perspective of the Indians and showing their struggle against imperialist aggression. *Die Söhne der grossen Bärin* (1966, *The Sons of the Great She Bear*), which tells the story of the proud and defiant Dakota nation, set the series into motion. That film was followed by *Chingachgook, die grosse Schlange* (1967, *Chingachgook, the Great Snake*) and all the other Indian films that, every summer season, regularly attracted more than two million viewers: *Die Spur des Falken* (*The Falcon's Trail*) in 1968, *Weisse Wölfe* (*White Wolves*) in 1969, *Tödlicher Irrtum* (*Deadly Error*) in 1970, *Osceola* in 1971, and *Tecumseh* in 1972. The Indian films contained many explicit and implicit references to the GDR's own struggles to preserve the traditions of working-class culture and resist the temptations of Western capitalism. Yet whereas the early films celebrated the Indians as figures of resistance, later contributions reflected on their oppression, an indication perhaps of the crisis of socialism in the early 1970s (Hahn 1995, Gemünden 1998).

Aside from the Indian films that led the studio's annual summer line-up, only three political prestige productions attracted more than two million viewers during the 1960s, namely *Die Abenteuer des Werner Holt* in 1965, *Ich war neunzehn* in 1968, and, finally in 1970, the German–Soviet co-production *Unterwegs zu Lenin* (*On the way to Lenin*), which was commissioned in commemoration of the centennial of Lenin's birth. With most hopes and expectations for an artistically and politically relevant cinema squelched, the studio from then on focused primarily on its younger audience and developed strategies aimed specifically at their interests and needs. For GDR youth, moviegoing offered an alternative to other group-oriented activities such as the obligatory FDJ (Freie deutsche Jugend) events, and the films provided pleasures ignored by official political culture and established high culture. The large percentage of adolescents and young adults in the motion-picture theatres caused some concern among studio and party officials, as these audiences represented a potential source, or indication, of growing dissent. Obviously, the notion of a national cinema that addressed all viewers as a collective could no longer be upheld, neither in social nor aesthetic terms. Later film-sociological studies would confirm this troubling trend towards audience segmentation by explaining the film-makers' preference for simple, linear narratives, clear moral oppositions, and powerful patterns of identifications through the cinema's growing domination by young audiences (Bisky and Wiedemann 1985).

Contributing further to the crisis of cinema, television began to pose a serious threat to the relationship between DEFA and its most faithful audiences. During the early 1960s, every citizen still went to the movies fourteen times a year; by the early 1980s, that number would fall to five times a year. Operating since 1952 under the direct control of the Central Committee, the Deutsche Fernsehfunk (DFF) had always been more hierarchical in its organisation but, for that reason, also more pragmatic in its programming decisions. In the late 1960s, DEFA began to experiment with more creative arrangements among film, television, broad-casting, and the recording industry. The studio's limited output made such arrangements both desirable and necessary. Actors and directors participated regularly in co-productions between DEFA and GDR Television, including ambitious multi-part television plays and highly publicised television premieres of big-budget feature films. Television also provided an important showcase for DEFA films and, sometimes, a refuge for ostracised directors. Contributing to the blurring of boundaries between film and television, the First Channel and, after 1969, Second Channel (then renamed DDR 1 and DDR 2) regularly showed popular successes from Italy and France, as well as film classics from other socialist countries. The demand for entertainment even extended to the old UFA films shown in nostalgia shows such as *Willi Schwabes Rumpelkammer* (*Junk Room*). Such diversity in programming helped to create a receptive and more diverse audience for DEFA films as well, an audience that included older citizens, mothers with young children, and viewers in remote rural areas. Moreover, these pragmatic arrangements responded to the growing competition from West German television and, most specifically, the endless stream of Hollywood films broadcast across the border and viewed regularly by many citizens, despite official prohibitions.

The Indian films and their close identification with the actor Goiko Mitic draw attention to the function of actors and actresses in East German cinema (Schenk 1995b). From the beginning, DEFA had rejected the profit-driven, market-based star system and its cult of celebrities. The studio found an alternative in topic-based approaches that favoured character actors with a background in the theatre and a talent for ensemble acting. Film-makers occasionally used the identification

129

of particular actors with particular genres to create recognisable screen personas, as in the case of comedian Rolf Herricht. But for the most part, directors paid little attention to the usual requirements of female beauty and sex appeal and focused instead on developing a particular physiognomy of class personified since the 1950s by Erwin Geschonnek in his signature roles as a resistance fighter and proletarian hero. Since then, DEFA actors and actresses were identified with a distinct physiognomy of class that found expression in particular body types, facial features, gestural codes, and individual mannerisms. Significantly, many actors looked unmistakably German and, with that elusive quality, resembled either the UFA stars of the Third Reich or the anti-stars of the New German Cinema. These similarities were particularly pronounced in older male actors such as Geschonnek, with his larger-than-life masculinity reminiscent of Heinrich George. At the same time, the more contemporary ideal of sensitive masculinity found expression in the comparable screen personas of East German Armin Mueller-Stahl and West German Bruno Ganz. The image of female beauty and eroticism projected by East German Angelika Domröse closely resembled that of West German Hanna Schygulla. Even the transition in DEFA productions from the cool modernist aesthetics of the 1960s to the intense personal explorations of the 1970s can be described through a noticeable change in the look of ideal-typical masculinity and femininity. Whereas the monochrome images of the 1960s remain associated with more reserved male actors such as the brooding Mueller-Stahl or the quiet Eberhard Esche, the colourful mise-en-scènes of everyday life evoked by the films of the 1970s cannot be separated from the intense performances by Jutta Hoffmann and Renate Krössner who combined female strength and independence with vulnerability and spontaneity.

Despite its opposition to the star system, DEFA produced one genuine screen idol: Manfred Krug. With his large frame, open face, and physical acting style, Krug came to represent the vitality and sensuality of the new society, qualities that made him a perennial favourite with male and female audiences. Repeatedly voted the most popular DEFA actor, Krug enjoyed impressive financial and social privileges. His first appearance in Ralf Kirsten's *Auf der Sonnenseite* (1962, *On the Sunny Side*), a love story between a steel welder-turned-actor and a female project manager, was partly autobiographical. Already his next role in *Beschreibung eines Sommers* (1963, *Description of a Summer*), about a similar romantic entanglement between an engineer and a party secretary working on a construction site, took advantage of the actor's appealing combination of brazenness and shyness, strength and tenderness, masculine aggression and maternal warmth. Krug's most famous role in *Spur der Steine* offered yet another contribution to the modern physiognomy of working-class masculinity, but this time in the heightened terms of unrequited love. Krug left the GDR in 1977 after the Biermann affair and pursued a successful career in West German film and television. Beyer's *Das Versteck* (1978, *The Hideaway*), a delightful comedy about a man hiding at his ex-wife's apartment under the pretence of being a fugitive from the law, turned out to be his last DEFA film.

Through their status as public figures, actors and actresses often functioned as telling indicators on the continuing back and forth between liberalisation and hard-line dogmatism that by the mid-1970s culminated in the imprisonment and expatriation of dissent thinker Rudolf Bahro and continued later with the so-called Biermann affair of 1976. Responding to the expatriation of Wolf Biermann, the popular singer, Eva-Maria Hagen and Armin Mueller-Stahl, as well as Jutta Hoffmann and Angelika Domröse, all left for the Federal Republic. Some, like author Thomas Brasch, would later reflect on their GDR experiences in West German productions like *Engel aus Eisen* (1981, *Angels of Iron*), a melancholy period piece about Berlin during the immediate postwar years. Others, like Mueller-Stahl, turned their performative otherness into an internationally recognisable trademark. The West German mass media sometimes exploited these emigration waves for their own political purposes. Meanwhile the more progressive regional television stations, or Third Channels, began to show DEFA films on a regular basis. After 1975, this gradual opening towards the East also made possible the occasional inclusion of a DEFA film in the main competition of the Berlin Film Festival.

Contributing to the building of an East German cinema, the 1960s and 1970s saw considerable improvements in the institutional support structures that had been established during the 1950s. Founded in 1955, the Staatliche Filmarchiv der DDR (State Film Archives of the GDR) continued to be responsible for the preservation and cataloguing of all German films and film-related materials. Its public theatre in the centre of Berlin, the Camera, functioned as an important showcase for new domestic and foreign releases. The training facilities in Potsdam-Babelsberg, established in 1954, were expanded and renamed in 1969 as the Hochschule für Film und Fernsehen der DDR 'Konrad Wolf'. Since the 1950s, the International Leipzig Festival for Documentary and Animated Film provided an important showcase for other film-producing nations, especially lesser known Third World cinemas. Like the Oberhausen Short Film Festival in the West, the Leipzig Festival during the 1960s often functioned as a forum for dissenting voices and sensibilities. For that reason, the organisers frequently experienced interference by the party leadership.

A new tradition of film criticism developed very slowly in the GDR and remained limited to mass dailies such as *Neues Deutschland*, popular magazines such as *Filmspiegel*, and more scholarly publications such as the *Deutsche Filmkunst* (1953–63); influential critics included Rolf Richter and Fred Gehler. The *Beiträge zur Film- und Fernsehwissenschaft* (formerly *Filmwissenschaftliche Mitteilungen and Filmwissenschaftliche Beiträge*) emerged as the main publication for film critics and scholars. The *Beiträge* produced an infamous suppressed issue in 1965 that confirmed the close familiarity of DEFA directors with the international New Waves. From the 1970s to the 1980s, the most influential journal was *Film und Fernsehen*, which published sophisticated reviews, of foreign as well as domestic films, and initiated critical debates on controversial topics, including the persistent problem of audience appeal (Stoff in Allan and Sanford 1999, 43–57). However, the pressure on film criticism and scholarship to participate in the advancement of socialist culture and its changing strategies of self-legitimisation prevented more extensive theoretical and historical investigations (Becker 1999).

The 1970s: the discovery of everyday life

Following the disillusionment of the Eleventh Plenary, the 1970s ushered in a period of relative normalisation. At DEFA, production increased from approximately twenty to twenty-five feature films in the 1960s to more than fifty feature films during the 1970s. A number of factors contributed to this process, beginning with the ascendancy of Erich Honecker as the new party leader; growing international recognition of the GDR through diplomatic relations with other countries and membership in the United Nations; and more relaxed relationships between the two Germanys after the official adaptation of the doctrine of the two German states. These developments had a profound influence on definitions of national identity and the place of socialism in cultural practices. In 1971, the Eighth Party Congress determined that the GDR was already a fully developed socialist society; hence, there would be no more taboos on artistic expression. Now film-makers were encouraged to engage with all socially relevant subject matter, including the kind of ordinary and typical problems widespread even in non-antagonistic class societies. Finally, the dogma of socialist realism, with its insistence on strong heroes and positive messages, could be replaced by the simultaneously more simple and more complicated stories of everyday life. Sustained by such developments, the relative degree of liberalisation reached during the Honecker period allowed artists and intellectuals to explore individual differences, personal perspectives, and alternative forms of consciousness. Yet these creative possibilities could be realised only within the clearly defined demarcations of public versus private, personal versus political, that have since been dismissed as *Scheinöffentlichkeiten* (illusory public spheres).

The situation at DEFA improved considerably after two phenomenal successes, *Der Mann, der nach der Oma kam* (1972, *The Man Who Came after Grandma*) and *Die Legende von Paul und Paula* (1973, *The Legend of Paul and Paula*). These new comedies and dramas about personal problems, especially those related to love, marriage, family, and the workplace, brought a more diversified older audience back to the theatres. Even more importantly, the films' close attention to everyday life opened up a space for the representation of individual desires, attitudes, and beliefs previously ignored in the insistence on typical situations and the search for positive solutions. Many of these films feature protagonists who stubbornly pursue their personal dreams against a conformist society intent on suppressing individual difference. The fact that their struggles are individual ones suggests a fundamental shift in a national cinema still committed to the ideals of collectivism. Moreover, the provocative ways in which the freethinkers, eccentrics, nonconformists, and individualists in these films expose the existing contradictions in society, especially in male–female relations, point to a growing awareness both of the limits of reason and rationality and of the elusiveness of desire. In the most positive terms, this

132

discovery of the personal brought a long-overdue examination and validation of those aspects of human existence that resist the determinations of class society and the history of class struggle. Yet seen in more negative terms, the retreat from politics in the traditional sense also meant a continuing marginalisation of cinema as part of the socialist public sphere.

The fundamental shift in the presentation of contemporary narratives from the notion of 'present time' (*Gegenwart*) to that of 'everyday life' (*Alltag*) has been described as a critique of the strict division between the personal and the political in Marxist ideology. Rebelling against that tradition, film-makers turned to the quotidian and the ephemeral to explore alternatives to the teleological models of history and narrative that, until that point, had constituted the present in relation to the past and the future (Leonhardt 1989, Feinstein 1995). With these implications, the so-called *Alltagsfilme* (contemporary dramas or films about everyday life) offered much more than a withdrawal to private life; they offered a radically different model of public life and social reality based on individual experiences and personal desires. Of course, behind many of the stories loomed the implicit question: to what degree were the films tacitly acknowledging socialist culture's failure to provide a unified national identity and coherent master-narrative for the German Democratic Republic?

The emergence of more films about everyday life – and an everyday life unmistakably marked by the social and economic structures introduced by socialism – coincided with the arrival of a new generation of film-makers who have often been identified with two very different approaches to the filmic medium. Committed to the ideals of 'documentary realism', the one group remained indebted to the Soviet films from the 1920s and the Italian neo-realists of the 1950s. Directors Lothar Warneke and Roland Gräf, the main representatives, often filmed on location, used lay actors, and preferred episodic narratives and a detached camera style. The other group, which included Heiner Carow, favoured a more dramatic approach and presented their often controversial subject matter through conventional narrative structures meant to solicit intense reactions. The difference between ambitious art films with limited appeal and a popular cinema of strong emotions was repeatedly thematised by contemporary reviewers who either denounced the second group of directors for their lack of formal innovation or attacked the first one for their lack of narrative talent.

Documentary realism prevailed in several films about the problems of the new managerial class, a theme that in itself marked a radical departure from the early DEFA films about the labour of reconstruction carried out by the nation's proverbial workers and peasants. More specifically, these social dramas offered a critique of the cult of productivity associated with socialist realism. The renewed interest in documentary styles developed partly in response to the enormously popular *Zeit zu leben* (1969, *Time to Live*), whose portrayal of a dying man's selfless efforts to turn a troubled factory into a competitive international concern owed much to idealised representations from the 1950s. Many reviewers rejected the film as socialist kitsch, and several film-makers set out to develop more differentiated approaches. Accordingly, *Im Spannungsfeld* (1970, *In the Area of Conflict*) focused on the different perspectives of workers and technocrats to examine the impact of technological progress on social relationships. Also set in the nationalised industries, *Netzwerk* (1970, *Network*) exposed the inevitable conflict between the fulfilment of production goals and the importance of technological innovation without offering any easy answers. And in *Bankett für Achilles* (1975, *A Banquet for Achilles*), which shows the barren industrial landscape near Bitterfeld, Gräf used the retirement of a model worker and the resultant change of generations to ask serious questions about the future of traditional working-class culture. Besides revealing the limits and limitations of institutional change, these contemporary dramas drew attention to the ongoing negotiation of work, career, and private life and the all-important question of personal happiness. By returning to the problem of alienation first addressed by the proponents of the New Waves, the film-makers committed to the program of 'documentary realism' took a clear political stance but they did so through the filmic language of objectivity.

The problems of succeeding in the workplace and of finding personal fulfilment in a career also spilled over into other genres, moods, and styles. Humorous and farcical treatments proved ill-suited to the kind of critique of institutional power attempted in *Nelken in Aspik* (1976, *Carnations in Aspic*). More effective was the dramatic approach taken in *Die Flucht* (1977, *The Escape*), about a respected East Berlin paediatrician who decides to leave his job for better research conditions in the West but dies tragically during his escape attempt; this film remained one of the few to address directly the growing problem of *Republikflucht* (flight from the republic). The adventurous life of a resourceful car mechanic allowed Günter Reisch in *Anton, der Zauberer* (1978, *Anton the Magician*) to further explore the possibility, or necessity, of individual survival strategies under the conditions of socialism. In their choice of farcical, dramatic, and picaresque elements, these three films brought into view the difficult balancing act between critique and compliance performed by many DEFA film-makers during the 1970s and made clearly visible in the actions of those protagonists resisting external determinations.

Generic conventions predominated in comedies about everyday life that presented their critique within a basic acceptance of the *status quo*. Usually, these comedies introduce one specific problem – lack of childcare, a new family car, a weekend house under construction – to test the resourcefulness of GDR citizens in dealing with the inevitable problems. Thus the above-mentioned *Der Mann, der nach der Oma kam* brings a male nanny into the household of an artistic dual-career couple, the source of many humorous complications. In *Einfach Blumen aufs Dach* (1979, *Just Flowers on the Roof*), when the birth of twins prompts a proud father to buy a second-hand Chaika, the stately limousine issued to East European diplomats, many farcical and ridiculous situations follow. Realising his dream of a summer house, Herricht in the hilarious *Der Baulöwe* (1980, *The Contractor*) is forced to deal with the material and labour shortages that sustain the barter economy in 'real existent socialism'. Similar problems preoccupy a middle-aged, single mother who, in *Dach überm Kopf* (1980, *A Roof over the Head*), moves to

Berlin to begin a new life in what turns out to be a dilapidated garden shed. As these examples show, criticising the economic structures and social institutions was possible as long as the basic assumptions about socialism as a shared ideology and historical fact remained unchallenged, an approach realised best in the conciliatory terms and harmonising effects of contemporary comedy.

More provocative contributions to the discovery of everyday life took the perspective of young adolescents, focusing in particular on their first sexual experiences. *Du und ich und Klein-Paris* (1970, *You and I and Little Paris*), a homage to the city of Leipzig, still presented the budding romance between a high-school student and a philosophy student in conventional gendered terms. By contrast, *Für die Liebe noch zu mager?* (1974, *Still Too Skinny for Love?*), about the sexual coming of age of a young textile worker, created a much more realistic atmosphere by taking the female point-of-view. *Sabine Wulff* (1978), by newcomer Erwin Stranka, and Gräf's rather depressing *P. S.* (1979), two films about young adults growing up in state homes, introduced even more confrontational tones. Both films document the experiences of social outsiders who resist all efforts at integration and repeatedly clash with the philistine attitudes in their environment. Contributing to the controversial reception of these films, film-makers frequently used the situation of the nation's youth as a measure of the future of socialism. Accordingly, not only did the youthful rebellion depicted in these stories threaten mainstream society but also the latter threatened the process of renewal and change embodied by these adolescent protagonists.

A significant number of films about everyday life featured strong women characters and focused on 'typical' female problems such as marriage, divorce, pregnancy, single parenthood, and the conflicting demands of love and career (Bahr in Frieden et al. 1993, vol.1: 125–40). The influential *Der Dritte* (1972, *The Third*), about a single woman with a career and two children, revealed the fundamental discrepancy between gender equality in the workplace and the enduring inequalities in male–female relationships. Despite the superficial similarities with the New Subjectivity in the New German Cinema, the meaning of these new sensibilities, including in sexual matters, remained quite specific to East Germany. For the characters' personal quests reflected less a politicisation of the private sphere than a growing dissatisfaction with the provincialism, conformity, and hypocrisy of public life. In this situation, the validation of the personal was meant to counteract, if not overcome, the shortcomings of the political and, in so doing, uphold the original vision of fully developed individuals living under socialism. In other words, the critique still functioned as a corrective, and not, as it would later during the 1980s, as a gesture of withdrawal and resignation.

Film-makers also turned to rebellious women characters to test the limits of the utopian promise of happiness against oppressive social conventions and to explore the corrosive effect of normative definitions of gender and sexuality on personal and professional relationships. The growing interest in films about women and, by extension, the private sphere has been interpreted as resignation about the political situation and a necessary reorientation in cultural matters (Schütz 1990). On the most obvious level, the many strong female characters confirmed the accomplishments of women's rights in the areas of higher education, employment, reproductive rights, family law, and free childcare. More subtextually, however, in revealing the continuing problems in love relationships, the women became a measure of the successes and, more often, the failures of socialism. Setting the tone for an entire decade, Carow's *Die Legende von Paul und Paula* turned a young woman's intensely romantic notions about love, and life, into a powerful parable about the pursuit of individual happiness and the social and psychological obstacles to its realisation. The phenomenal success of this countercultural fantasy hinged on the representation of experience as a value in itself, which found expression in the celebration of female sexuality as a primordial force. Wolf's surprise hit *Solo Sunny* (1980), with Renate Krössner in the title role, was both more sobering in its attention to the external constraints on sexual and artistic self-expression and more provocative in its conclusions about the psychological mechanisms behind social conformity and hypocrisy.

In response to social and artistic developments that, precisely through their countercultural visions, only highlighted the fundamental crisis of legitimisation in society, DEFA turned again to literary adaptations to formulate new answers to the question of national identity, cultural legacy, and the role of the classical tradition. As in the so-called literary adaptation crisis in the Federal Republic, literature came to function once more as a stabilising force, institutionally as well as ideologically. In terms of preferences, the long-established realist tradition at DEFA produced two new Fontane adaptations, the television film *Effi Briest* (1969) and *Unterm Birnbaum* (1973, *Under the Pear Tree*), which indicated a new appreciation for psychological treatments. Other adaptations (for example, of Eichendorff and E. T. A. Hoffmann) contributed to the ongoing reassessment of romanticism, a process that continued well into the early 1990s with several films about, or based on, Hölderlin and Novalis.

The leading practitioner of literary adaptations since the 1970s, Egon Günther, took full advantage of the critical potential inherent in literature. While also interested in modern authors such as Arnold Zweig and Johannes R. Becher, Günther focused specifically on the monumental work of Goethe to demonstrate the contemporary relevance of the classics but also to question their elevated official status in GDR culture. Thus *Lotte in Weimar* (1975, *Lotte in Weimar*), based on the Thomas Mann novel, allowed the director to deliver a biting critique of the Goethe genius cult and its oppressive effects (Mahoney in Rentschler 1986, 246–59). Yet Günther also gave a conventional class-based interpretation of *Die Leiden des jungen Werther* (1976, *The Sorrows of Young Werther*) in place of the cancelled adaptation of Plenzdorf's provocative novel/play *Die neuen Leiden des jungen W.* (*The New Sorrows of Young W*) that had emphasised the rebellious individualism of this quintessential 'Storm and Stress' hero.

All Goethe films from the mid-1970s were part of the elaborate 225th birthday celebrations for the main representative of German classicism (Stoff in Allan and Sanford 1999, 43–57). At best, the different approaches, from faithful adaptations to contemporary versions, confirmed the relevance of the classics for the present, especially as regards the advancement of enlightenment principles and the utopian idea of the fully developed individual. At worst, these literary adaptations contributed to the grandiose self-representations of the political leadership and its manipulation of the humanistic legacy. Some of these problems surfaced in Siegfried Kühn's attempt to infuse the complicated interpersonal relationships in *Wahlverwandtschaften* (1974, *Elective Affinities*) with vaguely contemporary references. Similar strategies of appropriation appeared in the related genre of the artist film that, like *Beethoven – Tage aus einem Leben* (1976, *Beethoven – Days from a Life*), tried to update traditional notions of genius, in this case by having the dishevelled composer make an appearance in modern-day East Berlin. Resisting such tendencies, Wolf's contribution to the artist films, *Goya* (1971), traced Goya's development from court painter to ally of the people and thereby examined the inherent conflict between an innovative artist and the existing power structures. Wolf continued his reflections on the public role of the artist in *Der nackte Mann auf dem Sportplatz* (1974, *The Naked Man on the Playing Field*) and its sobering conclusions about the difficulties of reconciling artistic ambitions with social expectations.

In the same way that the literary adaptations and artist films allowed film-makers to reflect on the conditions of contemporary cinema, the historical films about the Third Reich and the Second World War permitted them to reconsider the place of the anti-fascist tradition in the founding myths of nation. As a result, a number of films returned to the question of resistance during the Third Reich. Based on historical material about the group around Arvid Harnack, *KLK an PTK – Die Rote Kapelle* (1971, *KLK to PTK – The Red Chapel*) commemorated the bourgeois resistance movement and showed the importance of solidarity and co-operation beyond social and political differences. In the highly acclaimed *Mama, ich lebe* (1977, *Mama, I Am Alive*), Wolf explored the difficulties of national identity and political ideology through the individual choices of four German soldiers fighting against fascist aggression on the side of the Soviet Union. Focusing on the home front, Kirsten's *Ich zwinge dich zu leben* (1978, *I Am Forcing You to Live*) showed the desperate attempts of a politically disillusioned father to save his son after the mobilisation of the Hitler Youth during the last months of the war. Rücker and Reisch's *Die Verlobte* (1980, *The Fiancée*), a successful co-production with GDR television, similarly avoided the usual heroic rhetoric in depicting the suffering of an imprisoned woman communist during the Third Reich. Challenging another aspect of the anti-fascist mythology, Ulrich Weiss's *Dein unbekannter Bruder* (1982, *Your Unknown Brother*) used the discovery of a traitor in a communist resistance group to ask provocative questions about the ethos of solidarity and its continued relevance for the present. Finally, Beyer's *Der Aufenthalt* (1983, *Turning Point*), based on the well-known Hermann Kant novel, enlisted the wartime experiences of a German soldier in a Warsaw prison in a compelling reflection on collective guilt and national identity.

Furthermore, film-makers began to investigate the complicated relationship between history and narrative from the perspective of anti-Semitism. In contrast to the DEFA films from the late 1940s, the contributions from the 1970s and 1980s used the history of anti-Semitism to initiate a fundamental revision of the categories of class, race, ethnicity, and nation. Thus, in *Jakob der Lügner* (1974, *Jacob the Liar*), Beyer's adaptation of the famous Jurek Becker novel and the only DEFA film ever nominated for an Oscar, the possibility of hope and resistance becomes inextricably linked to conflicting definitions of reality and the meaning of truth. After all, Jacob's lying about advancing Soviet troops not only acknowledges the complexities of human behaviour but also highlights the importance of narrative as a reclaiming, a production of history, a process bound to be of central relevance to the antifascist narrative as well. Extending this revisionist process to other historical periods, the adaptation of the Johannes Bobrowski novel, *Levins Mühle* (1980, *Levin's Mill*), about an anti-Semitic incident in late nineteenth-century West Prussia, identifies the changing alliances (for example, between Gypsies and Jews) that can give rise to individual acts of political resistance.

The 1980s: the decline of cinema as a public sphere

Politically, the 1980s brought a series of dramatic changes originating in the Soviet Union under Gorbachev but affecting all East European countries. Poland, Hungary, and Czechoslovakia led the move towards democratisation. The GDR leadership resisted fundamental reforms and made only a few concessions. These included the liberalisation of travel restrictions and greater tolerance towards the various church groups that would later play a key role in the freedom movement. Glasnost and perestroika raised many hopes for a fundamental renewal of the socialist model and brought a wave of heightened cultural activity; yet political developments in East Germany took a different turn. The official return to more dogmatic positions increased the separation between ordinary citizens and the political elites and contributed to an overall sense of disillusionment and disempowerment. Adding to the frustration, the SED leadership refused to be consistent in its cultural policies. Repeated calls for more films with uplifting stories and real heroes coexisted with more open discussions about innovative forms and styles. General declarations about the central role of cinema in establishing models of social behaviour, and about film-makers as active participants in the building of socialist society, alternated with more specific complaints about DEFA films' persistent lack of popular appeal.

The controversial banning in the GDR of several new films from the Soviet Union confirmed widespread suspicions that the political system had reached a point of complete stagnation and fossilisation. Abandoning its dreams of a unified, and unifying, socialist cinema, DEFA had to accept not only the predominance of Western imports in the movie theatres but also the diminished role of cinema in popular culture. Throughout the decade, the studio concentrated on strengthening its existing ties with middle-class viewers attracted to certain genres (for instance, literary adaptations or contemporary dramas) and those political and cultural elites interested in GDR-specific topics (for instance, the relationship between the individual and the collective); both of these groups included a growing number of dissidents. On the one hand, the fragmentation of audiences contributed to the diversification of filmic practices. Far removed from the cultural bureaucracies, young film artists rediscovered experimental and avant-garde styles and created new outlets for their work through the founding of small film clubs and collectives. This alternative film culture was strongly influenced by contemporary painting and performance art and, with centres in Dresden and Berlin, functioned as a manifestation of countercultural life and political subversion (Fritzsche and Löser 1996). On the other hand, in the area of feature film production, first-time directors worked in painful awareness of their films' irrelevance to larger social and cultural developments, which was particularly troubling in light of the promising trends in other East European cinemas and the noticeable liberalisation in GDR literature and the visual arts. Frequently, controversial DEFA films were released under conditions (limited art-house runs, few prints in circulation, bad newspaper reviews) guaranteeing that they would never reach their intended audience; a critical debate no longer took place.

In this context, foreign films became increasingly important in providing mainstream entertainment. Since the 1970s, two-thirds of all new releases had come from socialist countries, including the GDR. However, the one-third imported from capitalist countries regularly attracted the largest audiences. Rather than fighting these tendencies, the studio leadership tried to reach a workable compromise between the conventional genre films imported from the West and the prestige productions by DEFA and other socialist countries. Major box-office successes included Italo-Westerns by Sergio Leone and slapstick farces with the French comedian Luis de Fumes, as well as a large number of Hollywood block-busters such as *Towering Inferno*, *Tootsie*, *Star Trek*, *Beverly Hills Cop*, *E.T.*, and *Dirty Dancing*. Most of these films attracted more than two million viewers. The popular reception of West German films covered the entire range from old-style professionals such as Hoffmann and popular comedians such as Otto Waalkes with his *Otto* films to politically committed directors such as Peter Lilienthal and Margarethe von Trotta. For the most part, the influence of New German Cinema remained negligible, even in the case of Rainer Werner Fassbinder or Wim Wenders. In the metropolitan areas, the European art cinema of the 1970s and 1980s led by Ingmar Bergmann, Damiano Damiani, Louis Malle, and Claude Lelouch often found a receptive audience. The same held true for the directors of the New American Cinema, including Martin Ritt, Arthur Penn, and Sidney Lumet (Jacobi and Janssen 1987).

During these years, DEFA usually provided one-fourth of all new feature film releases. The biannual national film festival in Karl-Marx-Stadt (Chemnitz) functioned as a showcase for these domestic productions. The few that reached more than one million viewers included the Wolf film *Solo Sunny* in 1980 and a re-released *Regalfilm, Jahrgang 45*, in 1990; but more indicative of prevailing tastes were the light-hearted Hungarian vacation comedy *Und nächstes Jahr am Balaton* (1980, *Next Year at Lake Balaton*) and the sensationalist drama of corruption in the West German pharmaceutical industry, *Ärztinnen* (1984, *Women Doctors*). The last two examples confirm that popular cinema during the 1980s offered above all a diversion from, and compensation for, social, cultural, and economic deficits (lack of travel opportunities, consumer goods, and career choices). In light of such functions, the return of generic conventions should not be surprising. The films about everyday life continued to celebrate the virtues of individualism, but now within a pervasive atmosphere of apathy, resignation, and non-involvement. The everyday had lost much of its provocative force, providing little more than an excuse for the affirmation of entrenched petty-bourgeois tastes and attitudes. Similarly, the preoccupation with mundane things, especially when combined with narrow-mindedness, often amounted to little more than an aesthetic and ideological accommodation to the *status quo* (Hoff and Wiedemann 1992).

Nonetheless, the marginalisation of cinema within GDR culture opened up a space for the different voices of women directors and for taboo subject matter such as homosexuality and religious faith. Until the 1980s, the function of femininity in classical narrative cinema and the role of women as the purveyors of sexual and emotional satisfaction had never been examined in feminist terms. Nor had the studio produced any female directors during a period that saw the rise of feminist film-making in the West. Until the arrival of Evelyn Schmidt and Iris Gusner, female authorship had remained limited to screenwriting. Moreover, their films revealed considerable differences between women film-makers in East and West Germany, beginning with the approach to the representation of sexuality and its function in definitions of female emancipation. Following rather conventional narrative patterns, Gusner in *Kaskade rückwärts* (1984, *Leap Backwards*) followed the adventures of a middle-aged woman as she changes jobs, moves to the city, and sets out to find love and romance. Taking a much more critical position, Schmidt in *Das Fahrrad* (1982, *The Bicycle*) documented the daily struggles of a young single mother and factory worker without much hope or interest in anything. In contrast to the contemporary dramas of the 1970s, no attempts at mediation and integration take place; even everyday life, it seems, has become meaningless. While largely ignored in the GDR, Schmidt's film became a critical success abroad, especially in the Federal Republic.

In the same way that the 1980s saw more realistic approaches to the woman's question, the new contemporary dramas about love, marriage, and family life avoided simplistic explanations in favour of more complex, open-ended treatments. Through their respective directorial styles, Heiner Carow and Hermann Zschoche infused harsher tones into the filmic representation of male–female relationships. Relying on melodramatic elements, Carow in *Bis dass der Tod euch scheidet* (1979, *Till Death Doth Thee Part*) presented the problems of a young married couple from the woman's perspective, but without any symbolic investments or didactic intentions; the result: a disillusioned commentary on people's inability to change their lives. With *Coming Out* (1989), Carow made the first DEFA film that directly addressed the discrimination against homosexuals in the GDR. Opening on the night of the fall of the Wall, the film and its important contribution were eclipsed

140

by political events. Continuing in the documentary tradition of the 1970s, Zschoche in *Bürgschaft für ein Jahr* (1981, *Bond for One Year*) told the story of a young single mother fighting to keep custody of her children. By resisting the rhetoric of uplift and reform, the figure of the outsider gave rise to a sobering reflection on the double standards still prevalent in socialist society. Zschoche's critically acclaimed films about adolescents and young adults were defined by a similar refreshing lack of didacticism. Already *Sieben Sommersprossen* (1978, *Seven Freckles*) stood out through its nuanced treatment of the sexual awakening of two teenage sweethearts at a youth summer camp. The boy and the girl returned to the screen in a sequel, *Grüne Hochzeit* (1988, *Green Wedding*), as overwhelmed young parents dealing with real-life problems. Earlier, in *Insel der Schwäne* (1983, *Island of Swans*), the experiences of a young boy who moves from an idyllic village to the satellite city of Berlin-Marzahn allowed Zschoche to trace a similar process of disillusionment through architectural metaphors indicating that the socialist homeland had become inhospitable and uninhabitable.

Taking a more conciliatory approach, Lothar Warneke in his symbolically charged stories about love, friendship and faith defended the possibilities of a fulfilled life by emphasising its spiritual and religious dimensions. In *Unser kurzes Leben* (1981, *Our Short Life*), a free adaptation of Brigitte Reimann's *Franziska Linkerhand*, an ambitious young woman architect on her first assignment confronts the problems in building public housing but eventually learns to be satisfied with small solutions and workable compromises. Similarly, in *Die Beunruhigung* (1982, *The Uncertainty*), a possible diagnosis of cancer persuades a successful divorced woman with a teenage son to re-examine her life and take seriously her emotional need for more meaningful relationships; the hopeful ending rewards her with a more supportive new lover. Warneke's last DEFA film, *Einer trage des anderen Last* (1988, *Bear Ye One Another's Burdens*), about the friendship between two patients, a Christian and a Marxist, in a lung sanatorium, brings together many of these elements: the power of hope and belief, the need for tolerance and understanding, and the importance of reconciliation and forgiveness.

In contrast to Carow, Zschoche and Warneke, whose critical and aesthetic sensibilities found foremost expression in their complex women characters, a growing number of younger directors returned to established generic formulas to reaffirm more traditional attitudes towards gender and sexuality. Thus *Der Doppelgänger* (1985, *The Double*) offered a variation on the marital dramas of the 1970s by showing how a woman changes her mind about divorce after a few months with her husband's more charming secret double. *Rabenvater* (1986, *Bad Father*) examined the impact of divorce on children from the perspective of a father who, despite his irresponsible behaviour, is allowed to participate in raising his son. The strong women characters from the 1970s also seemed to have produced a backlash in the form of buddy films that, almost deliberately, reduced the female characters to sexual objects. As evidenced by Peter Kahane's *Ete und Ali* (1985, *Ete and Ali*), the rituals of male bonding and youthful rebellion allowed for a return to misogynist attitudes, beginning with the equation of femininity with oppressive domesticity. Even Erwin Stranka's *Zwei schräge Vögel* (1989, *Two Weird Guys*), about two computer programmers in what must be regarded as the GDR's most backward industry, cultivated its defiant tone and eccentric attitude at the expense of the women characters.

The only genre that continued to flourish in the 1980s was the children's film, one of the studio's traditionally strong areas (König et al. 1996). Approaching the problems of childhood and early adolescence with humour and understanding, the children's films possessed all the qualities – social relevance, formal experimentation, and popular appeal – missing from many contemporary dramas and comedies. The fantastic elements allowed talented directors such as Zschoche and Rolf Losansky to explore the miraculous in everyday life but also to address social problems through unusual (i.e., fantastic or surrealistic) perspectives. Thus in Zschoche's *Philipp der Kleine* (1976, *Philipp the Small*), the possession of a magic flute allows a shy small boy to gain more self-confidence, initially through trickery but eventually on his own accord. *Das Schulgespenst* (1987, *The School Ghost*), directed by Losansky, acknowledges the special expectations placed on little girls when the film's unruly heroine exchanges places with a ghost and causes a lot of confusion among her parents, teachers, and friends. Taking a more serious approach to the problems of adolescent girls, *Hasenherz* (1987, *Hare's Heart*) revolves around a shy tomboy who is cast as the male lead in a fairy-tale film, an experience that, after a series of difficulties, leaves her more self-assured and accepting of herself.

In the wake of DEFA's fortieth anniversary in 1986, and in anticipation of the fortieth anniversary of the GDR in 1989, the studio experienced one last outpouring of productivity. Just as the myth of anti-fascism and the history of anti-Semitism had already posed important challenges to the definition of national identity, the filmic representations of postwar history now provided a conceptual framework for working through the self-representation of the GDR, including through the filmic images provided by the DEFA studio since its beginnings (Byg 1991). This process had started in the early 1960s with irreverent parodies of early reconstruction films (for example, in *Karbid und Sauerampfer*) and continued during the 1970s in the subversive registers of the picaresque (for example, in *Anton der Zauberer*). With *Das Luftschiff* (1983, *The Dirigible*), Rainer Simon returned to the possibilities of the fantastic to tell the story of an eccentric inventor of dirigibles drawn into the turmoil of twentieth-century German history. In *Märkische Forschungen* (1982, *Explorations in Brandenburg*), Gräf used the competing research projects of a respected history professor and an amateur local historian to contemplate the dangers of the past for the present. Based on the novel by Günter de Bruyn, the film suggested that the meaning of history could no longer be reduced to simplistic oppositions of true versus false, right versus wrong, but instead involved more complicated processes of rereading. Laying the foundation for the normalisation of German history that would continue in post-unification cinema, a few films intentionally, or even unintentionally, reduced the Third Reich to a mere backdrop for personal stories held together by such universal themes as love, friendship, family, and community. The perspective of children in *Kindheit* (1987, *Childhood*) allowed its director to relativise the historical events by emphasising the simple pleasures of country life even under conditions of war, a tendency also found in the West German *Heimat* series. In *Die Schauspielerin* (1988, *The Actress*), Corinna Harfouch appeared as a famous theatre actress who, in the 1930s, takes on a Jewish identity to be reconciled with her Jewish lover. By linking Jewishness and, by extension, anti-Semitism to questions of performance and masquerade, the film contributed to the postmodern simulations of history and historicity that, after 1989, would become a distinguishing mark of postunification cinema.

In the same way that the building of the Berlin Wall gave clear contours to the East German cinema, so its fall on 9 November 1989 brought about that cinema's institutional and ideological demise. Again, a number of *Überläuferfilme*, films begun as DEFA projects but released in another, united Germany, shed light on the wider implications for questions of cinema, nation, and history (Dalichow 1993). Michael Gwisdek's melancholy *Treffen in Travers* (1989, *Meeting in Travers*) revisited an episode from the life of the radical eighteenth-century naturalist Georg Forster in a desperate effort to make sense of the failure of love and revolution. In his adaptation of a well-known Christoph Hein novel, *Der Tangospieler* (1991, *The Tango Player*), Gräf returned to the purges of the 1960s to explain the decision of an academic banned from his profession to refuse all offers of social and political rehabilitation. Relying on spatial metaphors, Kahane in *Die Architekten* (1990, *The Architects*) turned the architectural competition for a community centre in a large public housing estate near Berlin into a compelling allegory of spiritual homelessness and the death of socialism. However, where Kahane still adhered to the DEFA tradition of using architecture as a metaphor of society, other film-makers emphatically rejected all forms of utopian thinking. Instead, in *Motivsuche* (1990, *Search for a Topic*), Dietmar Hochmuth offered troubling insights into the documentary practices celebrated during DEFA times as the quintessence of socialist ethics and aesthetics. Starting the difficult process of writing film history, the release of previously banned films such as *Die Russen kommen*, *Sonnensucher*, and *Berlin um die Ecke* in 1988 and 1989 already gave some indication to cinephile audiences of what could have been. Shortly after the fall of the Wall, several other shelved films had their belated premieres and were received with a similar mixture of surprise, sadness, and anxious anticipation. Then, in 1990, the Berlin Film Festival dedicated an entire festival segment to the *Regalfilme*. Yet, while the retrospective confirmed DEFA's important contribution to German cinema, it also threw into relief the studio's uncertain future.

6

WEST GERMAN CINEMA
1962–89

If the building of the Wall in August of 1961 formalised the division between cinema in East and West, the Oberhausen Manifesto announced a radical break with the cinema of the postwar period. On 28 February 1962, a group of young film-makers at the Oberhausen Short Film Festival proclaimed: 'The old film is dead. We believe in the new.' Signed by Edgar Reitz and Alexander Kluge, among others, the Oberhausen Manifesto sought to accomplish three things: to offer a critique of conventional genre cinema, to lay out the future of German film, and to present a list of demands on the government. The twenty-six film-makers called for public policies and subsidies that would finally acknowledge film as an art form similar to the other arts. While the signatories shared some basic understanding of film authorship, their manifesto clearly emphasised institutional rather than aesthetic concerns. Unlike the directors of the French *nouvelle vague*, who rebelled against an existing tradition of quality, the representatives of the Young German Cinema first had to create an art cinema with social relevance. Their contribution to the European New Waves of the 1960s and their relationship to the New German Cinema of the 1970s reflected these structural problems in the acute awareness of cinema as a social and political practice (Koch 1985, Reichmann and Schobert 1991).

The international reception of the New German Cinema has profoundly influenced the historiography of West German cinema after Oberhausen (Rentschler 1984). Despite the close affinities with new social movements, this cinema has been studied primarily as an *Autorenkino* (author's cinema) dominated by the work of famous directors such as Rainer Werner Fassbinder, Wim Wenders, Werner Herzog, and Volker Schlöndorff (Sanford 1980, Franklin 1983, Phillips 1984). While the emphasis on authorship has helped the critical reception of experimental film-makers such as Jean-Marie Straub and Danielle Huillet, writer-activists such as Alexander Kluge, and controversial figures such as Hans-Jürgen Syberberg, it has contributed to the neglect of those directors or producers specialising in certain genres. In general, women directors such as Margarethe von Trotta, Helke Sander, and Helma Sanders-Brahms have received most attention in the context of feminist film scholarship (Möhrmann 1980, Fischetti 1992, Knight 1992, Majer O'Sickey and von Zadow 1998). Approaching feature film as a reflection of society, some scholars have focused on topics such as the crisis of the family and the conflict among the generations; the changes in public institutions and the workplace; the impact of the sexual revolution and female emancipation; and the problems of everyday life in the cities and the provinces (Pflaum and Prinzler 1983, Pflaum 1990). Throughout, special attention has been paid to films about the Third Reich and their contribution to the rewriting of German history (Reimer and Reimer 1992). Moving beyond such thematic approaches, cultural-studies oriented scholars have explored the affinities among feminism, postmodernism, and the filmic and literary practices associated with New Subjectivity (McCormick 1991, Kosta 1994); yet others have used close readings of individual films to follow the continuing German dialogue with America (Corrigan 1994). Even the category of art cinema and its different modes of production and reception have been analysed in relation to the larger problems of a national cinema struggling against the economic and aesthetic dominance of Hollywood (Elsaesser 1989).

With the exception of a few passing references in feature films made after 1962, the German division played a surprisingly small role in the self-presentations of Young German Cinema. This also accounts for the limited West German reception of East German films, despite the often surprising parallels in thematic choices and stylistic preferences. Obviously, the ideological orientation of the Federal Republic towards Western Europe and the United States affected all aspects of cinema culture after 1962 and left a strong impact on the two main areas of contestation, namely the aesthetic revolution associated with the New Waves and the political revolution initiated by the student movement. The Great Coalition of 1966 between the conservative Christian Democrats (CDU) and the more progressive Social Democrats (SPD) institutionalised the historical compromise between tradition, innovation, and reform that guaranteed continuous economic growth but, after 1969, also brought more progressive policies under SPD Chancellors Willy Brandt and Helmut Schmidt. Also known as the APO (extra-parliamentary opposition), the radical student movement mobilised in the early 1960s around demands for school and university reform but soon expanded its political opposition into a more fundamental critique of postwar society and the capitalist system. In conflating the political and the personal, the programmatic calls for radical change gave rise to a heterogeneous counterculture, often summarised under the label 'the sixties'. Defining itself against an oppressive bourgeois society, the counterculture pursued social and cultural alternatives that culminated in sexual liberation, social experimentation, and individual self-discovery, including with the help of drugs, music, therapy, and alternative lifestyles. By the 1970s, all such alternatives – from dogmatic and unorthodox leftist groups and the terrorist underground under the aegis of the RAF (Red Army Faction) to various feminist initiatives, alternative projects, and ecological groups, including the Greens – posed a serious challenge to the political institutions and social structures identified with the generation of the fathers.

In this context, the convergence of cinema, aesthetics, and politics was inevitable, especially given the young generation's desire for new forms of self-expression beyond the traditional high–low culture divide. Participating in these larger developments, filmic practices after 1962 thrived on a number of oppositions: the fascination with American mass culture versus the critique of American cultural imperialism; the interest in formal experimentation versus the commitment to an alternative public sphere; the association with literature versus the search for other filmic traditions; and the opposition to existing definitions of German culture versus the demand for public funding and support (Petermann and Thoms 1988).

The Oberhausen Manifesto and the Young German Cinema

The innovative films made after 1962, often as a result of more funding opportunities, shared some important formal characteristics. Most of them offered an implicit or explicit critique of genre cinema and its stabilising functions within postwar society. The programme of a politicised modernism gave rise to unconventional images and narratives that facilitated the analysis of repressive social structures. Articulated through a range of thematic concerns, this provocative alliance between radical aesthetics and radical politics influenced the discourse of art cinema throughout the 1960s and, with considerable modifications, during the 1970s and 1980s as well, until the return to genre cinema in the 1990s. Whereas the European New Waves were distinguished by a provocatively direct approach to political subject matter, German film-makers in East and West usually preferred a more mediated approach. They channelled their awareness of the contradictions within society and the constraints on representation into one of the master-narratives of German identity, the conflict among the generations and its impact on family structures and gender roles. While both German cinemas used these paradigmatic conflicts to uncover contradictions in the existing power structure, and the underlying historical models, Young German Cinema concentrated on the destabilising effect of these conflicts on bourgeois notions of subjectivity and, with few exceptions, neglected both the political legacies of German history and the economic determinants of class.

In response to the Oberhausen Manifesto, but also in full awareness of the film industry's structural problems, the government created an infrastructure of federal offices, funding agencies, and training facilities more conducive to the proposed convergence of film and art. Founded in 1964, The Kuratorium Junger Deutscher Film (Board for the New German Film), which initially operated under the auspices of the Ministry of the Interior, proved very effective in supporting new film projects. The Kuratorium provided interest-free loans based on a committee review of submitted screenplays. After 1969, individual states administered this programme, with Bavaria and North-Rhine Westphalia leading the effort to use film funding as a form of regional development. While the Kuratorium gave first-time directors much-needed support, it failed to resolve many other problems such as the unwillingness on the part of distributors and exhibitors to show difficult films and the lack of an established film culture able to support formal innovation and experimentation. Responding to requests by industry representatives, the Film-förderungsanstalt (Film Subsidy Board), which was overseen by the Ministry of Economics, began to offer loans to companies with a record of box-office successes. This system benefited the so-called 'weepies cartel' and led to a short-lived increase in production – cheaply made sex education films, among others. The conditions for more long-term changes improved with the founding of two film schools in 1966 and 1967, respectively, the Deutsche Film- und Fernsehakademie (DFFB) in Berlin and the Hochschule für Film und Fernsehen (HFF) in Munich. Whereas the Berlin school developed into a centre of documentary film-making, the Munich school became known for cultivating new aesthetic sensibilities. Contributing to this slowly emerging cinephile culture, journals such as *Filmkritik* and *Film* provided an important forum for theoretical debates during the 1960s and 1970s. Frieda Grafe and Hans C. Blumenberg, who wrote for national newspapers, performed a similar function through their insightful reviews of films.

Already the first wave of films released in 1966 attested to the creative energy of Young German Cinema. In *Abschied von gestern* (1966, *Yesterday Girl*), Kluge enlisted episodic narrative structures, analytical montage techniques, and extended documentary sequences in a compelling analysis of contemporary problems and the solutions available in bourgeois society. Schlöndorff examined the socio-psychology of violence in his critically acclaimed adaptation of the Robert Musil novella in *Der junge Törless* (1966, *Young Törless*). Set in an upper-class milieu, Peter Schamoni's *Schonzeit für Füchse* (1966, *Closed Season on Fox Hunting*) displayed the symptoms of alienation through the lethal combination of modern youth and social privilege. Above all, the aesthetics of political modernism allowed young directors to shed light on the contradictions within German society through formal as well as thematic means. Accordingly, Ulrich Schamoni in *Alle Jahre wieder* (1967, *Year After Year*) turned the festivities during a typical Christmas holiday into an almost clinical study on the hypocrisies of bourgeois life. Others focused on the structures and institutions that defined social and sexual identities in the Federal Republic. A number of directors used the perspective of youth to introduce a new point-of-view on social practices and conventions. Individual gestures of youthful rebellion invaded the liberal upper-class milieu of Johannes Schaaf's *Tätowierung* (1967, *Tattoo*), whereas more collective forms of resistance prevailed among the high-school students of Peter Zadek's *Ich bin ein Elefant, Madame* (1969, *I Am an Elephant, Madame*). May Spils's light-hearted comedies with Werner Enke, most notably *Zur Sache, Schätzchen* (1968, *Let's Get Down to Business, Darling*) and *Nicht fummeln, Liebling* (1969, *No Petting, Darling*), advertised Schwabing's bohemian milieu of daydreamers and good-for nothings. Yet already the problems of the carefree young unmarried couple in *Es* (1965, *It*) revealed the limits of free sexuality through the woman's pregnancy and abortion. Questions of gender and sexuality also informed Ula Stöckl's *Neun Leben hat die Katze* (1968, *The Cat Has Nine Lives*), a contribution that, with its close attention to questions of female identity, remained the exception until the rise of feminist film-making in the mid-1970s. The same might be said about Stöckl's collaboration with Reitz, the *Geschichten vom Kübelkind* (1969/70, *Stories of the Bucket Baby*), which consisted of twenty-three independent episodes about a rebellious young woman shown in various combinations.

The Young German Cinema thrived on a number of productive contradictions. Many film-makers shared an intense frustration with the Federal Republic and its oppressive social structures. Some used formal means to convey their vision of a different world, while others turned to narrative to criticise the existing conditions. Some were driven by the desire for self-expression, while others set out to realise film's inherent potential as an instrument of communication. Some focused on developing a new filmic language, while others devoted themselves to creating an alternative public sphere. Some chose innovative forms and techniques to express their political ideas, while others reinterpreted established forms in new and creative ways. Ultimately, however, all film-makers channelled their deeply felt alienation from the culture of economic liberalism and social conservatism into two equally important thematic concerns: the conflict among the generations and the battle between sexes. Unlike in the postwar period, the films could no longer articulate and contain these conflicts through traditional forms; instead they had to examine them through new ways of telling, or not telling, stories. Here the historical avant-gardes and their modernist conception of film proved very influential; equally important were the challenges to classical narrative by the European New Waves, and the films of François Truffaut, Jean-Pierre Melville, and Jean-Luc Godard in particular. The extensive German reception of the French and Italian New Waves can be traced in film-makers' rediscovery of social realism and documentary forms, the critical appropriation of generic conventions, and the transformation of film into a political weapon. These diverse influences allowed a new generation of film-makers to approach the relationship between social reality and filmic reality as a more open, dynamic, and interventionist one. Frequently they used black-and-white cinematography to counter the effects of verisimilitude, experimented with anti-psychological acting styles, and opened up critical perspectives through montage, voice-over, and stream-of-consciousness.

It has become a commonplace to credit Young German Cinema and New German Cinema for a two-pronged attack on the repressive social and political structures in the Federal Republic and the conventional genre cinema associated with both the Hollywood studio system and the pre-Oberhausen era. But in fact, the radicalisation of film form and the aestheticisation of the political would not have been possible without earlier developments in German film and literature. The myth of a new beginning served only to distract from the considerable con- tinuities between the 1950s and 1960s. In the cinema, the critical engagement with social problems had already produced the compelling reflections on urban alienation offered by Ottomar Domnick in *Jonas* (1957). Will Tremper's Berlin films, including *Die endlose Nacht* (1963, *The Endless Night*) about one ordinary, and yet also extraordinary, night spent at Tempelhof airport, evoked the uncanny atmosphere that for him permeated all aspects of daily life in the Federal Republic. Moreover, many of the contemporary sensibilities captured by the Young German

Cinema were already prefigured in the looks, gestures, and attitudes promoted by the young actors and actresses of the late 1950s, such as Karin Baal and Horst Buchholz, who combined classic star attributes like beauty and sex appeal with the cool detachment perfected by the androgynous anti-stars of the Munich scene, Uschi Obermaier and Marquard Bohm.

The Young German Cinema profited furthermore from the intense interest in modernist experimentation cultivated by many postwar writers, including those involved with literary groups such as Gruppe 47. The ongoing politicisation of cinema built directly on the example of the public intellectual personified by Heinrich Böll and Günter Grass. Not surprisingly, both authors inspired a number of acclaimed film adaptations. Confirming the status of Böll as the most influential author of the postwar period, Herbert Vesely's *Das Brot der frühen Jahre* (1962, *The Bread of the Early Years*) followed the story's central character in his difficult journey from social conformity to individual freedom. Straub and Huillet's *Nicht versöhnt* (1965, *Not Reconciled*), based on *Billiard um halb zehn*, explored the complicated relationship between German past and present through the sympto-matic story of a family of architects. For *Katz und Maus* (1965, *Cat and Mouse*), Hansjürgen Pohland relied on similar critical intentions in adapting Grass's autobiographical account about a group of high-school friends from Danzig during the Second World War. Significant as works of art in their own right, these films established a pattern of cultural transfer from literature to film that would dominate the process of *Vergangenheitsbewältigung* throughout the 1970s and 1980s. In addition to these contemporary authors, it was Bertolt Brecht who exerted the strongest influence on filmic practices both through his reflections on epic theatre and through his theory of progressive mass media. Especially the provocative writings of Hans Magnus Enzensberger about the consciousness industry confirmed Brecht's relevance to the politicisation of film during the 1960s (Mueller 1989).

In terms of filmic styles, Young German Cinema can be identified with three basic tendencies: the return to social realist forms and documentary influences; the revival of avant-garde and experimental practices; and the critical engagement with popular culture and other modern mass media. The creative impulses received from documentaries forced many film-makers to deal with problems of social and economic inequality and to question their preconceived notions about politically responsible film-making in the confrontation with often difficult subject matter. The documentary tradition in film and literature provided an important model for turning film into an instrument of social analysis. Film-makers adopted approaches first tested by contemporary writers (for example, in protocol literature) to give a voice to marginalised social groups. But their films also questioned the conventions of reportage, and its tacit assumptions about objectivity and authenticity, by presenting a more subjective, and often more differentiated, point-of-view. Erika Runge's *Warum ist Frau B. glücklich?* (1968, *Why Is Mrs B Happy?*), about an ordinary working-class woman, is the best-known example of this productive exchange between literature and film.

149

The Young German Cinema profited also from the renewed interest in experimental and avant-garde film-making. Never part of the mainstream, Peter and Birgit Hein, Werner Nekes, Dore O, and Vlado Kristl experimented with the basic elements of the filmic medium, including the inherent tension between image and narrative and their competing notions of the real. Straub and Huillet emerged as the main representatives of an avant-garde cinema radical in its aesthetic and political vision (Byg 1995). The austerity of their filmic vision prevented a more extensive reception but guaranteed their enduring influence on other film-makers. Straub and Huillet's *Chronik der Anna Magdalena Bach* (1968, *Chronicle of Anna Magdalena Bach*) illustrated their programmatic refusal to assume a position of narrative authority but also established a conceptual model for more formal inquiries into the spatio-temporal relationships unique to the filmic medium. Similar strategies of detachment informed their engagement with literary texts, from Brecht in the case of *Geschichtsunterricht* (1972, *History Lesson*) to Kafka in the case of *Klassenverhältnisse* (1983, *Class Relations*). Some of the more politically oriented members of the avant-garde used filmic techniques for direct critical interventions. Hellmuth Costard caused a scandal at the 1968 Oberhausen Film Festival with *Besonders wertvoll* (1968, *Rating: Especially Valuable*) and its close-up of a speaking penis. Throughout the 1970s and 1980s, Costard relied on techniques such as slow motion and time-lapse photography to explore the relationship between the filmic image and the visible world, most recently in the whimsical *Aufstand der Dinge* (1992, *The Revolt of Things*). As one of the main representatives of a radical political cinema, Harun Farocki commented extensively on the overdetermined politics of representation and the elusive dynamics between knowledge and experience in modern societies, from early experimental shorts to ambitious essay films such as *Etwas wird sichtbar* (1981, *Something Becomes Visible*), about the role of mass media during the Vietnam War. A compilation of instructional films, titled *Leben: BRD* (1990), has been released under the revealing English title: *How to Live in the Federal Republic*.

Perhaps most importantly, the Young German Cinema developed a unique filmic style through both the critical re-interpretation of classical Hollywood genres, especially the crime thriller, and the self-conscious references to popular culture, from pop music to Pop Art. Responding to the New Wave appropriation of the American gangster myth, Klaus Lemke's *Achtundvierzig Stunden bis Acapulco* (1967, *Forty-eight Hours to Acapulco*) and Rudolf Thome's *Rote Sonne* (1970, *Red Sun*) presented their scenarios of sex and murder with mechanical precision and ritualistic detachment. However, the isolated nature of such attempts at ironic appropriation also underscored the lack of an established iconography, especially of crime and violence, in German film history. With much more flair and finesse, Robert van Ackeren, Rosa von Praunheim, and, of course, Rainer Werner Fassbinder combined melodramatic excess, ironic detachment, and formal stylisation in order to measure the reverberations of the sexual revolution in certain psychological dispositions. Inspired by Andy Warhol, Praunheim in *Die Bettwurst* (1970, *The Bedroll*) and Ackeren in *Harlis* (1972) relied on extreme theatricalisation to explore the spectacle of modern sexuality and its preferred scenarios of submission and domination. Both directors moved beyond purely aesthetic categories, including those of high and low camp, in order to explore the relationship between affective dispositions such as melancholy, aggression, and indifference and the social and political practices that define social and sexual identity in often normative terms. In so doing, these directors also preserved the aesthetic provocations of the 1960s for the identity-based sexual politics of the 1970s.

A literary author, critical writer, and political activist, Alexander Kluge must be considered the film-maker most closely identified with the political, institutional, and theoretical programme of the Young German Cinema. By developing further the analytical possibilities of montage, he preserved the original vision of the Oberhausen group throughout the 1970s and 1980s. Kluge formulated many of his ideas about the role of experience in a society dominated by modern mass media in a study co-authored with Oskar Negt, *Öffentlichkeit und Erfahrung* (1972, *Experience and the Public Sphere*). The book confirmed Kluge's intellectual debt to critical theory which, from Horkheimer and Adorno's critique of the culture industry to Habermas's writings on the public sphere, influenced an entire generation of critics and scholars committed, like the director himself, to rethinking the relationship between theory and praxis. Consequently, Kluge's approach to film-making brought together two artistic impulses: the transformation of film into a means of critical inquiry and the transformation of cinema into an alternative public sphere. This process requires the active participation of the audience in creating what Kluge once described as 'the real film in the mind of the spectator'. As a technique of deconstructing and reconstructing meaning, montage in his films offers the most effective strategy for developing such an approach. As a discursive device, montage establishes a principle for combining documentary footage, voice-over commentary, legal terminology, and political speeches with diverse references to painting, literature, folklore, mythology, and classical music. Together these elements give rise to an anti-illusionist narrative structure resistant to conventional patterns of identification. With such investments, already *Die Artisten in der Zirkuskuppel: ratlos* (1968, *Artists in the Big Tent, Perplexed*) offered an allegorical self-representation of Young German Cinema in a moment of doubt about the social relevance of film and a passionate affirmation of the power of the imagination.

During the 1970s, Kluge continued to critique social institutions and public discourses through the productive power of fantasy and its ability to advance the utopian promise of a society committed to the fulfilment of human desires. The search for more authentic forms of experience linked the episodic documentary style of *Abschied von gestern*, his most famous film, and the conceptual approach of *Gelegenheitsarbeit einer Sklavin* (1974, *Occasional Work of a Domestic Slave*) to the dream-like montage sequences in such later works as *Die Patriotin* (1979, *The Patriot*) and *Die Macht der Gefühle* (1983, *The Power of Emotions*). Frequently, the director relied on women as the representatives of a tradition of human productivity presumably less damaged by the existing power structures. His aesthetic choices confirmed the ability of high culture (e.g., opera, classical literature) to resist commodification; but, in truly dialectical fashion, Kluge made this point most forcefully through a modern mass medium like film.

Despite the provocation of the Young German Cinema, genre cinema remained a formidable force throughout the decade. The ageing stars and directors of the 1950s continued to rely on established conventions to engage with contemporary problems as well as with new styles and sensibilities, especially those attributed to the young generation. Offering German alternatives to rock 'n' roll, the *Schlagerfilme* featured popular singers such as Freddy Quinn who, like his predecessor Albers, sought adventures on foreign shores, or Udo Jürgens who, in a paradigmatic scene of 1960s youth culture, appeared as the embodiment of maturity among the rockers and mods from *Siebzehn Jahr, blondes Haar* (1966, *Blond and Seventeen*). The world of teenagers inspired several high school comedies in the style of *Die Lümmel von der ersten Bank* (1967, *The Brats from the First Row*) that reduced the threat of youthful insurrection to harmless pranks and adventures. Just as the comedies about free-spirited youth guided younger audiences in their choice of fashion styles, status symbols, and the appropriate vernacular, the films about the sexual revolution supplied older audiences with more lurid fantasies about adolescent sexuality. The controversial *Helga* series (1967–68) and the various sequels to the *Schulmädchenreport* (1970, *School Girl Report*) resorted to the documentary format to conceal their lascivious intentions. By contrast, the enormously successful *Oswald Kolle: Das Wunder der Liebe* (1968, *Oswald Kolle: The Miracle of Love*) relied on the rhetoric of public health to enlighten the spectator about various sexual practices.

The hybridisation of genres gave rise to the arbitrary combinations of crime caper, action adventure, vacation comedy, and detective thriller that show post-Oberhausen cinema at its worst. Mixing suspense, humour, romance, and eroticism, these films engaged with contemporary lifestyles on a level of formal conventionality that unintentionally revealed the underlying social and cultural fantasies. Foreign locations, different nationalities, and unusual local customs gave film-makers licence to experiment with the most bizarre plot combinations, involving jewellery heists, fashion shows, adulterous affairs, fake kidnappings, and so forth. The model for this sort of generic eclecticism was established by the rewriting of German history as picaresque in *Es muss nicht immer Kaviar sein* (1961, *It Doesn't Always Have to Be Caviar*), based on the best-seller by Johannes Mario Simmel. From then on, French characters and locations acquainted German audiences with the customs of *savoir vivre*, whereas English country settings provided an imaginary space for the celebration of old-fashioned eccentricity. Nostalgic tendencies prevailed in the *Pater Brown* series that cast Heinz Rühmann in the role of the inquisitive country priest and amateur detective created by G. K. Chesterton.

The popular Edgar Wallace films combined elements of the murder mystery, Victorian melodrama, and Gothic tale of horror to indulge its lurid fascination with the passions and perversions behind the façade of British propriety and reserve. Produced by Constantin, the series started with *Der Frosch mit der Maske* (1959,

The Frog with the Mask) and continued with countless sequels up through the 1970s, propelled forward by the same formulaic plot elements and populated by a familiar cast of thieves, murderers, forgers, addicts, lunatics, and eccentric aristocrats. Cult classics from the series include *Die toten Augen von London* (1961, *The Dead Eyes of London*) and *Das Gasthaus an der Themse* (1962, *The Inn on the Thames*), two Alfred Vohrer films that brought together many of the regulars, including Joachim Fuchsberger as the inspector from Scotland Yard and Eddi Arent as his comic sidekick. The performative and representational excess and the ironic self-awareness in the Edgar Wallace films have contributed to their enduring status as (postmodern) cult movies. Reviving one of the great villains of Weimar cinema, CCC's *Mabuse* series failed to achieve similar effects, despite an initial contribution by Lang himself, *Die tausend Augen des Dr. Mabuse* (1960, *The Thousand Eyes of Dr Mabuse*).

Meanwhile, the German love–hate relationship with Hollywood continued. America remained an integral part of the German imagination through its double identification with the image of urban jungle and primordial wilderness. On the one hand, the fascination with crime and violence – and the awareness of their infinite marketability – stood behind the formulaic *Jerry Cotton* series and similar low-budget productions based on the dime novels published by Bastei. On the other hand, the mythical American West inspired romantic dreams about a reconciliation between good and evil through the figure of the noble savage. Based on Karl May, *Der Schatz im Silbersee* (1962, *The Treasure of Silver Lake*) became the most successful German film from that year and was followed by other May adaptations in the famous *Winnetou* trilogy (1963–65). Produced for Rialto-Film, directed by Harald Reinl, and usually shot in Yugoslavia with lead actors Pierre Brice and Lex Barker, these Westerns allowed for a displacement of German history into the mythological spaces of the New World; therein the May adaptations fulfilled a similar socio-psychological function as the DEFA Indian films. The transposition of these regressive patterns into the world of Germanic myth and legend, as attempted by Reinl in the two-part *Die Nibelungen* (1966–67, *The Nibelungs*), proved much less successful, an indication perhaps of the continuing need for a clear distinction between American popular culture and German high culture.

The 1970s: the emergence of New German Cinema

The transition from the first to the second generation after Oberhausen has been described in terms of short-lived improvements on the institutional level; old structural problems in the organisation of the film industry; and, perhaps most problematically, an abiding sense of belatedness, or separateness, in comparison to other New Wave cinemas. The inherent contradictions in an art cinema that combined aesthetic innovation and political critique, and did so primarily within the discourses of national cinema, found a resolution in the unifying concept of film authorship through which the New German Cinema distinguished itself from the

Young German Cinema. From the perspective of the 1960s, the *Autorenfilm* and its emphasis on individual creativity contributed to the depoliticisation of cinema as a public sphere. Yet from the perspective of the 1980s, the notion of authorship represented a logical continuation of earlier debates about the oppressive effects of classical narrative and the need for radically subjective visions both of cinema and society. During the decade itself, the identification of New German Cinema with the contribution of individual directors provided a workable compromise between changing political and economic exigencies, on the one hand, and new aesthetic sensibilities and critical agendas, on the other. The film-maker's desire for political relevance betrayed a continuing belief in film as a reflection of, and intervention into, social reality. At the same time, the innovative styles allowed for more fluid relationships between reality and representation that, according to these young directors, made film an integral part of contemporary life, if not a more authentic form of experience.

Politically, the 1970s were defined by the ambitious reform initiatives (for example, liberalisation of family laws, changes in the educational system, improvements in East–West relations) started under the Social Democratic government of Chancellor Brandt. As an outcome of, and a reaction to, these developments, the emergence of radical leftist and autonomous groups culminated in a wave of terrorist activities in the late 1970s. In response, the government passed several measures – including an emergency decree – to restore law and order. These measures only deepened the citizens' suspicion about the return of authoritarian structures. Widespread disillusionment with traditional politics added to the appeal of alternative movements, including the early ecology movement. But the turn towards the private sphere also gave rise to a heterogeneous counterculture committed both to the defence of traditional civil rights and to new forms of identity politics that, among other things, brought consciousness-raising and alternative therapies, autonomous projects and New Age religions, feminist and gay rights groups, and the various cultural movements – from punk to new wave – that connected the postmodern culture of narcissism to the most advanced forms of artistic expression in literature, theatre, painting, dance, music, and film.

Sharing basic ideas with the political elites about the possibility of social change and the importance of critical debate, the New German Cinema in some ways functioned as an integral part of SPD cultural policy. Economically and politically, the movement can be described as a strategy of production differentiation and foreign policy that proved particularly successful abroad, both in the traditional art-house venues and as part of the cultural mission of federal agencies such as the Goethe Institutes. Under these conditions, the concept of *Autorenfilm* promised not only a new artistic programme but also, and more crucially, a discursive and institutional model for marketing the Federal Republic – a modern democracy, a social welfare state, and a liberal middle-class society – both to its citizens and to its political allies. The notion of authorship left an impact on a wide range of practices, from the celebrity cult surrounding the most famous directors to the founding of new distribution and production companies (for example, the

Filmverlag der Autoren). Yet outside these discourses of art cinema, the film industry continued to struggle for economic survival, despite all public subsidies, tax breaks, regional initiatives, and so forth. Faced with the double competition of public television and Hollywood entertainment, producers found most of the available solutions ineffective. Feature-film production had increased from fewer than a hundred films in 1960 to 121 films in 1969, a result primarily of the Film Subsidy Law. During the 1970s, the numbers fell again from a hundred to fifty new releases per year. Some producers, such as the Munich-based Franz Seitz, subsidised more ambitious projects through crassly commercial films. Alois Brummer emerged as the most successful producer of pornography, specialising in sex films with Bavarian *Heimatfilm* settings. Even the once powerful distribution companies experienced problems. By the late 1960s, Constantin had been sold to the publishing house Bertelsmann, only to be reconstituted as Neue Constantin in the 1970s by Bernd Eichinger and Leo Kirch, the two men whose ascendancy after 1989 would coincide with the demise of the *Autorenfilm*.

The three directors usually associated with New German Cinema – Fassbinder, Herzog, and Wenders – emerged from the social and political movements of the 1960s but each responded with a filmic style that combined generic traditions, literary influences, and countercultural sensibilities in new and innovative ways. Fassbinder's *Liebe ist kälter als der Tod* (1969, *Love is Colder than Death*) resembled the gangster films of other Munich directors such as Thome and Lemke but moved beyond the formal allusions to Hollywood to reconstruct a specifically German mise-en-scène of violence. Reflecting critically on the preceding decade of political utopias, Herzog in *Auch Zwerge haben klein angefangen* (1970, *Even Dwarfs Started Small*) used documentary techniques to study group interactions and assess the aggressive side of human behaviour. And taking advantage of the long tradition of Americanism, Wenders in *Summer in the City* (1971) captured his generation's sense of disillusionment by playing optimistic pop tunes over images of wintry German cityscapes.

The integrative myth of authorship, including its affinities with auteurism, and the artistic collaborations and patterns of influence that sustained that myth invested these directors' filmic inquiries with an aura of authenticity and legitimacy. Their work as writers, critics, and celebrities secured Fassbinder, Wenders, and Herzog the rank of public figures, even if controversial ones. Moreover, their professional experiences abroad (for instance, Wenders's work in Hollywood) and their deliberate allusions to other filmic oeuvres (for instance, Sirk in the case of Fassbinder) guaranteed their films a strong international reception and made them part of the established traditions of art cinema. In developing their signature styles, all three directors depended to a large degree on a steady group of collaborators, beginning with those actors who assumed the function of muses or doubles (for instance, Hanna Schygulla for Fassbinder, Rüdiger Vogler for Wenders, Klaus Kinski for Herzog). The contribution of the country's leading cinematographers proved equally decisive, with Michael Ballhaus and Xaver Schwarzenberger creating tightly composed frames for Fassbinder; Robby Müller developing elaborate long takes in his work with Wenders; and Thomas Mauch lending his fluid camera style to the on-location shoots preferred by Herzog. Similar influences, this time in the approach to editing and montage, can be traced in the work of Juliane Lorenz for Fassbinder and of Beate Mainka-Jellinghaus for Herzog and, of course, Kluge.

Rainer Werner Fassbinder was not only the most prolific but also the most talented, influential, and controversial director of the New German Cinema. His oeuvre includes thirty-three feature films, as well as numerous television series, radio plays, and theatre productions. Such phenomenal creativity over fourteen years was possible only through the kind of involvement by colleagues, friends, and lovers depicted, with shocking openness, in *Warnung vor der heiligen Nutte* (1970, *Beware of the Holy Whore*). In his thematic interests and concerns, Fassbinder remained preoccupied with the individual's (often futile) struggles against the social and economic forces that preclude the realisation of his or her desires. The director pursued this veritable obsession through a creative engagement with the German filmic tradition that included social dramas such as *Warum läuft Herr R. Amok?* (1970, *Why Does Herr R. Run Amok?*), critical *Heimatfilme* such as *Wildwechsel* (1972, *Jailbait*), and chamber play films such as *Die bitteren Tränen der Petra von Kant* (1972, *The Bitter Tears of Petra von Kant*), as well as acclaimed literary adaptations such as Fontanes *Effi Briest* (1974). Likewise his almost compulsive explorations of power and violence in personal relationships included – to mention only three films from one single year – *Faustrecht der Freiheit* (1974, *Fox and His Friends*), one of the most provocative treatments of gay life and class prejudice; *Angst essen Seele auf* (1974, *Ali – Fear Eats the Soul*), a melodramatic study on the destructive effect of racism and ageism; and *Martha* (1974), a chilling portrayal of the oppression of women in bourgeois marriage.

Selfishness, greed, lust, and the need for control emerged as the driving impulses that, time and again, triumphed over all expressions of yearning, compassion, and despair and that laid the foundation for the director's more politicised reflections on the emotional landscape of postwar society. During the 1970s, Fassbinder resisted the general trend towards self-reflexive interiority and further sharpened his inquiries into the micro-politics of power and desire through a provocatively anti-psychological conception of characters; a marked preference for theatrical conventions and melodramatic effects; and a deliberately anti-realist use of interiors, objects, and settings. For Fassbinder, formal and emotional excess provided the most compelling expression of modern alienation and the most effective defence against the corrupting effects of authenticity; hence the director's ritualistic approach to interpersonal relationships. The resistance of Fassbinder's work to interpretative categories such as modernist detachment and postmodern reflexivity culminated in his obsessive approach to film, and film-making, as a more intense form of life. With these implications, the possibilities and the limitations of extreme stylisation found full articulation in the director's last film, an adaptation of Jean Genet's *Querelle* (1982).

More conventional narratives allowed Fassbinder to engage with the political controversies of the 1970s through the melodramatic effects that, through his eyes, only highlighted the contradiction between public discourse and the national imaginary. His films about left-wing radicalism in *Mutter Küsters Fahrt zum Himmel* (1975, *Mother Küsters Goes to Heaven*) and of left-wing terrorism in *Die dritte Generation* (1979, *The Third Generation*) diagnosed the inevitable corruption of political idealism and revolutionary fervour. From such a position of disillusionment, Fassbinder embarked on his most famous project, the so-called FRG trilogy, in which he rewrote the postwar years in the allegorical terms of female melodrama. From *Die Ehe der Maria Braun* (1979, *The Marriage of Maria Braun*), about the period of reconstruction, and *Lola* (1981), about the years of the Economic Miracle, to *Die Sehnsucht der Veronika Voss* (1982, *Veronika Voss*), about the tragic life of a former UFA star, Fassbinder used these highly gendered stories in order to examine the emotional investments in the writing of national history. *Lili Marleen* (1980), which recounts the story of the most famous song from the Second World War, also belongs to this group of films that makes sense of Germany in terms of specific libidinal structures, including the structures of repression that for Fassbinder defined postwar society from the 1950s to the 1970s (Elsaesser 1996b).

Among the group of film-makers emerging during the 1970s, Werner Herzog must be considered the most German in his aesthetic sensibilities and thematic pursuits, which also meant that he went furthest in exploring uncharted territories and seeking extreme situations (Corrigan 1986). Styling himself as a romantic hero, Herzog was influenced by Weimar directors such as Murnau – to whom he paid homage in *Nosferatu, Phantom der Nacht* (1978, *Nosferatu*) – and remained indebted to the legacies of German romanticism, including the sublime. These aesthetic traditions found expression in the director's heavy reliance on religious and mythological references and his intense preoccupation with notions such as fate, destiny, and redemption. The romantic tradition gave rise to the main concerns in his work: the motif of the journey and the search; the opposition of nature and culture; and the fascination with outsiders and foreigners. Significantly, it is usually a position on the margins, defined in spatial or temporal terms, that in Herzog reveals the power of the romantic imagination and expands the boundaries of reality, and experience, to include myth and history, fantasy and reality. From the old folk legend told in *Herz aus Glas* (1976, *Heart of Glass*) to the colonialist adventures shown in *Aguirre, der Zorn Gottes* (1972, *Aguirre, the Wrath of God*) and *Fitzcarraldo* (1981), Herzog insistently evokes images, visions, and dreams in order to overcome the poverty of contemporary existence. During the 1980s, the director continued these inquiries in films with a more pronounced anthropological and ethnographic interest.

Not surprisingly, the figure of the outsider functions as a recurring motif in Herzog's films, from the handicapped and dwarfs of his early allegories of the Federal Republic and the legacies of German romanticism to the Aborigines and Saharan Nomads who inspire his later sojourns to the few remaining areas in the world still untouched by capitalism and consumerism. Setting the tone, *Jeder für sich und Gott gegen alle* (1974, *The Enigma of Kaspar Hauser*) uses the fate of the famous nineteenth-century foundling to show the inherent violence of Western civilisation. The futile search by three outsiders in *Stroszek* (1977) for a better life in Wisconsin and a soldier's descent into madness in *Woyzeck* (1978), based on the Büchner play, follow the same tragic trajectory. In most of Herzog's films, heroic gestures of conquest lead to disaster and death, and desperate attempts of liberation only highlight the limits of progress and change. But the figure of the outsider not only sheds light on specific German compulsions, including a historical affinity for nihilism, mysticism, and romanticism. The failed stories of civilisation – or the stories of failed civilisation – also give rise to a powerful dynamic of creation and destruction, domination and subordination, which suggests a world beyond moral principles. By taking such an anti-humanist position, Herzog's films offer a radical critique of enlightenment rationality and classical modernity.

The films of Wim Wenders explore a similar tension between the search for authenticity, immediacy, and belonging and the desire for freedom and self-discovery. But in his films the resultant psychological conflicts find a privileged expression in the love–hate relationship with American popular culture. Influenced by New Subjectivity, Wenders set out in the mid-1970s to address the dilemmas of modern masculinity through a number of recurrent themes: the alienation from contemporary society and the search for new experiences; the bonds of male friendship and the impossibility of romantic love; the power of popular culture and the corrosive effect of modern mass media on the very notion of the real. Frequently, the episodic, open-ended narratives of his films are structured around a journey. Formally, the link between motion and emotion finds articulation in the contemplative long takes, elaborate camera movements, and composed still images that distinguish his filmic style. Through the characters' own fascination with images and perceptions, the journeys also draw attention to the hidden connection between the crisis in male–female relationships and the impossibility of story and history. Whereas *Falsche Bewegung* (1975, *Wrong Movement*) uses the Goethean motif of the educational journey to examine a society paralysed by post-1960s disillusionment, *Im Lauf der Zeit* (1976, *Kings of the Road*) already considers the possibility of visual perception as a redemptive experience. These possibilities are developed further in Wenders's intensely romantic films about America, the melancholy *Alice in den Städten* (1978, *Alice in the Cities*) and the more sentimental *Paris, Texas* (1984), which won the Palme d'Or at Cannes.

During the 1980s, Wenders continued his inquiries into the redemptive power of the filmic image along three axes: the return to storytelling as the prerequisite of romantic love; the rediscovery of place, and *Heimat*, as the foundation of identity; and the reaffirmation of film as the most important visual medium. His homages to the classical metropolis as the perfect compromise between freedom and belonging inspired several films about Lisbon, Tokyo, and Los Angeles and found full expression in two critically acclaimed films set in Berlin, first as the divided city of *Himmel über Berlin* (1987, *Wings of Desire*) and then as the unified German capital in *In weiter Ferne, so nah!* (1993, *Faraway, so Close*). After the noirish *Der Stand der Dinge* (1981, *The State of Things*), Wenders repeatedly used self-referential stories about film-making and image production to juxtapose the emotional power of film with the various models of simulation provided by the electronic and digital media that dominate the dystopian, post-apocalyptic world of *Bis ans Ende der Welt* (1991, *Until the End of the World*). These continuing reflections on the nature of images and perceptions and their relationship to memory, history, and desire reveal the strong influence of postmodern thought on Wenders's work, but they sometimes also suggest a more essentialist view of the filmic image as the locus of some transcendental truth (Geist 1988, Kolker and Beicken 1993, Cook and Gemünden 1997).

The international reception of New German cinema in the mid-1970s focused on individual directors and their elevated status as representatives of a different Germany (Rentschler 1984). The films assumed symbolic functions by offering aesthetic alternatives to Hollywood and by making a break with the cultural and political traditions associated with the Third Reich. The fact that such patterns of reception still relied on national stereotypes confirmed the role of the national as a category of difference even within the larger trends towards standardisation, globalisation, and hybridisation. In Germany, the popular and critical reception of the *Autorenfilm* turned out to be equally complicated. While often denounced as pretentious and self-indulgent, the films in fact helped to redefine the terms of national cinema by linking the search for more authentic (German) stories and images to definitions of Germanness unburdened by the ideology of nationalism. Accordingly, the relevance of cinema as an aesthetic, sensual, and social experience was demonstrated through its affinities with diverse social movements and cultural phenomena. Thus based in alternative forms of identity politics, the film-makers' search for more open narrative forms and fluid visual styles was driven and sustained by the widespread desire for a radically different relationship between subjective experience and social reality. This quality, which New German Cinema shared with postmodernism, manifested itself in the passionate commitment of its leading directors to develop alternatives to the enlightenment tradition, whether through the power–desire nexus evoked by Fassbinder, the liminal places and states explored by Herzog, or the redemptive moments of vision and visuality pursued by Wenders.

The difference between the international and the national reception of New German Cinema is nowhere more pronounced than in the critical assessment of Hans Jürgen Syberberg. Attacked in Germany for his reactionary views and elitist attitudes, this director frequently won praise in the United States for his willingness to confront the irrational forces in German culture and history. Relying on a panoply of visual, literary, musical, and philosophical effects, Syberberg transformed cinema into a *Gesamtkunstwerk* in order to perform what he called a necessary labour of mourning – that is, a working through the legacies of German romanticism and nationalism and their central role in the traumas of German history. Revisiting key personages, legends, and myths in the national imagination, Syberberg began with feature films about *Ludwig, Requiem für einen jungfräulichen König* (1972, *Ludwig, Requiem for a Virgin King*) and *Karl May* (1974) and continued in the documentary mode for *Winifred Wagner und die*

Geschichte des Hauses Wahnfried von 1914 bis 1975 (1975, *The Confessions of Winifred Wagner*). Confirming his fascination, if not identification, with the composer, Syberberg later directed the opera film Wagner's *Parsifal* (1982). The director's search for the libidinal foundation of National Socialism culminated in the monumental, almost seven-hour-long *Hitler – ein Film aus Deutschland* (1977, *Our Hitler*). This controversial film explores the collective fantasies surrounding Hitler through a mixture of modernist montage and postmodern citation, with a heavy reliance on parody and pastiche and an almost fetishistic use of icons, symbols, and myths. According to Syberberg, these formal elements and rhetoric moves only confirm the continuing relevance of the question of nation for the present conjuncture.

The international reception of New German Cinema revolved around the contested meaning of 'Germany' in the aftermath of the Third Reich. Yet during the same period that American audiences praised Syberberg and Herzog for confronting the emotional investments in the fantasy of German nation, German audiences rediscovered their interest in films that dealt with the less politicised but equally problematic notion of *Heimat*. Through its rural settings and characters, the critical *Heimatfilm* engaged with some of the more problematic generic legacies of the 1950s. But through filmic styles inspired by the international avant-gardes of the 1960s, its also opened up new perspectives on the Federal Republic and its anachronisms. *Jagdszenen aus Niederbayern* (1969, *Hunting Scenes from Lower Bavaria*), *Mathias Kneissl* (1971), and *Jaider, der einsame Jäger* (1971, *Jaider, the Lonely Hunter*) offered new interpretations on the familiar figure of the outsider, including as someone destined to unite and lead the community against an external power. With a clear view towards then-ongoing struggles, Schlöndorff in *Der plötzliche Reichtum der armen Leute von Kombach* (1971, *The Sudden Wealth of the Poor People of Kombach*) reconstructed an actual historical incident to reflect on the possibility of social action and political resistance. The critical *Heimatfilm* provided one of the few contexts in which film-makers after Oberhausen could reflect on questions of community, society, and nation, and do so without recourse to the reactionary discourses of folk and community. Moreover, the passionate defence of regional against national interests, of rural against urban culture, and of traditional against modern society gave rise to counter-narratives of community that remained relevant throughout the 1980s and 1990s (Schacht 1991).

The heavy reliance on literature marked the New German Cinema as a middle-class phenomenon propelled by the desire, first expressed during the 1910s, of moving beyond the high–low culture divide and of elevating film to the level of the other arts. The director most closely identified with this disposition or tendency was Volker Schlöndorff. Known for skilled adaptations of twentieth-century authors such as Marcel Proust, Max Frisch, and Arthur Miller, Schlöndorff repeatedly enlisted conventional narratives in formal explorations and utilised canonical works for critical rereadings. From *Der junge Törless*, his first feature film, to the later *Der Fangschuss* (1976, *Coup de Grâce*), Schlöndorff's modernist sensibilities found expression in a marked preference for analytical narrative strategies, minimal dramatic effects, reserved acting styles, and, at least in the early films, a stark black-and-white cinematography. Schlöndorff's greatest commercial and critical successes, his adaptation of the Böll story *Die verlorene Ehre der Katharina Blum* (1975, *The Lost Honour of Katharina Blum*) and the Grass novel *Die Blechtrommel* (1979, *The Tin Drum*), both featured individuals who find themselves confronted with powerful political forces and dramatic historical events. Whereas the earlier film focuses on an innocent victim of the police brutality and public hysteria generated by the terrorist activities of the 1970s, the later one revisits the German past from the perspective of a young boy who, like the nation itself, refuses to grow (up) and confront reality. *Die Blechtrommel* received the Palme d'Or and the Oscar for Best Foreign Film. Throughout the 1980s and 1990s, Schlöndorff would continue to rely on his belief in the values of humanism to explore difficult topics – the abuses of power, the possibility of resistance, and the importance of individual responsibility – without sacrificing popular appeal.

The increase in literary adaptations was not always an expression of directorial preferences but often also a response to diminished funding opportunities and the literary biases of a selection process based on submitted screenplays. Known as the literature adaptation crisis of the mid-1970s, the sudden increase in films inspired by canonical authors such as Goethe, Fontane, Storm, and Ibsen contributed to a more general change in filmic styles and, by extension, critical sensibilities. The modernist aesthetics of formal innovation and political critique gradually gave way to psychologically motivated, dialogue-driven narratives with clear patterns of identification – a process that, in turn, cannot be separated from the larger developments, in literature and in public debate, known as the conservative *Tendenzwende*. Only the writers of German romanticism sustained a creative engagement with the tradition of irrationalism and its relevance for definitions of national identity. Especially the figure of the romantic genius inspired several projects about the life and work of Heinrich von Kleist, including Eric Rohmer's critically acclaimed *Die Marquise von O.* (1975, *The Marquise of O*).

Offering a workable solution to the declining public support for, and the limited popular success of, New German Cinema, public television during the early 1970s emerged as a leading supporter of more innovative film-makers and controversial projects. The active involvement of WDR (West German Radio) gave rise to the *Arbeiterfilm* (workers' film) that offered realistic portrayals of working-class life in films such as *Liebe Mutter, mir geht es gut* (1972, *Dear Mother, I Am Well*) by Christian Ziewer and Klaus Wiese, and *Die Wollands* (1972, *The Wollands*) by Marianne Lüdcke and Ingo Kratisch. By continuing in the Weimar tradition of political film-making, the workers' film offered film-makers a rare opportunity for reflecting on the importance of solidarity as an individual and collective virtue (Collins and Porter 1981). The active involvement by various regional television channels in promoting difficult subject matter, on the one hand, and the public's gradual acceptance of the 'amphibian' styles dictated by the television format, on the other hand, further strengthened the ties between film and television. In 1974, their relationship was formalised in the Television Framework Agreement between public television and the Film Subsidy Board, which helped to generate more than DM30 million in funds between 1974 and 1978. Ambitious cultural series such as ZDF's *Das kleine Fernsehspiel* (*The Short Television Play*) provided an important showcase for first-time directors. At the same time, the programming structure of television accommodated large-scale literary adaptations of works by Thomas Mann, Hans Fallada, and Jakob Wassermann in the form of mini-series. These possibilities proved particularly important to ambitious projects such as Fassbinder's fourteen-hour-long adaptation of Döblin's *Berlin Alexanderplatz* (1979–80) and Reitz's sixteen-hour project *Heimat* (1984), along with its twenty-six-hour sequel, *Die zweite Heimat* (1992, *Second Heimat*).

The founding of new film museums and the launching of new book series contributed further to the institutionalisation of art cinema as the dominant model of national cinema during the 1970s. Modelled after the Cinémathèque Française, the Stiftung Deutsche Kinemathek was founded in Berlin in 1971 as an important film archive and centre for research. The Freunde der Deutschen Kinemathek started the famous Arsenal cinema, Berlin's premier location for film retrospectives, and organised the International Forum of the New Film at the Berlin Film Festival. Even the Bundesarchiv/Filmarchiv, originally founded in 1953 with the goal of preserving films as historical documents, expanded its holdings in 1978 to become the central national archives for all feature and non-feature films. The Federal Film Archives subsequently moved most of their operations from Koblenz to Berlin; after 1989, it incorporated the holdings of the GDR's State Film Archives. Confirming cinema as an essential part of national culture, film museums opened in the country's major cities, including the Deutsches Filmmuseum in Frankfurt am Main, as well as several smaller museums in Munich and Düsseldorf. The proliferation of regional film festivals, all with their own competitions and awards, further underscored film's indispensability to the revitalisation of regional culture. Responding to a growing interest in film as a subject of critical study, several publishing houses began to put out both general film histories and encyclopaedias and more specific books about German film history and theory. Hanser launched a 'famous directors' series under the editorship of Wolfram Schütte and Peter W. Jansen, Fischer until recently produced the informative Film Almanac yearbooks, and Heyne started a successful monograph series devoted to popular genres and stars. The ambitious film historical projects undertaken by the *Cinegraph* group under Hans-Michael Bock and several new scholarly journals and monograph series contributed greatly to the emergence of German film studies during the 1970s and 1980s. Supporting this development, Karena Niehoff for the *Süddeutsche Zeitung* and above all Karsten Witte for the *Frankfurter Rundschau* maintained the high quality of film criticism in national newspapers and played a key role in promoting the German *Autorenfilm* as part of an international art cinema.

The 1970s have often been described as a retreat to the politics of the personal associated with the literary movement of New Subjectivity and its clear validation of psychological reflection over political action. One of its main representatives, the author Peter Handke, collaborated with Wenders on *Die Angst des Tormanns beim*

Elfmeter (1971, *The Goalie's Fear at the Penalty Kick*) and directed his own film adaptation of *Die linkshändige Frau* (1978, *The Left-handed Woman*). In these paradigmatic works, the reconfiguration of identity in terms of ambivalence and ambiguity also gave rise to the prevailing moods of the decade: melancholy, hypersensitivity, reflexivity, and a deep sense of self-alienation. Pointing to a pervasive crisis of masculinity, the films' male leads seemed compelled to act out the guilt of their fathers through their unwillingness, or inability, to make decisions and take responsibility. The resultant cult of interiority had a profound effect on narrative and visual styles (for example, episodic structures, essayistic forms), but it resonated also in the physical appearance and performance style of the decade's leading actors and actresses. Rüdiger Vogler, Bruno Ganz, and Hanns Zischler regularly played characters caught amidst obsessive contemplation, heightened awareness, and unmitigated narcissism. The social typology of the sensitive but also completely self-centred male contrasted sharply with the image of the strong, independent woman conveyed by Hanna Schygulla, Eva Mattes, and Barbara Sukowa. The fact that this gendered imbalance of power, including in erotic matters, also appeared in many DEFA films from the 1970s confirms its narrative function as a displacement of more deep-seated psychological traumas related to the body of German nation.

The new sensibilities conveyed by these actors, and, of course, directors, contributed to the revival of cinema as an alternative public sphere and implicated moviegoing more directly in the search for new experiences. After years of cinema closings, especially in smaller towns and rural areas, their numbers during the 1970s stabilised at 3,300 or so cinemas throughout the country. The proliferation of porn cinemas in downtown areas stopped. At the same time, the number of tickets sold was now regularly above 110 million per year. The rising attendance figures reflected the increased interest in film among students, artists, and intellectuals, as well as the educated middle class. German and European art films never seriously threatened the popular appeal of Hollywood films, which dominated the market with almost 80 per cent of all new releases. Nonetheless, the art films gave rise to a small but influential counterculture sustained, among other things, by new exhibition venues. In 1971, Hilmar Hoffmann opened the first Kommunale Kino (communal cinema) in Frankfurt am Main; many cities started similar projects under municipal supervision. Functioning like art houses, these cinemas organised historical retrospectives and often showed films from lesser-known national cinemas and avant-garde traditions. Responding to the changing expectations about moviegoing as a social activity, commercial theatre-owners, including the entrepreneurial Hans-Joachim Flebbe, built a number of multi-screen theatres that showed a mixture of difficult and entertaining films and often included cafés, bars, and bookshops on their premises. All of these initiatives responded to the 'hunger for experience' (M. Rutschky) that drove the spectator's emotional involvement with different identities, new sensations, and presumably more authentic situations. In the light of such aesthetic, sensory, and psychological investments, German cinema culture by the end of the 1970s found itself both on the forefront of a postmodern cult of pure perception and in sharp opposition to the aesthetics of the simulacrum.

Of course, New German Cinema can be defined also through the topics and themes that dominated German culture and society during the 1970s and 1980s, a fact that is often forgotten by auteurist readings. Often made by lesser-known directors, these topical films combined social relevance and popular appeal in order to address a wide range of pressing problems such as the brutality of public life, the alienation of youth, the disappearance of regional culture, the power of large corporations, and the threat of ecological disasters. Many stories revolved around the tension between the characters' desire for belonging, as captured in the notion of *Heimat*, and a deep need for independence that often found expression in their desperate or violent opposition to family, community, and the state. Young protagonists seemed ideally suited to articulate this tension in narrative terms. Thus Hark Bohm, the main representative of the critical youth film, showed the alienation of adolescent boys in *Nordsee ist Mordsee* (1975, *The North Sea Is Murderous*) and *Moritz, lieber Moritz* (1977, *Moritz, Dear Moritz*), two top-grossing films from the decade. In one of the earliest films about the problems in Turkish immigrant families, *Yasemin* (1988), Bohm explored the same problematic from the perspective of a female high-school student. Its conciliatory mood remained the exception among the many depressing stories about Germany's troubled, alienated youth. Still committed to the critical force of negativity, Uwe Friessner in *Das Ende des Regenbogens* (1979, *The End of the Rainbow*) consciously avoided all didactic impulses in his sobering portrayal of a West Berlin youth involved in street prostitution and petty theft. By contrast, the cautionary tale of a young girl's descent into a world of hard drugs and sexual tricks in Ulrich Edel's *Christiane F. – Wir Kinder vom Bahnhof Zoo* (1981, *Christiane F*) catered primarily to sensationalist impulses and, because of these qualities, became a great commercial success.

The many films about social outsiders all shared a similar sense of anger, fear, and paranoia and often used violence as a metaphor of contemporary life. Action, suspense, and high drama emerged as the preferred modalities for examining social problems such as the dehumanising conditions in the prison system depicted in Reinhard Hauff's *Die Verrohung des Franz Blum* (1974, *The Brutalisation of Franz Blum*), the criminalisation of homosexuals in Wolfgang Petersen's *Die Konsequenz* (1977, *The Consequence*), and the spectre of epidemics raised by Peter Fleischmann's *Die Hamburger Krankheit* (1979, *The Hamburg Disease*). Political thrillers such as *Messer im Kopf* (1978, *Knife in the Head*) and *Kamikaze* (1982) offered cautionary tales about the immense power of state institutions and large corporations. Despite the politicisation of the public sphere during the 1960s, only a few film-makers addressed the problem of political persecution, such as Sohrab Shahid Saless in *In der Fremde* (1975, *Far from Home*), a moving portrayal of Iranians exiled by the Shah regime, and Ziewer in *Aus der Ferne sehe ich dieses Land* (1977, *From a Distance I See This Country*), about Chilean refugees escaping from the Pinochet regime. However, the voice of international solidarity sounded loud and clear in Peter Lilienthal's films about Latin America, from *Es herrscht Ruhe im Land* (1975, *Calm Prevails in the Country*), which showed the reality of everyday life under a totalitarian regime, to *Der Aufstand* (1980, *The Uprising*), which reflected on the possibility of resistance under conditions of political oppression.

Sometimes, the figure of the outsider inspired more humorous treatments, especially in stories set among disenfranchised social groups or in declining industrial regions. With considerable commercial success, Adolf Winkelmann in *Die Abfahrer* (1979, *On the Move*) and *Jede Menge Kohle* (1981, *Lots of Dough*) developed his stories of individual rebellion against the backdrop of the declining steel industry in the Ruhr region. A similar combination of obstinacy and sentimentality characterised the surprise hit *Die Interessen der Bank sind nicht die Interessen, die Lina Braake hat* (1975, *Lina Braake*), about the struggle of a feisty old woman against a powerful bank, and *Das Brot des Bäckers* (1976, *The Baker's Bread*), about the hopeless fight of a small-town bakery against mechanisation and mass production. But such light-hearted approaches remained the exception in a decade committed to more serious investigations of the constraints on social and sexual identity.

It was under such conditions that the so-called *Frauenfilm* (woman's film) emerged as a logical continuation of, and a powerful challenge to, the New German Cinema. The not unproblematic term *Frauenfilm* usually refers to films by women directors, films about 'women's issues' (for example, sexuality, pregnancy, motherhood), and films with a pronounced feminist orientation. The critical reception of the woman's film in the mainstream press was dismissive, with 'one-sided', 'self-indulgent', 'boring', and 'depressing' frequent complaints that, in a way, only confirmed the underlying provocation. Many of the early women directors developed their filmic visions through the critical engagement with the student movement of the 1960s and the women's movement of the 1970s. The feminist agenda shared by Helke Sander, Helma Sanders-Brahms, Jutta Brückner, and Margarethe von Trotta was to move beyond the narrow understanding of politics prevalent even in the radical left and to focus on personal relationships as the real point of departure for fundamental change. For these women, film-making represented a form of self-expression, consciousness-raising, and political activism. Some directors enlisted their stories of discrimination and oppression in a radical critique of patriarchal society, whereas others focused on typical women's problems (for example, unequal pay, job discrimination, sexual violence, reproductive rights), and yet others explored intimate relationships among women, including lesbianism, as a valid personal and political alternative. The diagnosis of institutional sexism and the critique of the sexual revolution sometimes gave way to a not unproblematic essentialist celebration of women's otherness. Thus by the 1980s, the growing divisions within the women's movement (socialist versus feminist, heterosexual versus lesbian, reformist versus autonomous) began to marginalise the women's film as an influential genre, notwithstanding the continuing successes of individual women directors. The anti-feminist backlash in the early 1990s further diminished the core audience for these films, except within the feminist and lesbian subcultures found in many major cities.

Most women's films shared a number of characteristics, beginning with the preference for autobiographical forms, for stories of everyday life, and for what some critics have referred to as a female aesthetic. The feminist movement remained a ubiquitous reference point by providing the actual and intended audience for these films, by functioning as the model of a different public sphere, and by serving as a source of critical impulses. The basic feminist tenet that 'the private is political' guided the film-makers' search for, and exploration of, alternative filmic forms and styles. Their radical programme extended to various autonomous film and media activities, organisations for women film professionals, and feminist film festivals such as the Cologne Feminale. Founded in 1974, the feminist film journal *Frauen und Film* contributed actively to the emergence of an autonomous women's film culture and, later, to the advancement of feminist film theory (Riecke 1998). The international orientation of the feminist and lesbian movements was largely responsible for the positive reception of German women directors in other countries (for example, Monika Treut in the United States). The productive exchanges between feminist and avant-garde practices extended to the work of video artists such as Austrian Valie Export and helped to cultivate film's affinities with painting, video, and performance art. Unfortunately, the documentary tradition started by Stöckl and Runge during the 1960s proved of little relevance to the discourse of identity shared by the feminist movement with other social and cultural phenomena of the 1970s.

Many of the early women's films combined a traditional narrative structure with provocative subject matter in order to achieve two equally important goals: to tell different stories, and to tell stories differently. The preference for melodramatic forms helped film-makers to reaffirm emotionality as a female strength, but this time under female authorship. Autobiographical and biographical approaches allowed them to validate personal perspectives and individual experiences, to formulate a new ethos and erotics of authenticity, and to explore the gendered body as a locus of female identity with positive as well as negative implications. In the early years, women directors often emphasised the liberating power of female solidarity, as did Sanders-Brahms through the arguments of the troubled couple depicted in *Unter dem Pflaster liegt der Strand* (1974, *Below the Pavement Lies the Beach*) and Sander through the problems of a single working mother in *REDUPERS: Die allseitig reduzierte Persöhnlichkeit* (1977, *The All-round Reduced Personality*). Instead of offering social or political explanations, both films explored the difficult situation of women through the prohibitions on female sexuality and creative expression. Working within a feminist framework, Sander continued with *Der subjektive Faktor* (1980, *The Subjective Factor*) and *Der Beginn aller Schrecken ist Liebe* (1983, *The Beginning of All Horror Is Love*). Resisting such overt politicisation, Sanders-Brahms pursued more subjective visions. She moved from the sense of social responsibility that informed the tragic story of a Turkish woman in Germany, *Shirins Hochzeit* (1976, *Shirin's Wedding*), to the highly allegorical interweaving of family story and national history in what became her most famous, and most controversial film, *Deutschland – bleiche Mutter* (1979, *Germany, Pale Mother*).

In the early 1980s, feminist film-makers also began to examine the relationship between autobiography and historiography and to pay closer attention to the suppression of female voices in the master-narratives of German history and cultural identity (Weinberger 1992, Linville 1998). The discovery of forgotten historical figures such as the feminist and socialist Flora Tristan, who inspired Claudia Aleman's imaginative filmic journey in *Die Reise nach Lyon* (1980, *Blind Spot*), or von Trotta's moving portrait of *Rosa Luxemburg* (1986) as both a female revolutionary and a woman in love represented only one side in this process; the other side involved a fundamental reinterpretation of established modes of explanation. In confronting the Third Reich, some women film-makers moved beyond the available socio-psychological accounts that explained the rise of National Socialism and the postwar culture of denial solely through the crises of the authoritarian family. Challenging the implicit assumptions about traditional masculinity as the guarantor of political stability, and of stable sexual identities as the foundation of a healthy national culture, feminists emphatically insisted on a sharp distinction between the historical experiences of women and their allegorical status in historical narratives, including those offered by the representatives of New German Cinema.

Uncovering the past in the present, Jeanine Meerapfel in *Malou* (1981) showed a woman's increasingly desperate attempts to reconstruct the tragic life story of her mother and, in so doing, to come to terms with her own divided identity of being Catholic, Jewish, and Argentine in West German society. By focusing on the complexities of sexual, social, and national identity, women film-makers also opened up new perspectives on the postwar years. The mother–daughter relationship played a key role in these explorations, as did the often ambiguous relationship to the figure of the stranger and the experience of otherness. Thus Jutta Brückner in *Hungerjahre* (1980, *Hunger Years*) used a young girl's experience of growing up during the 1950s to trace the connection between sexual repression and the culture of the Economic Miracle. Taking a more playful approach (for example, through dream sequences, fantastic elements), Marianne Rosenbaum in *Peppermint Frieden* (1983, *Peppermint Peace*) returned to the sense of hope, confidence, and infinite possibility prevalent in the postwar years by assuming the perspective of an imaginative young girl.

As the most famous female director of the 1980s, von Trotta remained closely identified both with the specific concerns of the woman's film and with more general developments within New German Cinema. From the beginning, her films exhibited a remarkable consistency in their preference for middle-class settings and the intense conflicts between sisters or close friends. *Schwestern oder die Balance des Glücks* (1979, *Sisters or The Balance of Happiness*) and *Heller Wahn* (1982, *Friends and Husbands*) offered psychological insights into the complicated dynamics of closeness and distance and the underlying processes of identification and projection found in all relationships. In her most famous film, *Die bleierne Zeit* (1981, *The German Sisters/Marianne and Juliane*), von Trotta used the story of the Ensslin sisters to measure the effect of terrorism on everyday life and to explore the connection between revolutionary politics and individual biography. By combining psychological and political perspectives, von Trotta proved essential in conveying feminist concerns to a wider public; but she also contributed to the less noticeable transformations that made the films of the 1980s more conventional in form and content.

The 1980s: crises and transformations

The preoccupation with personal relationships as the primary site of power struggles reached a critical impasse when film-makers had to confront the political events of the late 1970s, encapsulated in the term 'German Autumn'. The wave of terrorism that shook the foundations of the state and resonated in all areas of public life forced many artists, intellectuals, and public figures to respond to the underlying political crisis. Following a wave of kidnappings, assassinations, and terrorist trials, several directors joined forces to produce an omnibus film, *Deutschland im Herbst* (1978, *Germany in Autumn*), that contemplated the far-reaching effects of terrorism on Germany society, including on new forms of censorship and self-censorship. Similar critical intentions informed a later project, *Der Kandidat* (1980, *The Candidate*), about the election campaign of conservative Franz-Josef Strauss. During the 1980s, film-makers continued to deal with the psychological causes and social consequences of left-wing terrorism, whether through the dramatic re-enactment of the RAF trials in *Stammheim* (1986) or the screen adaptation of Bernhard Vesper's autobiography, *Die Reise* (1986, *The Journey*). These films participated in the labour of mourning that connected the 'German Autumn' to the unresolved legacies of the Third Reich and the failed utopias of the student movement. The sense of failure, loss, and melancholia in most films about terrorism and the West German left resonated even in much later attempts to preserve, transform, and jettison the politicised discourses of cinema developed during the 1960s and 1970s.

Most historical overviews characterise the 1980s as a period of artistic decline, with the death of Fassbinder in 1982 marking the end of New German Cinema as a formally innovative and politically provocative cinema. After the elections in 1982, the CDU-dominated government under Chancellor Helmut Kohl brought about a conservative turn in social and economic policies as well as cultural tastes. The official approach to film funding found expression in provocative comments by the new Minister of the Interior about film as mere entertainment. The threat to the future of art cinema loomed in the further reduction of public subsidies on the national level and the denial of already approved loans to controversial projects. For the film industry, this loss of support coincided with an intensified competition for audiences after the introduction of home video and, later, cable television. Some companies such as the Kirch group diversified their holdings by buying the rights to old Hollywood films and television programmes. The pursuit of commercial success contributed to the exodus of yet another generation of German film-makers to Hollywood. After the phenomenal success of *Das Boot* (1981, *The Boat*), which depicts the heroic fight of a German submarine crew during the Second World War, Petersen went on to make *Die unendliche Geschichte* (1984, *The Never-ending Story*), based on Michael Ende's popular children's book, already with an eye towards international markets. In Hollywood, Petersen developed a reputation for suspenseful political thrillers. In the 1990s, Roland Emmerich had similar success with monster and science fiction films.

While some producers and directors turned to big-budget films to become more competitive, others took advantage of the many connections among film, television, and the recording industry to attract younger audiences and to do so in accordance with the established formulas that most accommodated their demand for films as, at worst, cheap diversion and, at best, good entertainment. The affinities between music and film proved particularly profitable, as evident in the success of *Panische Zeiten* (1980, *Panic Times*), with rock star Udo Lindenberg, or *Theo gegen den Rest der Welt* (1980, *Theo against the Rest of the World*), with singer Marius Müller-Westernhagen. The exploitation of regressive tendencies and parochial sensibilities in these commercial films was most noticeable in the registers of German humour. Comedians such as Otto Waalkes in *Otto – der Film* (1985, *Otto – the Film*) or Dieter Hallervorden with *Didi auf vollen Touren* (1986, *Didi in Full Form*) acquired a large cult following with their adolescent pranks and inane jokes. Among the few television personalities who made the successful transition to the screen was the eccentric Loriot (alias Vicco von Bülow), who appeared in two box-office hits, *Ödipussi* (1987) and *Pappa ante Portas* (1991).

Through the synergies between film and television, film-makers found more possibilities to reach larger audiences, including for difficult subject matter. Under these conditions, the return to generic conventions, especially those of melodrama, even opened up the history of the Third Reich to more detailed investigations into the possibility of individual resistance and the involvement of ordinary Germans in anti-Semitic atrocities. The central role of film and television in this process of remembering became overwhelmingly clear in two surprise successes: the retelling of the Holocaust as family melodrama in the American television series *Holocaust*, which sparked intense public debates in 1979; and, two years later, the tragedy of German wartime heroism commemorated by *Das Boot* through a careful avoidance of all political references. These developments continued in several German co-productions with Switzerland that produced two films about the Swiss involvement with the Third Reich, *Das Boot ist voll* (1980, *The Boat Is Full*) and *Glut* (1983, *Embers*). The renewed interest in the Nazi past during the 1980s cannot be separated from the so-called Historians Debate about the nature of National Socialism and the significance of the Holocaust. On the one hand, first signs of a normalisation of German history appeared in the changing rituals of public commemoration (for example, the fortieth anniversary of the end of the Second World War in 1985). On the other hand, the very fact of these revisionist tendencies brought additional urgency to the question of historical representation and the available narrative models and paradigms. The rewriting of German history in melodramatic terms contributed to the overwhelmingly positive reception of

Schindler's List (1993). An earlier Polish–German–French co-production, Agnieszka Holland's *Hitlerjunge Salomon* (1992, *Europa, Europa*) had a much more divided reception because of its allegedly frivolous portrayal of a German Jewish boy who miraculously survives the Third Reich by assuming different racial, national, and political identities.

The films about the Third Reich followed two basic models: studies of significant historical figures and events and more generic investigations into the fascism of everyday life. For a fictional account of the life of Rudolf Höss, the commandant of the Auschwitz concentration camp, in *Aus einem deutschen Leben* (1977, *From a German Life*), a detached documentary style was chosen in order to underscore the banality of evil. Chilling factuality also prevailed in *Die Wannseekonferenz* (1984, *The Wannsee Conference*), about the eponymous secret meeting in January 1942 concerning the Final Solution. However, similar claims to historical authenticity also stood behind the more dramatic reflections on art and politics, and the dangers of blind ambition, that informed the intense performances by Klaus Maria Brandauer in two Istvan Szabo films, *Mephisto* (1981), about the phenomenal career of actor Gustav Gründgens during the Third Reich, and *Hanussen* (1987), about a famous clairvoyant from the Berlin of the 1920s who fatally predicted the rise of the Nazis.

The second type of film about the Third Reich concentrated on average characters, typical situations, and ordinary lives. As illustrated by *David* (1979) and *Die Kinder aus Nr. 67* (1979, *The Children from No. 67*), some film-makers chose the perspectives of children to move beyond the official discourses of collective guilt and to disrupt familiar patterns of historical explanation. Others, such as Alf Brustellin and Bernhard Sinkel in *Berlinger* (1975), explored the possibility of individual choice in the face of political oppression through the very different careers of two friends, a calculating opportunist and a stubborn individualist – an approach reminiscent of Hoffmann's *Wir Wunderkinder* of 1958 and the DEFA production *Anton, der Zauberer* from the same year. These stories provided alternative points-of-view from which to confront the complexities of history beyond the dichotomies of guilt and innocence and, in so doing, to reconsider questions of agency and responsibility. Along similar lines, Bernhard Wicki's *Sansibar oder der letzte Grund* (1986, *Sansibar or the True Reason*), based on the novel by Alfred Andersch, offered a moving parable of reconciliation, with a communist man and a Jewish woman joining forces to save a Christian artefact from imminent destruction by the Nazis. Many of these new tendencies and arguments coalesced in the work of Michael Verhoeven, whose Third Reich Trilogy recounts paradigmatic instances of individual resistance based on historical figures and events. Whereas *Die weisse Rose* (1982, *The White Rose*), about the Munich student resistance group around Sophie and Hans Scholl, still followed a conventional narrative pattern, *Das schreckliche Mädchen* (1990, *The Nasty Girl*) presented a curious girl's school project about her hometown during the Third Reich through an imaginative combination of pseudo-documentary scenes, grotesque dream sequences, and other critical strategies inspired by Brechtian distanciation. The last film in the Verhoeven trilogy, *Mutters Courage* (1995, *My Mother's Courage*), used a not unproblematic mixture of grotesque, comedy, and burlesque to link George Tabori's account of his mother's survival during the Holocaust to larger questions about the decisive moments of life and death.

The renewed interest in the Third Reich arose from a long overdue confrontation with the historical implications of anti-Semitism and the Holocaust, on the one hand, and the growing awareness of their importance to then-current debates about German history and national identity, on the other. As part of this process, the rediscovery of *Heimat* served both to offer an alternative to the tainted history of nation and to provide an escape from the discourse of collective guilt to that other Germany identified with idyllic villages and beautiful landscapes. The ordinary story of one such village, Schabbach in the Hunsrück mountains, was thus elevated to a grand epic scale in one of the most ambitious German film and television projects, Reitz's 1980–84 production of *Heimat* and its 1988–92 sequel, *Die zweite Heimat*. Whereas the original *Heimat* tells the history of a small village from the 1920s to the 1950s through the coming-of-age story of its central character, the sequel follows the young man to Munich where he joins the bohemian milieu of artists and intellectuals during the 1960s. Criticised for its sentimental tendencies but also hailed for its close attention to the organisation of everyday life, *Heimat* inspired heated debates about the relationship among history, memory, narrative, and national identity. In particular, the television series was attacked for its affirmative reconstruction of Germanness outside the realities of anti-Semitism (Kaes 1989, Santner 1990).

Several directors during the 1970s and 1980s became closely identified with the uncanny, absurd, and humorous scenarios inspired by this critical re-evaluation of *Heimat*. Bringing an outsider's sensibility to familiar landscapes such as the Lüneburg Heath and the Rhine Valley, Swiss-born director Niklaus Schilling turned the cold idylls and beautiful still-lives of *Nachtschatten* (1971, *Night Shades*), *Rheingold* (1978, *Rhine Gold*), and *Der Willi Busch Report* (1979, *The Willi Busch Report*) into morbid allegories of the Federal Republic. The eccentric Herbert Achternbusch made a name for himself by celebrating the whimsical, scurrilous, and zany nature of everyday life in Bavaria with a mixture of anthropological detachment, confrontational techniques, and deeply felt personal ambivalence. From Munich films such as *Servus Bayern* (1977, *Bye-bye Bavaria*) and *Das Gespenst* (1982, *The Ghost*) to *Ab nach Tibet* (1993, *Gone to Tibet*), Achternbuch carried on in the tradition of anarchic humour started by Valentin during the 1920s. With almost compulsive regularity, Achternbusch combined elements of vaudeville, burlesque, passion play, and absurd theatre to work through his love–hate relationship with a city and a region ruled by the Catholic Church, haunted by the legacies of the Third Reich, and defined by the beer-drinking rituals of the infamous *Hofbräuhaus*. Introducing a more conciliatory perspective, Percy Adlon in the quirky *Zuckerbaby* (1985, *Sugar Baby*) and the enormously successful *Out of Rosenheim* (1987, *Baghdad Café*), realised the dream of self-expression through the figure of a buxom Bavarian woman, played by Marianne Sägebrecht, who finds personal happiness in defiance of all social and sexual stereotypes.

In less obvious ways, the rewriting of the Third Reich also made possible the acceptance, no matter how tentative, of the Federal Republic as a contemporary version of *Heimat*. The resultant reflections on identity, place, and belonging found their favourite protagonists among the urban counterculture of artists and intellectuals as well as the successful members of the educated middle class. Significantly, it was the growing dissatisfaction with the narcissistic cult of subjectivity that opened up a space for reclaiming romance, love, and sexuality as an essential, and essentially unchanged, human experience. Two directors from the 1960s played a key role in initiating this change in erotic sensibilities. Specialising in romantic comedies, Rudolf Thome during the 1980s presented his stories of ordinary men and women as an essential part of everyday life in West Berlin and, later, a reunited Berlin. However, the symptomatic shift from the public debates about gentrification that still complicated romantic love in *Berlin Chamissoplatz* (1980) to the sentimental images of couples and families in *Das Mikroskop* (1988, *The Microscope*) and *Liebe auf den ersten Blick* (1991, *Love at First Sight*) became possible only through the reaffirmation both of traditional notions of gender and of the private sphere as the locus of individual happiness. Focusing on the rituals of heterosexual desire, not least in the context of prostitution, Robert van Ackeren developed a more cynical tone and turned into an observant chronicler of the endless erotic constellations between strong women and weak men. From *Die Reinheit des Herzens* (1980, *The Purity of the Heart*) and *Die flambierte Frau* (1983, *The Woman in Flames*) to *Die wahre Geschichte von Männern und Frauen* (1992, *The True Story of Men and Women*), the spectacle of female sexuality allowed van Ackeren simultaneously to demonstrate the liberalisation in public attitudes towards sexuality and to measure the reverberations of the sexual revolution on erotic passions and perversions.

Last but not least, the dismantling of art cinema as the master discourse of national cinema opened up a space for the cultivation of more diverse audiences and marginal tastes. Resisting the overwhelming trend towards verisimilitude, two productive stylists/activists from the 1960s continued to probe the affinities between sexuality and aesthetics from an openly gay perspective. Beginning with *Der Tod der Maria Malibran* (1971, *The Death of Maria Malibran*), with cult star Magdalena Montezuma, Werner Schroeter relied on an eclectic mixture of opera, melodrama, religion, ritual, and performance art to explore the connection between beauty and desire in the sexually ambiguous terms of camp and kitsch. His most compelling reflection on gay aesthetics, *Der Rosenkönig* (1986, *The Rose King*), captured the erotics of the filmic image through the well-known fantasy of Italy as the embodiment of beauty and sensuality. Schroeter's earlier social melodramas about Italian guest workers, *Neapolitanische Geschwister* (1978, *Kingdom of Naples*) and *Palermo oder Wolfsburg* (1980, *Palermo or Wolfsburg*), were structured around the same convergence of reality and artifice that undermined the conventional patterns of compassionate identification with otherness.

Representative of a more activist stance on issues of gay rights, the work of the prolific Rosa von Praunheim can be divided into three groups: polemics about the discrimination against homosexuals in the style of *Nicht der Homosexuelle ist pervers, sondern die Situation, in der er lebt* (1970, *Not the Homosexual Is Perverted but the Situation in which He Finds Himself*) and *Die AIDS-Trilogie* (1992, *The AIDS Trilogy*); low-budget melodramas such as *Ein Virus kennt keine Moral* (1986, *A Virus Knows no Morals*) and *Anita, Tänze des Lasters* (1987, *Anita, Dances of Vice*) that imitate Weimar expressionism; and documentaries about the ordinary lives of extraordinary people like the elderly male cross-dresser of *Ich bin meine eigene Frau* (1992, *I Am My Own Woman*). In contrast to Schroeter and Praunheim, who remained committed to the aesthetic and political project of sexual liberation, the Berlin underground film-maker Lothar Lambert made a career for himself by celebrating gay tastes through the kind of misogynist overtones found in *Die Alptraumfrau* (1980, *The Nightmare Woman*) and *Was Sie nie über Frauen wissen wollten* (1989, *What You Never Wanted to Know about Women*). Similar conclusions concerning the politics of sex could be drawn about *Taxi zum Klo* (1981, *Taxi to the John*), a controversial depiction of the promiscuous gay scene in Berlin before the times of AIDS.

In what ways some films with gay and lesbian themes moved beyond expanding generic conventions to actually conveying a distinct queer sensibility – in other words, a challenge to established notions of gender, identity, and desire – became evident in the few films committed to sexual liberation and formal experimentation. During the 1970s, Ulrike Ottinger produced the visually most imaginative body of work by appropriating the means of postmodern citation, modernist defamiliarisation, and post-colonial ethnography for beautiful mise-en-scènes of female love and adventure. Whether caught on a junk in the Chinese Seas or drunk in the streets of Berlin, the women of *Madame X, eine absolute Herrscherin* (1977, *Madame X*) and *Bildnis einer Trinkerin* (1979, *Ticket of No Return*) articulated their otherness through the means of parody, theatricality, and artifice. Ottinger's ambition to reclaim visual pleasure for the cinema continued in the excursions of *Johanna d'Arc of Mongolia* (1988) and found expression in three discursive registers: erotic allegory, exoticism, and ethnography. Rejecting the essentialism of feminist identity politics, Monika Treut drew attention to the aesthetics of sadomasochism in *Verführung: Die grausame Frau* (1985, *Seduction: The Cruel Woman*), a highly stylised film shot in black-and-white by well-known cinematographer Elfi Mikesch. The later *Die Jungfrauenmaschine* (1988, *The Virgin Machine*), the coming-out story of a young German woman during a stay in San Francisco, allowed Treut to explore the performative nature of gender and sexuality in more playful tones, an indication also of the changing function of sexual politics in the postmodern politics of representation (Kuzniar 2000).

The only important director to emerge during the 1980s, Doris Dörrie, was also the one who most successfully enlisted the conventions of romantic comedy in new approaches to love and romance and the inevitable complications of female identity in a post-feminist world. Inspired by Hollywood genre cinema but with a distinct German sensibility, committed to the ideas of feminism but also surprisingly open about the messiness of ordinary life, Dörrie emerged on the scene after the phenomenal success of *Männer* (1986, *Men*). This rather conventional romantic comedy about the myth of the New Man and the power of traditional gender roles showed her talent of combining precise social observation and commentary with a deep understanding of human foibles. By presenting her quirky characters and their unusual lifestyles through familiar generic elements, Dörrie became an important transitional figure between the ethos of self-discovery cultivated by New German Cinema and the greater emphasis on entertainment in post-unification cinema. To a large degree, this transition hinged on the re-articulation of gender troubles through the new multiculturalism symbolised by the many on-screen friendships between single women and gay foreign men. Thus Dörrie in *Happy Birthday, Türke!* (1991, *Happy Birthday, Turk*) resorted to elements of film noir, including its myth of the urban jungle, to present the complications of German-Turkish identity – in, fact of all identities – in conscious opposition to the liberal rhetoric of integration. Likewise, references to black comedy in *Keiner liebt mich* (1994, *Nobody Loves Me*) and to the road movie in *Bin ich schön?* (1998, *Am I Beautiful?*) allowed Dörrie to explore productive alliances between various 'others' – women, gays, foreigners – while avoiding all too simplistic solutions to the central question of identity in a world of postmodern simulation.

The one significant political issue linking the West German cinema of the 1980s to the post-unification cinema of the 1990s was the growing awareness among film-makers of the many foreigners living in the Federal Republic. Their impact on culture and society resonated throughout filmic practices, from the familiar national stereotyping and the dynamics of self and other to various efforts at raising social tolerance and understanding. This process had already begun in the 1950s with the first cameo appearances by Italian and Spanish guest workers in the revue films, youth films, and *Heimatfilme*. It had continued during the 1970s with dramatic stories about Turkish men and women arriving in the Federal Republic and beginning the difficult process of social integration and cultural assimilation, a process often expressed through the problems in first- and second-generation immigrant families. Finally, this development culminated in the 1980s in the representation of more contemporary lifestyles that, in their tastes and sensibilities, implicitly acknowledged the existence of a culturally and socially more diverse society. The shifts in the representation of Germany's various 'others' did more than just reflect a change in public attitudes, however. Filmic representations also participated in the discourses of legitimisation necessitated by the growing pressure on traditional definitions of national identity in an increasingly multi-ethnic, multicultural world. Whereas the foreigners became an integral part of the self-representation of the Federal Republic, the Germans from the East continued to function as figures of otherness and difference. From *Berlin Mitte* (1980, *Central Berlin*) and *German Dreams* (1981) to *Der Mann auf der Mauer* (1982, *The Man on the Wall*), the East–West encounters in the films of the 1980s invariably ended in disorientation, dissatisfaction, and disillusionment. Little did the film-makers know that these paradigmatic moments would soon be surpassed by more momentous historical events.

15 Sabine Sinjen and Bruno Dietrich in *Es*. Courtesy of BFI stills, Posters and Designs.

16 Renate Blume and Eberhard Esche in *Der geteilte Himmel*. Courtesy of BFI stills, Posters and Designs.

17 Rainer Werner Fassbinder and Peter Chatel in *Faustrecht der Freiheit*. Courtesy of BFI stills, Posters and Designs.

18 Eva Mattes and Bruno S. in *Stroszek*. Courtesy of BFI stills, Posters and Designs.

19 Lutze and Tabea Blumenschein in *Bildnis einer Trinkerin*. Courtesy of BFI stills, Posters and Designs.

20 Uwe Ochsenknecht, Ulrike Kriener, and Heiner Lauterbach in *Männer*. Courtesy of BFI stills, Posters and Designs.

21 Bruno Ganz and Solweig Dommartin in *Der Himmel über Berlin*. Courtesy of BFI stills, Posters and Designs.

22 Franka Potente in *Lola Rennt* (Sony Pictures, 1999). Courtesy of the Kobal Collection.

7

POST-UNIFICATION CINEMA
1989–2000

The collapse of the Wall on 9 November 1989 marked the end of the postwar period. The difficult process of unification brought dramatic changes in all areas of society, and not only in the New States. Among other things, the heated debates about Germany's future role as an economic and political superpower directed attention again to the problematic legacies of the past and to the changing meaning of national culture in a unified Europe defined less by ideological differences than by economic inequity, social discord, and ethnic strife. The equally dramatic changes in the world economy, from the ascendancy of multinational corporations to the creation of new information technologies, only intensified such concerns, especially around issues of immigration, citizenship, and asylum laws. In 1998, after seventeen years of CDU rule, the new SPD/Greens coalition government led by Chancellor Gerhard Schröder began to initiate social and economic reforms intended to make the country more competitive on global markets and less inflexible on immigration, labour, and employment issues. These developments provided new opportunities but also raised a number of serious concerns: about the dismantling of the social welfare state and the erosion of a German *Leitkultur* (guiding culture); about the collapse of the old consensus model binding together big corporations, labour unions, political parties, and special interest groups; and about continuing problems in the New States (for example, unemployment, racial violence). After the government's move to Berlin, a number of architectural projects, from the new Reichstag and Potsdamer Platz to the planned Holocaust Memorial, generated intense public discussions about the changing meaning of nation, history, and identity and the possibility of normalising the discourses of Germanness.

The impact of these historical events on German cinema was traceable less in the few feature films that directly thematised unification than in the unexpected revival of popular cinema, a development that has been examined critically by some film scholars (Rentschler 2000). In their effort to address specific post-unification concerns, film-makers returned to the genres of the postwar period as a way of reclaiming the stabilising function of classical narrative and of utilising these effects in the making of another Zero Hour. This process found expression in the new generation's pronounced opposition to film movements with political or social ambitions, including New German Cinema. Younger producers and directors rejected its ethos of authorship and self-expression for a more workable, and profitable, compromise between artistic and commercial interests. In validating entertainment as the primary function of cinema, they aligned themselves with international trends in film-financing and marketing that had made the 1990s a particularly uninspired decade dominated by formulaic blockbusters and star vehicles. Yet responding to specific domestic concerns, film-makers also enlisted the harmonising effects of genre in the rewriting of the German past and the remapping of the German present within the cultural and geopolitical topography of post-Wall Europe. Addressing themselves explicitly to German audiences, the films of the 1990s sought to accommodate the audience's contradictory desire both for less complicated narratives of Germanness – including in terms of national identity – and for more optimistic visions of a multi-ethnic, multicultural society. In considering the wider implications of such ongoing revisionism for contemporary filmic practices and the writing of film history, film scholars have begun to reassess the prevailing critical models (for example, the emphasis on famous directors and canonical films) and to pay more attention to the continuities of German popular cinema and its function in competing definitions of the national (*Arachne* vol. 3, no. 2, *Seminar* vol. 33. no. 4, *Camera Obscura* no. 44, McCarthy and Halle 2002).

Elements of popular cinema: the return to genre

As part of the process of privatisation that affected all state-owned industries in the former GDR, the DEFA studio was sold in 1992 to a French Conglomerate, Compagnie Général Des Eaux. During Volker Schlöndorff's tenure as artistic director from 1992 to 1997, Studio Babelsberg turned the old DEFA facilities into a centre of European film and television production. Reflecting fundamental changes in film production, distribution, and exhibition, the old oppositions of film versus television, and of public versus private funding, gave way to more pragmatic approaches. Multimedia conglomerates such as the Kirch group, independent production companies such as X Filme Creative Pool, and various federal, regional, and local agencies started to form mutually beneficial relationships. After the privatisation of public broadcasting in the early 1980s, cable stations and media concerns played an increasingly important role in financing film projects, sponsoring new interesting work, and developing further the synergies among film, television, video, in addition to the existing ties with the recording and publishing industry. All of these initiatives contributed to what some welcomed as necessary professionalism and others denounced as excessive commercialism. Joining established German distributors like Constantin, such US distributors as Warner, Columbia, UIP, Fox, and Buena Vista developed an interest in domestic productions and promoted them through elaborate advertising campaigns. During the same period, German companies became involved in the financing of several Hollywood productions, including those by German-born directors such as Petersen and Emmerich.

The considerable flows of venture capital into film projects, made possible through the stock offerings on the New Market and fuelled by the rituals of celebrity culture (for instance, in talk-shows, award ceremonies, and charity events) confirmed the new German films not only as a viable commodity but also as a powerful symbol of the post-unification mentality of pragmatism, optimism, and hedonism. This compromise between art and commerce found perfect expression in the new Filmmuseum Berlin on Potsdamer Platz, the central location since 2000 for the Berlin Film Festival, the archival collections of the Deutsche Kinemathek, and a permanent exhibition on German film history.

The different systems of distribution identified with cinema, video, and television, and the changing alliances among public and private, national and international forms of financing profoundly affected the definition of film as a medium with distinct qualities. In the light of the seemingly unstoppable trend towards 'amphibian' forms and practices, a clear distinction between film and television was no longer feasible. Conventional films intended for theatrical release ended up being shown only on television, whereas innovative television plays received prestigious prizes. Usually known for its crass commercialism, RTL2 produced the critically acclaimed media thriller *Der Sandmann* (1996, *The Sandman*), and SAT 1 launched *German Classics*, a series of remakes from the 1950s that included *Das Mädchen Rosemarie*. While profiting from their exposure to a mass audience, the feature films made under such conditions remained aesthetic hybrids without a distinctive visual or narrative style. Their close adherence to the format of the television play is especially evident in the limited number of locations and characters, the heavy emphasis on dialogue, and the overarching concern with typicality, relevance, and a harmonising of social differences.

The rediscovery of German films as a marketable product was not just a response to the intense competition with electronic and digital media and the new alliances between public and private funding; it also reflected more worrisome developments in cinema culture as a whole. In the former East, unification had a devastating effect on local film exhibition. With higher admission prices and lower discretionary incomes, ticket sales plummeted – in some areas by almost 40 per cent – and many motion-picture theatres stopped operations. This wave of closings in the East coincided with a diminished public interest in the offerings of revival houses in the West and a general trend throughout the country towards large multiplexes. Showing mainstream Hollywood films in often spectacular settings, the multiplexes brought older and more diverse audiences back to the movies – namely as part of the new fun culture – but also contributed further to the levelling of popular tastes and the marginalisation of art cinema.

During the early 1990s, two kinds of films dominated the programmes: big-budget Hollywood productions and low-budget German productions. Hollywood continued to satisfy the need for blockbusters with famous stars, spectacular settings, and special effects. *Pretty Woman* headed the list of box-office hits in 1990, followed by *Home Alone* in 1991, *Basic Instinct* in 1992, *Jurassic Park* in 1993, *While You Were Sleeping* in 1994, *The Lion King* in 1995, *Independence Day* in

1996, *Men in Black* in 1997, and so forth. During the same period, domestic productions increased their market share from 10 to 20 per cent of all new releases. This division of labour between international tastes and preferences, as embodied by American popular culture, and regional and local sensibilities, as captured in the highly successful but basically unexportable filmic manifestations of German humour and sentimentality, left little room for the kind of formal innovation and critical reflection usually identified with art cinema. Many East and West German directors from the 1970s and 1980s continued to make films but with little commercial or critical success and virtually no international resonance, Wenders and Schlöndorff excepted. In a cultural climate that no longer identified filmic practices with cultural critique, but instead reassigned this function to literature and theatre, even Schroeter's ambitious adaptation of Ingeborg Bachmann's *Malina* (1991) attracted fewer than fifty thousand viewers. Outside urban centres such as Berlin, Munich, Hamburg, and Frankfurt, the relative lack of interest in other European cinemas among moviegoers further weakened those traditions that, since the 1920s, had provided alternatives to Hollywood by engaging with, and appreciating, difference as an aesthetic and intellectual category.

This division of labour between the global and the regional fostered a new *Erlebniskultur* (culture of diversion) that, in embracing commercialism with a vengeance, tried to move beyond the legacies of the 1960s and 1970s, including the credos of political radicalism and radical subjectivity. In some cases, the underlying anti-intellectualism produced expressions of crudeness and vulgarity uniquely German in the animosity towards high culture. In other cases, the postmodern culture of narcissism provided a convenient model for combining retrograde fantasies of family and community with (superficially) liberal attitudes towards alternative sexualities and hybrid identities. By validating individual ambition and self-interest, these films did not provide only models of identification for the new social and economic elites. The contemporary narratives also assigned different functions to socially marginalised groups, either by turning them into symbols of the new culture of tolerance and openness (for instance, in the case of immigrants and asylum seekers) or by enlisting them in a regressive defence of provincialism and parochialism (for instance, in the case of simple country folk). With such contradictory investments, the comedies and dramas from the early 1990s provided a convenient vehicle for the social attitudes and mentalities that, translated into political terms, characterised the Berlin Republic.

To a large degree, the formula for commercial success hinged on the adaptation of generic conventions to contemporary sensibilities, including an acute awareness of identity as a construction and a performance. The rediscovery of genre cinema, German style, began with a number of undistinguished but very influential romantic comedies by women directors. Director Sherry Hormann defined the main elements of the genre in several yuppie comedies about troubled marriages, relationships, and love triangles, including *Frauen sind was Wunderbares* (1993, *Women Are Something Wonderful*) and *Irren ist männlich* (1995, *To Err Is Masculine*). A number of films were based on novels by best-selling author Hera

Lind, including Peter Timm's *Ein Mann für jede Tonart* (1992, *A Man for Every Mood*) and Sönke Wortmann's *Das Superweib* (1996, *Superwoman*). The new female ideal found a perfect embodiment in blonde Katja Riemann who, whether as a newspaper cartoonist in *Abgeschminkt!* (1993, *Without Makeup!*) or a radio talk-show host in *Stadtgespräch* (1995, *The Talk of the Town*), combined professional competence with romantic incompetence, and pseudo-feminist arguments with traditionally female wiles.

Showing attractive young professionals in fashionable middle-class and upper-middle-class settings, these so-called *Beziehungskomödien* (relationship comedies) derived much of their comic appeal from the alleged discrepancy between the 'eternal' problems in male–female relationships and the contemporary culture of political correctness. Katja von Garnier's *Abgeschminkt!* set the tone for the young post-feminist generation by simultaneously evoking the lifestyle markers of the emancipated woman and demonstrating the inevitable collapse of feminist positions in the face of true love. Perhaps most disconcerting is the degree to which these comedies reduce the problems of modern femininity to that of sexuality, and, to add to the essentialist backlash, to motherhood (even if outside marriage). Sustained by this strange mixture of liberal, progressive, and conservative attitudes, even unconventional living arrangements and romantic constellations end up affirming the importance of love, friendship, and family as a refuge from the pressures of the workplace and public life. Following this narrative pattern, the lesbian comedy *Alles wird gut* (1997, *All Ends Well*) by Angelina Maccarone celebrates love, or the pursuit of love, as the penultimate expression of social harmony and cross-cultural understanding. The difference between such conciliatory visions and the insistence on radical otherness in the queer sensibility of Treut could not be more pronounced; as for the legacies of feminism, the same might be said about the difference between Hormann and an old-fashioned feminist such as Sander.

The typical romantic comedies from the 1990s involve young women who want it all: lovers, friends, children, and a successful career. Yet invariably, their professional ambition upsets the balance of power between the sexes; this point is usually made through the stereotypical figure of the unreconstructed male. The ensuing dramatic complications – arguments, fights, breakups, affairs, new attachments – aim at the restoration of traditional femininity and masculinity, but in more enlightened terms. The underlying message: that men must control their selfish and aggressive impulses without becoming overly feminised, and that women must embrace their feminine qualities without falling back into complete dependency. Most romantic comedies achieve this conciliatory effect by first diagnosing the excesses of male egotism and then documenting the miraculous transformation of self-centred leading men into mature, caring partners. In Wortmann's *Der bewegte Mann* (1994, *Maybe . . . Maybe Not*), the re-education of the arrogant macho comes about through his gay friend; a feminist commune performs the same task in *Allein unter Frauen* (1996, *Alone among Women*). Detlev Buck in *Männerpension* (1996, *A Boarding House for Men*) offers another variation on this theme by delivering male prisoners during a weekend on vacation to the women volunteers intent on rehabilitating them.

For one thing, the romantic comedies shed light on the modified versions of love, marriage, and family life considered the most compatible with changing middle-class attitudes towards career, marriage, and family life. For another, the films displayed and promoted the new lifestyle choices apotheosised in the trinity of hedonism, narcissism, and luxury consumption. Through young professionals typically working in consulting, advertising, private television, and investment banking, the comedies introduced the representatives of a post-unification society unburdened by ideology, politics, and history. However, the almost compulsive optimism also served as a defence against the frightening prospect of an adult world defined by responsibilities, compromises, and regrets. From Helmut Dietl's much-discussed *Rossini* (1996), about a fashionable Munich restaurant favoured by local celebrities from stage and screen, to *Workaholic* (1996), about the marital diffi-culties of a dual-career couple, these cautionary tales about the relentless pursuit of power, fame, and status rarely followed their own recommendations for moderation and modesty and remained intoxicated by the trappings of power and wealth. Perhaps it was the audience's desire for more substantial dramatic conflicts that contributed to the surprise success of Caroline Link's *Jenseits der Stille* (1996, *Beyond the Silence*), about a young woman who fulfils her dream of becoming a musician despite the opposition of her deaf-mute parents.

Perennial favourites with younger audiences, the petty-bourgeois comedies of the 1990s performed similar socio-psychological functions. They provided uplifting stories that reconciled individual desires with social realities, but this time from a disadvantaged or marginal position clearly defined in class terms. Frequently, the male protagonists in these films confront their diminished social or economic status and try to regain some degree of stability or control through the affirmation precisely of their class-based otherness in the context of job activities, hobbies, sports, and other recreational activities. Some contributions offer revealing vignettes of everyday life in the provinces, the kind depicted in the Northern flatlands of Buck's *Karniggels* (1991, *Rabbits*). Other films allow their protagonists to acquire a surrogate identity through their association with certain car brands, as demonstrated in the weekend activities of young Opel drivers in Peter Timm's *Manta, Manta* (1991) and the adventures of the East German family travelling in the modified Trabant from *Go Trabi, Go* (1991). Yet other protagonists, such as the fanatical soccer fans in Winkelmann's *Nordkurve* (1992, *North Curve*), rely on sports to preserve some of the traditions of working-class culture still found in the declining Ruhr industrial region.

Whereas a few comedies offered a critique to the upwardly mobile yuppie culture through their defiant affirmation of petty-bourgeois lifestyles, the vast majority expressed their opposition and resentment through extreme crudeness. Comedian Gerhard Polt established the simple formula for these so-called *Proll-Lustspiele* (proletarian comedies) with *Man spricht deutsch* (1987, *German Spoken Here*), about one of the 'typical' German families populating the beaches on the Adriatic

Coast, and he continued with a similar vacation farce about the drinking rituals of Majorca tourists in *Ballermann 6* (1997). Film adaptations of popular cartoons proved particularly effective in satisfying the younger audience's demand for shock value and vulgarity, whether in the juvenile humour of *Werner Beinhart* (1990), based on the books by Brösel, or in the gay humour of *Kondom des Grauens* (1996, *Killer Condom*), inspired by the work of Ralf König. The mockery of middle-class notions of normalcy also stood behind the infantile pranks of Tom Gerhardt in *Voll normaal* (1994, *Totally Normal*). This new group of actors and characters thrived on aggressive forms of humour that expressed loud if inarticulate opposition to the pressures of social and economic mobility.

The unwillingness of protagonists to enter adulthood and reach maturity was nowhere more striking than in the immensely popular road movies. Modelled on established Hollywood formulas but also inspired by the spatial and social topography of a unified Germany, the road movies articulated a growing frustration with available designs for living. Typical reactions by the characters include the renunciation of heterosexual love in favour of all-male or all-female groups; the flight from metropolitan centres to provincial towns and deserted landscapes; and the abandonment of comfort and stability for the kind of makeshift alliances forged by circumstance. Structured around these choices, the road movies provided dream images of a new homeland in which all differences and difficulties could be overcome through the shared opposition to middle-class values. In *Wir können auch anders* (1993, *No More Mr Nice Guy*), Buck used two goofy brothers and a Red Army deserter to introduce a grotesquely distorted perspective on the former East. Yet beginning with *Bunte Hunde* (1995, *Wild Guys*), which was inspired by an actual prison break/hostage drama, the adventures of the road exhausted themselves in romantic and sentimental clichés. The last trip taken by two terminally-ill young men in *Knockin' on Heaven's Door* (1996) remained fraught with symbolic references to travelling as a form of self-discovery. An exception at least in terms of gender dynamics, *Burning Life* (1994) presented two young women who find new meaning in life by robbing banks and distributing their loot among the people. Less convincing in her take on girl power, von Garnier in *Bandits* (1997) followed four escaped female convicts from their dramatic prison break to their media-driven fame as punk stars and folk heroines.

While the return to genre cinema owed much to directors such as Wortmann and Buck, the popular appeal of the new films depended even more on their attractive stars. Again the similarities to the postwar years are pronounced, with heartthrob Til Schweiger a contemporary version of Horst Buchholz and perky Katja Riemann a combination of Lieselotte Pulver and Sabine Sinjen. The leading German stars of the 1990s also modelled themselves on then-current Hollywood versions of youthful masculinity and femininity, with Schweiger as a German Tom Cruise and Riemann a German Meg Ryan. Less famous actors and actresses became closely identified with particular dramatic registers and social types. Whereas Thomas Heinze revived the tradition of charming rogues, Kai Wiesinger convinced in the role of the eternal boy. Joachim Król built an impressive career by playing sensitive, thoughtful, and often slightly quirky characters. Maria Schrader performed the traditional dramatic heroine with a touch of *femme fatale*, while Meret Becker combined elements of the classical *ingénue* with some punk sensibilities. Similarly, Franka Potente convinced as a modern version of the girl next door, and Veronica Ferres succeeded as a blonde bombshell with ambition.

The typical characters played by the new stars of post-unification cinema are well-adjusted, upwardly mobile, reasonably happy, but also incredibly self-centred men and women in their twenties and thirties. Many are making the difficult transition to the kind of modern adulthood symbolised no longer by changed family status (marriage, parenthood) but by an acute awareness of the limits of individual self-gratification. The inevitable conflicts are articulated through personal relationships and, more specifically, the main character's competing needs for complete independence and a sense of belonging. At times, these problems erupt in the context of corporate takeovers, society intrigues, family crises, and criminal activities. At other times, stressful summer vacations, endless traffic jams or ambitious house renovations provide some much-needed comic relief. Yet in the obligatory happy endings, the diverse and colourful characters – the foreigners, immigrants, and asylum seekers; the gays, feminists, yuppies, and skinheads; and the stereotypical *Wessies* and *Ossies* (West and East Germans) – all come together through their belief in new economic and social possibilities and the ideology of progressive liberalism that sustains them.

Despite the habitual references to the global economy, the stock market, and the information age, most films contemplated the consequences of globalisation only in social and psychological terms, beginning with the changing definition of marriage, family, and community. In the light of such tendencies, it should not surprise that the revival of popular traditions bypassed those political genres underrepresented in German cinema since 1933: thrillers about national and international crises and dramas set in the world of high finance and multinational corporations. Perpetuating the division between the 'large' stories covered by big-budget Hollywood films and the 'small' stories provided by inexpensive German productions, film-makers continued to avoid political subject matter – with one exception: films about the Third Reich and the former GDR.

Once again: coming to terms with the past(s)

Sustained by the renewed interest in the Third Reich and, more generally, the question of German national identity, the most ambitious projects of the 1990s were reserved for historical narratives, including many based on real-life stories and events. The old distinction between those periods instantly available to sentimental or sensationalist treatments and those periods requiring special considerations yielded to more fluid constellations. As if to confirm the diagnosis by postmodern theoreticians of a gradual disappearance of history into simulation and spectacle, the new attempts at coming to terms with the past seemed at once more conventional in their reliance on the identificatory effects of classical narrative and more conservative in their validation of the personal in opposition to the political. Two tendencies prevailed in narratives set during the period of classical modernity from 1871 to 1933: a continuous preference for the type of literary adaptations, primarily of canonical authors, which had sustained the industry since the 1970s, and a growing interest in nostalgic milieu studies that presented the past as a paradise lost. Literary adaptations profited immensely from the synergies between film and television that made possible expensive multi-part adaptations of novels by Thomas Mann, Joseph Roth, and Lion Feuchtwanger. Whereas middle-brow authors such as Erich Kästner, Kurt Tucholsky, and Vicki Baum allowed audiences to indulge their desire for visions of mass culture and modernity presumably untainted by politics, the adaptations of East German authors Erwin Strittmatter and Erich Loest showed a concerted effort by several former DEFA directors to keep other literary traditions alive, especially in the genre of historical fiction. Adding to the gradual transformation of German history into a fantasy effect, many stories were set in the entertainment world, from the Berlin of the roaring 1920s depicted in *Die Tigerin* (1992, *The Tigress*) and the *demimonde* of Wilhelmine Berlin revived by *Rosenemil* (1993) to the last years of silent film evoked nostalgically in *Der Kinoerzähler* (1993, *The Movie Commentator*), a veiled comment also on the crisis of cinema in the age of electronic media.

Revealing insights into the new approach to German history can be found in the work of Joseph Vilsmaier, the most commercially successful director-producer-cinematographer of the 1990s. Vilsmaier started out with *Herbstmilch* (1989, *Autumn Milk*), which recounts the life-story of a peasant woman from Lower Bavaria, and *Rama dama* (1990), which depicts the travails of a young mother in Munich after the war. Evoking the tradition of German romanticism, *Schlafes Bruder* (1996, *Sleeper's Brother*) allowed the director to adapt the popular Robert Schneider novel about a nineteenth-century musical prodigy to his own grand vision of a national cinema reborn through the convergence of history, mythology, and entertainment. Vilsmaier continued this revisionist project with three films about the Third Reich: *Stalingrad* (1996), a graphic war spectacle about the senseless sacrifice of the Sixth Army in the Second World War; *Die Comedian Harmonists* (1998), a musical biography of the famous *a capella* group torn apart by anti-Semitism; and, most recently, the biopic *Marlene* (2000), with Katja Flint in the role of the quintessential German star.

Significantly, Vilsmaier's films about the Third Reich offer no social or political explanations for the origins of National Socialism. Moreover, the narratives avoid established forms of historical explanation except those based on individual behaviour. The heavy reliance on production design contributes further to the normalisation of German history by reducing the recent past to a visual spectacle. The broader implications can been seen in a comparison with two very different films about the Third Reich that directly address the dependency of historical representation on media-produced images and stories. Thus in *Der olympische Sommer* (1992, *The Olympic Summer*), Gordian Maugg invited critical reflection through his choice of equipment: by shooting the love story between an older woman and a young man during the 1936 Olympic Games with an old Askania camera, he produced an uncanny resemblance that effectively defamiliarised the material. Schlöndorff, on the other hand, used highly stylised settings and melodramatic effects in recreating an uncanny, dream-like hallucination of the Third Reich in the German–French co-production of *Der Unhold* (1996, *The Ogre*), based on the controversial Michel Tournier novel.

Equally significant to these revisionist tendencies were the many contemporary narratives that used historical inquiries to assess the meaning of the past for the present – that is, for Germany after unification. The process began with Dietl's *Schtonk!* (1992), a political satire with the indefatigable Götz George about the fascination with Nazi memorabilia that fuelled the media frenzy around the forged Hitler diaries. Combining historical interests with contemporary concerns, several film-makers developed their dramatic conflicts on the geographical and ideological terrain identified with the former GDR. *Die Spur des Bernsteinzimmers* (1992, *The Trail of the Amber Room*) brings together three very different people in a detective-like search for the legendary treasure lost during the war. The protagonists in Schilling's *Die blinde Kuh* (1994, *Project Blind Cow*) find important historical documents about early television research by the Nazis in the crumbling military installations left behind by the Red Army. Blurring the boundaries between past and present, even Mueller-Stahl's Hitler film *Gespräch mit dem Biest* (1997, *Conversation with the Monster*) and George's *Nichts als die Wahrheit* (1999, *Nothing but the Truth*), about Josef Mengele, define their historical projects in contemporary terms by presenting their main characters as old, ailing, but unmistakably and frighteningly alive in the present.

However, the tension between historical detachment and contemporary relevance was most pronounced in a group of new films about anti-Semitism and the Holocaust. These films often revealed as much about the increased German interest in Jewish culture as about the hidden yearning for essentialist categories of identity that, in a strange reversal of terms, gave rise to sentimental and nostalgic images of Jewishness. The underlying desire for the symbolic reconciliation of self and other – German and Jew – found expression in the heightened terms of romantic love. Accordingly, *Aimée und Jaguar* (1998, *Aimée and Jaguar*), based on the memoirs of Erica Fischer, rewrites the history of everyday life during the Third Reich from the perspective of a lesbian love story. *Meschugge* (1998, *The Giraffe*), a collaboration by Dani Levy and Maria Schrader, similarly relies on sexual desire to move beyond the family dynamics of victims and perpetrators and to work through the historical events haunting German–Jewish relations. In both cases, romantic love is confirmed as the driving force behind individual gestures of resistance and subversion and later efforts at coming to terms with the past. Yet in the process, all social and political processes, including those exposing the origins of anti-Semitism, are reduced to a background effect, a diminishment also found in *Comedian Harmonists*.

For the most part, the films about German unification used classical narrative structures in presenting historical events and in measuring their impact on public and private lives. In recounting the process, most film-makers preferred typical figures and ordinary situations and relied heavily on socio-psychological models of explanation. In the two-part television production *Nikolaikirche* (1995, *Nikolai Church*), based on the Erich Loest novel, Beyer focused on a middle-class family from Leipzig to show the possibility of individual choice even under an oppressive regime. Based on a true story, *Der Blaue* (1993, *The Informer*) examined the power structures that allowed an informer for the East German secret police to become a state secretary in the unified Germany. In many of these films, a profound sense of loss, failure, and regret coexists with the kind of fearless pragmatism shown by the old woman from *Der Brocken* (1993, *The Brocken Mountain*), who defends her idyllic life on the island of Rügen against old and new enemies, and the less assured efforts by the young heroine of Helke Misselwitz's *Herzsprung* (1992), who tries to build a new existence in a small town located near the nation's (new) geographical centre. More often than not, the victims of history were forgotten in favour of more forward-looking narratives of radical change and its liberating possibilities; hence the painful belatedness of such a film as Michael Gwisdek's *Abschied von Agnes* (1993, *Farewell to Agnes*). Rather than succumbing to melancholia, the last generation of GDR citizens began to relive their experience of growing up in East Berlin during the 1970s through the cheerful tones and tunes from *Sonnenallee* (1999) and through the gestures of ironic appropriation invited by re-releases of DEFA classics and post-communist compilation films such as *East Side Story* (1997).

It may still be too early to expect any feature films about the political elites in the GDR, the power of the secret police, the work of political dissidents, and the role of artists and intellectuals. In fact, the crude sensationalism of Christoph Schlingensief's unification farce, *Das deutsche Kettensägenmassaker* (1990, *The German Chain Saw Massacre*), and his equally bizarre *Terror 2000* (1992), about right-wing terrorism in the former East, only highlight these political topics' uncomfortable closeness to the present. Nonetheless, in the same way that the first films about unification repeated narrative formulas from the postwar period (for example, compare *Der Blaue* with *Mein Schulfreund*), so the first films about the GDR drew upon established models of explanation about an all-powerful regime and its anonymous power structures; the excesses of the party leaders and the essential decency of ordinary people; and, to introduce a more critical perspective, the continuities of authoritarianism across the ideological divides of modern German history. Illustrating some of these points, von Trotta in *Das Versprechen* (1995, *The Promise*) presents the postwar division as the tragic story of two young lovers divided by ideology but meant to be united; the happy ending for the nation comes with the post-ideological identity of a unified Germany. In a significant departure from earlier West and East films about the German division, the gendered division now involves a West German woman and an East German man. Yet in accordance with allegorical representations of nation, the outcome still (or again) confirms the female principle (that is, of Germania) as the victorious one. Focusing on the period from the 1970s to the 1980s, Schlöndorff in *Die Stille nach dem*

Schuss (2000, *The Legends of Rita*) combines the underground experiences of several RAF terrorists to offer a more nuanced portrayal of everyday life in the GDR that acknowledges the losses and losers on both sides of the border.

During the same period, a number of documentary film-makers began to examine the impact of unification on everyday life in the former GDR. Indeed, documentaries, essay films, and other non-narrative forms proved very effective in addressing such social problems as unemployment, youth violence, and xenophobia and in providing a visual memory of the GDR, not least through long-term projects like *Die Kinder von Golzow* (*The Children of Golzow*), started by Winfried Junge in 1980 (Alter 2002). The increase of neo-Nazi activities in the East was the main focus of Winfried Bonengel's *Beruf Neonazi* (1992, *Occupation Neo-Nazi*), as well as of Thomas Heise's feature *Stau – jetzt geht's los* (1992, *Now It's Boiling Over*), which attracted controversy because of its sensationalist style. Responding to the public's fascination with the images generated by, or associated with, fascism, a number of documentary film-makers decided to approach the legacies of the Third Reich through the complicated relationship among film, aesthetics, and history. The best-known contribution is Ray Müller's *Die Macht der Bilder* (1991, *The Wonderful, Horrible Life of Leni Riefenstahl*), about the work and life of the most famous film-maker from the Third Reich. The affinities between cinema and modern warfare also inspired such essayistic reflections on the limits of visual representation as in *Mein Krieg* (1990, *My Private War*), a compilation film made up of home movies by German soldiers. Taking a feminist approach with *BeFreier und Befreite* (1992, *Liberators Take Liberties*), Helke Sander made a much-debated documentary about the mass rapes of German women by Soviet soldiers during the last months of the war in which she relied primarily on historical documents, personal interviews, and critical commentary to challenge prevailing views on gender, power, and history (*October* no. 72).

Whereas comedies provided a useful vehicle of self-representation for the new social and economic elites, melodramas emerged as the preferred form for presenting the concerns not only of the victims of German history but also of its marginalised others in the present. Here film-makers often focused on the ethnic and sexual minorities in order to challenge official images of an enlightened German nationhood. Setting the mood, Peter Sehr's *Das serbische Mädchen* (1990, *The Serbian Girl*) used the troubles of a young Serbian woman searching for her German boyfriend to probe the meaning of displacement and migrancy in post-wall Europe. The same dynamics between the centre and the margins structured the growing number of films about Turkish immigration, from the experiences of economic hardship in Anatolia to the problems of social integration in the Berlin Republic. In the contributions by German-Turkish film-makers, two tendencies prevailed: the affirmation of an essential difference located in ethnicity and the exploration of new forms of cultural hybridity. The encoding of otherness in melodramatic form, including conventional gendering, was particularly evident in films that articulated their dramatic conflicts through the spatial terms of evictions, deportations, and illegal border crossings. This trend began with the claustrophobic scenario of female confinement in *Vierzig m2 Deutschland* (1986, *Forty Square Metres of Germany*), directed by Tevfik Baser, one of the first German-Turkish directors, and it continued with his elegiac reflections on the meaning of exile in *Lebe wohl, Fremde* (1991, *Farewell, Stranger*). Similarly concerned with experiences of displacement, Kadir Sören in *Winterblume* (1996, *Winter Flower*) showed the failed attempts of a group of deportees to re-enter the Federal Republic. In *Yara* (1998), Yilmaz Arslan recounted the sad story of a young woman equally homeless in Turkey and Germany. In many of these contributions, the identification of Turkishness with essential qualities allowed for the displacement of German guilt into stories of ethnic discrimination and oppression that, quite problematically, revolve around the Turkish woman as the quintessential victim.

Reaching out to other audiences, a younger generation of directors in the late 1990s began to offer more complex, and often also more controversial, views on the situation of first- and second-generation immigrants. For instance, in *Ich Chef, Du Turnschuh* (1998, *Me Boss, You Gym Shoe*), Hussi Kutlucan portrays a group of illegal workers on a construction site for the new government buildings in Berlin but eschews the liberal rhetoric of social tolerance and cultural diversity sometimes found in comparable German films about foreigners. Similarly, Fatih Akin's *Kurz und schmerzlos* (1998, *Short Sharp Shock*) evokes the conventions of the gangster genre to show how three good friends – a Turk, a Serb, and a Greek – succumb to a life of crime, violence, murder, and death. These noirish urban thrillers contributed to an investigation of diasporic and hybrid identities that, since Lars Becker's haunting *Schattenboxer* (1992, *Shadow Boxer*), turned to Hollywood genres to explore different and often aggressively masculinist attitudes to capture post-unification Germany and its new social, ethnic, and national constellations. In a sharp departure from earlier representations, compassion is often replaced by aggression, and the promise of integration undercut by more disillusioned observations about the emergence of a new social underclass (Göktürk 2000).

Berlin's proximity to Eastern Europe inspired a number of innovative film dramas that confirmed the city's central position within the changing routes of mass migration after 1989, beginning with the journey from Poland to New York via Berlin in Michael Klier's *Überall ist es besser, wo wir nicht sind* (1989, *Things Are Always Better Elsewhere*) and the return of Polish-Americans to Warsaw via Berlin in Jan Schütte's *Auf Wiedersehen, Amerika* (1993, *Goodbye, America*). Already an earlier film by the same director, *Winckelmanns Reisen* (1990, *Winckelmann's Travels*), evoked a similar spiritual homelessness through the figure of a travelling salesman, suggesting that even 'natives' found themselves moving through familiar cities and landscapes as if in a foreign country. The extent to which this sense of detachment reflected more fundamental problems became very apparent in the growing number of films about social outcasts and outsiders. The same sense of disengagement also characterised the filmic styles that – from poetic realism to magic realism, from monochrome tones to artificial colour schemes – proved most conducive to visualising the provisional, improvised designs for living in post-unification Germany. Precisely this affinity to subcultural sensibilities distinguished one of the more noteworthy films from the late 1990s, Wolfgang Becker's *Das Leben ist eine Baustelle* (1996, *Life Is All You Get*), its title a telling reference to Berlin as the construction site of nation and identity. With similar intentions, Andreas Dresen in *Nachtgestalten* (1998, *Night Shapes*) drew attention to the underclass of urban derelicts and their difficult existence on the edges of prosperity. Extending these reflections on homelessness into the world of new information technologies, Hans-Christian Schmid offered a chilling portrayal of 1980s hacker subculture with *23* (1998). Taking a more playful approach, the scenarios of simulated murder played out in the virtual-world thriller *killer.berlin.doc* (1999), conceived by Tina Ellerkamp and Jörg Heitmann for *Das kleine Fernsehspiel*, introduced yet another generation of young Berliners moving very comfortably among global cities, social cliques, and information networks.

Undoubtedly, the most innovative Berlin films of the late 1990s was *Lola rennt* (1999, *Run Lola Run*), written and directed by Tom Tykwer. Praised for its multi-layered narrative structure and its profoundly filmic sense of movement and space, this MTV-inspired city symphony with Franka Potente in the title role received several film prizes and became the most commercially successful German film internationally since *Das Boot* in 1982. With its playful references to popular music, modern fashion, and contemporary lifestyles, *Lola rennt* appealed to national and international audiences as the quintessential postmodern film. It also confirmed Tykwer, together with Becker and Schütte, as a frontline innovator among several younger directors determined to move beyond the conventional styles of the mainstream dramas and comedies and develop uniquely filmic styles. In the case of Tykwer, his self-reflexive play with visual symbols and filmic ciphers and his strong interest in relations of temporality and causality was already evident in *Die tödliche Maria* (1993, *Deadly Maria*) and *Winterschläfer* (1997, *Winter Sleepers*). Yet as the last decade of the twentieth century showed, the future of German cinema requires more than the creative contribution of a few talented directors. Above all, the survival of this particular filmic tradition needs the productive and dynamic interplay among the constitutive elements that have characterised German national cinema from the very beginning. In other words, the validity and vibrancy of this important cinematic tradition depends upon a workable compromise between art cinema and popular cinema; between generic tradition and formal innovation; between political intentions and social fantasies; between private investment and public funding; and between a real appreciation for the local and the regional and a critical examination of the national as a new/old category of cultural identity within an increasingly streamlined global media landscape.

SELECT BIBLIOGRAPHY

The following is a selection of books and articles on German cinema or relevant to the study of German cinema. Preference has been given to monographs and anthologies; articles have been included only where few other sources are available. More extensive bibliographies on individual periods can be found in the following English-language monographs and anthologies: in Elsaesser 1996a for Wilhelmine cinema; in Elsaesser 2000b for Weimar cinema; in Rentschler 1996 and Reimer 2000 for Third Reich cinema; in Fehrenbach 1995 for postwar cinema; in Allan and Sanford 1999 for East German cinema; and in Elsaesser 1989 and Corrigan 1994 for West German cinema. The statistical data are taken from the chronology in Prinzler 1995; the dates in the filmography are based on Bock 1984.

Reference Works

Bock, H.-M. (ed.) (1984ff.) *Cine-Graph: Lexikon zum deutschsprachigen Film*, Munich: edition text + kritik.

Bock, H.-M. and Jacobsen, W. (eds) (1997) *Recherche: Film. Quellen und Methoden der Filmforschung*, Munich: edition text + kritik.

Cramer, T. (ed.) (1995) *Reclams Lexikon des deutschen Films*, Stuttgart: Reclam.

Elsaesser, T. and Wedel, M. (eds) (1999) *The BFI Companion to German Cinema*, London: bfi Publishing.

Heinzlmeier, A. and Schulz, B. (2000) *Lexikon der deutschen Film- und TV-Stars*, Berlin: Lexicon.

Holba, H. et al. (eds) (1984) *Reclams deutsches Filmlexikon: Filmkünstler aus Deutschland, Österreich und der Schweiz*, Stuttgart: Reclam.

Jacobsen, W. et al. (1993) *Die Geschichte des deutschen Films*, Stuttgart: Metzler.

Prinzler, H. H. (1995) *Chronik des deutschen Films 1895–1994*, Stuttgart: Metzler.

Smith, D. C. (2000) *The German Filmography 1895–1949*, Jefferson: McFarland.

List of Works Cited

Agde, G. (1987) *Kurt Maetzig – Filmarbeit: Gespräche, Reden, Schriften*, Berlin: Henschel.

Agde, G. (ed.) (1991) *Kahlschlag: Das 11. Plenum des ZK der SED 1965*, Berlin: Aufbau.

Albrecht, G. (1969) *Nationalsozialistische Filmpolitik: Eine soziologische Untersuchung über die Spielfilme des Dritten Reiches*, Stuttgart: Enke.

Albrecht, G. (ed.) (1979) *Der Film im 3. Reich*, Karlsruhe: DOKU.

Allan, S. and Sanford, J. (eds) (1999) *DEFA: East German Cinema, 1946–1992*, New York: Berghahn Books.

Alter, N. (2002) *Projecting History: Non-fiction German Cinema 1967–2000*, Ann Arbor: University of Michigan Press (forthcoming).

Alter, N. and Koepnick, L. (eds) (2002) *Sound Matters: Essays on the Acoustics of German Cinema* (forthcoming).

Amend, H. and Bütow, M. (eds) (1997) *Der bewegte Film: Aufbruch zu neuen deutschen Erfolgen*, Berlin: VISTAS.

Arnheim, R. (1957) *Film as Art*, Berkeley: University of California Press.

Arnheim, R. (1977) *Kritiken und Aufsätze zum Film*, ed. H. H. Diederichs. Munich: Hanser.

Aurich, R. and Jacobsen, W. (eds) (1998) *Werkstatt Film: Selbstverständnis und Visionen von Filmleuten der zwanziger Jahre*, Munich: edition text + kritik.

Baird, J. W. (1974) *The Mythical World of Nazi War Propaganda 1933–1945*, Minneapolis: University of Minnesota Press.

Balázs, B. (1982–84) *Schriften zum Film*, 2 vols, eds. H. H. Diederichs et al., Berlin: Hanser.

Barkhausen, H. (1982) *Filmpropaganda für Deutschland im Ersten und Zweiten Weltkrieg*, Hildesheim: Olms.

Barlow, J. D. (1982) *German Expressionist Film*, Boston: Twayne.

Barsam, R. M. (1975) *Filmguide to 'Triumph of the Will'*, Bloomington: Indiana University Press.

Bartetzko, D. (1985) *Illusionen in Stein: Stimmungsarchitektur im deutschen Faschismus. Ihre Vorgeschichte in Theater- und Film-Bauten*, Reinbek: Rowohlt.

Barthel, M. (1986) *So war es wirklich: Der deutsche Nachkriegsfilm*, Munich: F. A. Herbig.

Bechdolf, U. (1992) *Wunsch-Bilder? Frauen im nationalsozialistischen Unterhaltungsfilm*, Tübingen: Vereinigung für Volkskunde.

Becker, D. (1999) *Zwischen Ideologie und Autonomie: Die DDR-Forschung und die deutsche Filmgeschichte*, Münster: LIT.

Becker, W. (1973) *Film und Herrschaft: Organisationsprinzipien und Organisations- strukturen der nationalsozialistischen Filmpropaganda*, Berlin: Spiess.

Becker, W. and Schöll, N. (1995) *In jenen Tagen . . . Wie der deutsche Nachkriegsfilm die Vergangenheit bewältigte*, Opladen: Leske + Buderich.

Behn, M. (ed.) (1994) *Schwarzer Traum und weiße Sklavin: Deutsch-dänische Filmbeziehungen 1910–1930*, Munich: edition text + kritik.

Belach, H. (ed.) (1979) *Wir tanzen um die Welt: Deutsche Revuefilme 1933–1945*, Munich: Hanser.

Belach, H. (1986) *Henny Porten: Der erste deutsche Filmstar 1890–1960*, Berlin: Haude & Spener.

Belach, H. and Jacobsen, W. (eds) (1990) *Richard Oswald: Regisseur und Produzent*, Munich: edition text + kritik.

Belach, H. and Prinzler, H. H. (eds) (1983) *Exil: Sechs Schauspieler aus Deutschland*, Berlin: Stiftung Deutsche Kinemathek.

Benzenhöfer, U. and Eckart, W. U. (eds) (1990) *Medizin im Spielfilm des National- sozialismus*, Tecklenburg: Burgverlag.

Berg, J. (1993) *Am Ende der Rolle: Diskussion über den Autorenfilm*, Marburg: Schüren.

Berger, J. et al. (eds) (1977) *Erobert den Film: Proletariat und Film in der Weimarer Republik*, ed. Neue Gesellschaft für Bildende Kunst und Freunde der deutschen Kinemathek, Berlin: NGBK.

Berger, J. et al. (eds) (1989) *Zwischen gestern und morgen*, Frankfurt am Main: Deutsches Filmmuseum.

Bergfelder, T. et al. (eds) (2002) *The German Cinema Book*, London: bfi Publishing (forthcoming).

Berg-Ganschow, U. and Jacobsen, W. (eds) (1987) *. . . Film . . . Stadt . . . Kino . . . Berlin . . .*, Berlin: Argon.

Bertram, T. (ed.) (1998) *Der rote Korsar: Traumwelt Kino der fünfziger und sechziger Jahre*, Essen: Klartext.

Bessen, U. (1989) *Trümmer und Träume: Nachkriegszeit und fünfziger Jahre auf Zelluloid. Deutsche Spielfilme als Zeugnisse ihrer Zeit. Eine Dokumentation*, Bochum: Studienverlag Dr. N. Brockmeyer.

Beyer, F. (1991) *Die Ufa-Stars im Dritten Reich*, Munich: Heyne.

Birett, H. (1980) *Verzeichnis in Deutschland gelaufener Filme: Entscheidungen der Filmzensur 1911–1920*, Munich: Saur.

Birett, H. (1991) *Das Filmangebot in Deutschland 1895–1911*, Munich: Winterberg.

Birett, H. (1994) *Lichtspiele: Das Kino in Deutschland bis 1914*, Munich: Q-Verlag.

Bisky, L. and Wiedemann, D. (1985) *Der Spielfilm – Rezeption und Wirkung. Kultursoziologische Analysen*, Berlin: Henschel.

Bliersbach, G. (1989) *So grün war die Heide: Die gar nicht so heile Welt im Nachkriegsfilm*, Weinheim: Beltz.

Blum, H. R. and Blum, K. (1997) *Geschichte des neuen deutschen Films*, Berlin: Parthas.

Blunk, H. (1984) *Die DDR in ihren Spielfilmen: Reproduktion und Konzeption der DDR-Gesellschaft im neueren DEFA-Gegenwartsspielfilm*, Munich: Profil.

Blunk, H. and Jungnickel, D. (eds) (1990) *Filmland DDR: Ein Reader zu Geschichte, Funktion und Wirkung der DEFA*, Cologne: Verlag Wissenschaft und Politik.

Bock, H.-M. and Behn, M. (eds). (1988) *Film und Gesellschaft in der DDR*. Material-Sammlung, Hamburg: Cinegraph.

Bock, H.-M. and Lenssen, C. (eds) (1992) *Joe May: Regisseur und Produzent*, Munich: edition text + kritik.

Bock, H.-M. and Töteberg, M. (eds) (1992) *Das Ufa-Buch: Kunst und Krisen, Stars und Regisseure, Wirtschaft und Politik*, Frankfurt am Main: Zweitausendundeins.

Bongartz, B. (1992) *Von Caligari zu Hitler – von Hitler zu Dr. Mabuse? Eine 'psychologische' Geschichte des deutschen Films von 1946 bis 1960*, Münster: MAkS.

Borgelt, H. (1993) *Die UFA – ein Traum: Hundert Jahre deutscher Film. Ereignisse und Erlebnisse*, Berlin: edition q.

Brady, M. and Hughes, H. (1995) 'German Film after the *Wende*', in Lewis, D. and McKenzie, J. R. P. (eds) *The New Germany: Social, Political and Cultural Challenges of Unification*, Exeter: Exeter University Press.

Brandt, H.-J. (1987) *NS-Filmtheorie und dokumentarische Praxis: Hippler, Noldan, Junghans*, Tübingen: Niemeyer.

Bredow, W. von and Zurek, R. (eds) (1975) *Film und Gesellschaft in Deutschland: Dokumente und Materialien*, Hamburg: Hoffmann & Campe.

Brennicke, I. and Hembus, J. (1983) *Klassiker des deutschen Stummfilms 1910–1930*, Munich: Goldmann.

Bretschneider, J. (ed.) (1992) *Ewald André Dupont: Autor und Regisseur*, Munich: edition text + kritik.

Bretschneider, J. et al. (ed.) (1999) *Leni Riefenstahl*, Berlin: Henschel.

Bromley, R. (2001) *From Alice to Buena Vista: The Films of Wim Wenders*, Westport: Praeger.

Bronner, B. and Brocher, C. (1973) *Die Filmemacher: Zur neuen deutschen Produktion nach Oberhausen*, Munich: Bertelsmann.

Budd, M. (ed.) (1990) *The Cabinet of Dr. Caligari: Texts, Contexts, Histories*, New Brunswick: Rutgers University Press.

Bulgakowa, O. (ed.) (1995) *Die ungewöhnlichen Abenteuer des Dr. Mabuse im Land der Bolschewiki*, Berlin: Freunde der Deutschen Kinemathek.

Bruns, K. (1995) *Kinomythen 1920–1945: Die Filmentwürfe der Thea von Harbou*, Stuttgart: Metzler.

Byg, B. (1980) 'The anti-fascist tradition and GDR film', in *Proceedings, Purdue University Fifth Annual Conference on Film*, West Lafayette: Purdue University.

Byg, B. (1990) 'What might have been: DEFA films of the past and the future of German cinema', *Cineaste* vol. 17, no. 4.

Byg, B. (1991) 'Two approaches to GDR history in DEFA films', *Studies in GDR Culture and Society* vol. 10.

Byg, B. (1995) *Landscapes of Resistance: The German Films of Danièle Huillet and Jean-Marie Straub*, Berkeley: University of California Press.

Coates, P. (1991) *The Gorgon's Gaze: German Cinema, Expressionism, and the Image of Horror*, Cambridge: Cambridge University Press.

Collins, R. and Porter, V. (1981) *WDR and the Arbeiterfilm: Fassbinder, Ziewer and Others*, London: British Film Institute.

Cook, R. and Gemünden, G. (eds) (1997) *The Cinema of Wim Wenders: Image, Narrative, and the Postmodern Condition*, Detroit: Wayne State University Press.

Corrigan, T. (ed.) (1986) *The Films of Werner Herzog: Between Mirage and History*, London: Methuen.

Corrigan, T. (1994) *New German Film: The Displaced Image*, rev. and exp. ed., Bloomington: Indiana University Press.

Courtade, F. and Cadars, P. (1975) *Geschichte des Films im Dritten Reich*, Munich: Hanser.

Crofts, S. (1993) 'Reconceptualizing national cinema/s', *Quarterly Review of Film & Video* vol. 14, no. 3.

Dahlke, G. and Karl, G. (eds) (1988) *Deutsche Spielfilme von den Anfängen bis 1933: Ein Filmführer*, Berlin: Henschelverlag.

Dalichow, B. (1993) 'Die jüngste Regiegeneration der DEFA – Aufbruch oder Abgesang?', *Augenblick* vol. 14.

Davidson, J. E. (1999) *Deterritorializing the New German Cinema*, Minnesota: University of Minnesota Press.

Diederichs, H. H. (1986) *Anfänge deutscher Filmkritik*, Stuttgart: Robert Fischer & Uwe Wiedlerroither.

Dillmann-Kühn, C. (1990) *Artur Brauer und die CCC: Filmgeschäft, Produktionsalltag, Studiogeschichte 1946–1990*, Frankfurt am Main: Deutsches Filmmuseum.

Donner, W. (1995) *Propaganda und Film im 'Dritten Reich'*, afterword Andreas Kilb, Berlin: TIP-Verlag.

Dost, M. et al. (1973) *Filmwirtschaft in der Bundesrepublik Deutschland und in Europa: Götterdämmerung in Raten*, Munich: Hanser.

Downing, T. (1992) *Olympia*, London: British Film Institute.

Drawer, C. (ed.) (1996) *So viele Träume: DEFA-Film-Kritiken aus drei Jahrzehnten von Heinz Kersten*, Berlin: VISTAS.

Drewniak, B. (1987) *Der deutsche Film 1938–1945*, Düsseldorf: Droste.

Eisner, L. (1977) *The Haunted Screen*, trans. R. Greaves, Berkeley: University of California Press.

Eisner, L. (1979) *Murnau*, Frankfurt am Main: Kommunales Kino.

Elsaesser, T. (1982) 'Social mobility and the fantastic: German silent film', *Wide Angle* vol. 5, no. 2.

Elsaesser, T. (1984) 'Film history and visual pleasure: Weimar history', in Mellencamp, P. and Rosen, P. (eds) *Cinema Histories, Cinema Practices*, Los Angeles: American Film Institute.

Elsaesser, T. (1989) *New German Cinema: A History*, New Brunswick: Rutgers University Press.

Elsaesser, T. (ed.) (1996a) *Early German Cinema: The First Two Decades*, Amsterdam: Amsterdam University Press.

Elsaesser, T. (1996b) *Fassbinder's Germany: History Identity Subject*, Amsterdam: Amsterdam University Press.

Elsaesser, T. (2000a) *Metropolis*, London: bfi Publishing.

Elsaesser, T. (2000b) *Weimar Cinema and After: Germany's Historical Imaginary*, London: Routledge.

Esser, M. (ed.) (1994) *Gleissende Schatten: Kamerapioniere der zwanziger Jahre*, Berlin: Henschel.

Fassbinder, R. W. (1992) *The Anarchy of the Imagination: Interviews, Essays, Notes*, ed. M. Töteberg and L. A. Lensing, Baltimore: Johns Hopkins University Press.

Fehrenbach, H. (1995) *Cinema in Democratizing Germany: Reconstructing National Identity after Hitler*, Chapel Hill: University of North Carolina Press.

Feinstein, J. I. (1995) 'The triumph of the ordinary: depictions of daily life in the East German cinema, 1956–66.' Ph.D. Diss., Stanford University.

Feldmann, S. et. al. (eds) (1980) *Werner Schroeter*, Munich: Hanser.

Fischer, R. and Hembus, J. (1981) *Der neue deutsche Film 1960–1980*, Munich: Goldmann.

Fischetti, R. (1992) *Das neue Kino – Filme von Frauen. Acht Porträts von deutschen Regisseurinnen*, Dülmen-Hiddengsel: tende.

Fox, J. (2000) *Filming Women in the Third Reich*, Oxford: Berg.

Franklin, J. (1983) *New German Cinema: From Oberhausen to Hamburg*, Boston: Twayne.

Frieden, S. et al. (eds) (1993) *Gender Perspectives in German Cinema*, 2 vols, Providence, R.I.: Berg Publishers.

Fritzsche, K. and Löser, C. (eds) (1996) *Gegenbilder: Filmische Subversion in der DDR 1976–1989*, Berlin: Janus press.

Gandert, G. (1993) *Der Film der Weimarer Republik: Ein Handbuch der zeitgenössischen Kritik 1929*, Berlin: de Gruyter.

Gehler, F. and Kasten, U. (1990a) *Friedrich Wilhelm Murnau*, Berlin: Henschel.

Gehler, F. and Kasten, U. (1990b) *Fritz Lang: Die Stimme von Metropolis*, Berlin: Henschel.

Geiss, A. (ed.) (1994) *Filmstadt Babelsberg: Zur Geschichte des Studios und seiner Filme*, Berlin: Nicolai.

Geist, K. (1988) *The Cinema of Wim Wenders: From Paris, France to Paris, Texas*, Ann Arbor: UMI Research Press.

Gemünden, G. (1998) 'Between Karl May and Karl Marx: The DEFA "Indianerfilme" (1965–85)', *Film History* vol. 10, pp. 399–407.

Georgi, R. and Hoff, P. (eds) (1990) *Konrad Wolf: Neue Sichten auf seine Filme*, Berlin: VISTAS.

Gersch, W. (1975) *Film bei Brecht: Bertolt Brechts praktische und theoretische Auseinandersetzung mit dem Film*, Munich: Hanser.

Ginsberg, T. and Thompson, K. M. (eds) (1996) *Perspectives on German Cinema*, New York: G. K. Hall.

Glass, P. (1999) *Kino ist mehr als Film: Die Jahre 1976–1990*, Berlin: AG-Verlag.

Goergen, J. (ed.) (1989) *Walter Ruttmann: Eine Dokumentation*, Berlin: Freunde der Deutschen Kinemathek.

Göktürk, D. (2000) 'Migration und Kino – Subnationale Mitleidskultur oder transnationale Rollenspiele?', in Chiellino, C. (ed.) *Interkulturelle Literatur in Deutschland: Ein Handbuch*, Stuttgart: Metzger.

Greffrath, B. (1995) *Gesellschaftsbilder der Nachkriegszeit 1945–1949*, Pfaffenweiler: Centaurus.

Gunning, T. (2000) *The Films of Fritz Lang: Modernity, Crime and Desire*, London: bfi Publishing.

Güttinger, F. (1984a) *Kein Tag ohne Kino: Schriftsteller über den Stummfilm*, Frankfurt am Main: Deutsches Filmmuseum.

Güttinger, F. (1984b) *Der Stummfilm im Zitat der Zeit*, Frankfurt am Main: Deutsches Filmmuseum.

Habel, F.-B. (2001) *Das grosse Lexikon der DEFA-Spiefilme*, Berlin: Schwarzkopf & Schwarzkopf.

Hagener, M. (ed.) (2000) *Geschlecht in Fesseln: Sexualität zwischen Aufklärung und Ausbeutung im Weimarer Kino 1918–1933*, Munich: edition text + kritik.

Hagener, M. and Hans, J. (eds) (1999) *Als die Filme laufen lernten: Innovation und Tradition im Musikfilm 1928–1938*, Munich: edition text + kritik.

Hahn, F.-B. (1995) *Goiko Mitic, Mustangs, Marterpfähle: Die DEFA-Indianer Filme*, Berlin: Schwarzkopf & Schwarzkopf.

Hake, S. (1990) 'Chaplin reception in Weimar Germany', *New German Critique* no. 51.

Hake, S. (1992a) *Passions and Deceptions: The Early Films of Ernst Lubitsch*, Princeton: Princeton University Press.

Hake, S. (1992b) 'Self-Referentiality in early German cinema', *Cinema Journal* vol. 31, no. 3.

Hake, S. (1993) *The Cinema's Third Machine: Writing on Film in Germany 1907–1933*, Lincoln: University of Nebraska Press.

Hake, S. (2002) *Popular Cinema in the Third Reich*, Austin: University of Texas Press.

Hanisch, M. (1991) *Auf den Spuren der Filmgeschichte: Berliner Schauplätze*, Berlin: Henschel.

Hansen, M. (1983) 'Early silent cinema, whose public sphere?', *New German Critique* no. 29.

Happel, H. G. (1984) *Der historische Spielfilm im Nationalsozialismus*, Frankfurt am Main: R. G. Fischer.

Hardt, U. (1996) *From Caligari to California: Eric Pommer's Life in the International Film Wars*, Providence: Berghahn.

Hasenberg, P. and Thull, M. (eds) (1991) *Filme in der DDR 1987–90*, Cologne: Verlag Katholisches Institut für Medieninformation.

Hauser, J. (1989) *Neuaufbau der westdeutschen Filmwirtschaft 1945–1955 und der Einfluss der US-amerikanischen Filmpolitik*, Pfaffenweiler: Centaurus.

Heath, S. (1978) 'Questions of property: film and nationhood', *Cinetracts* vol. 1, no. 4.

Heimann, T. (1994) *DEFA, Künstler und SED-Kulturpolitik: Verständnis von Kulturpolitik und Filmproduktion in der SBZ/DDR 1945 bis 1959*, Berlin: VISTAS.

Heller, H.-B. (1984) *Literarische Intelligenz und Film: Zu Veränderungen der ästhetischen Theorie und Praxis under dem Eindruck des Films 1910–1930 in Deutschland*, Tübingen: Max Niemeyer.

Helt, R. C. and Helt, M. E. (1987) *West German Cinema since 1945: A Reference Handbook*, Metuchen: Scarecrow Press.

Helt, R. C. and Helt, M. E. (1992) *West German Cinema 1985–1990: A Reference Handbook*, Metuchen: Scarecrow Press.

Hembus, J. (1981) *Der deutsche Film kann gar nicht besser sein: Ein Pamphlet von gestern. Eine Abrechnung von heute*, Munich: Rogner & Bernhard.

Hickethier, K. (1986) *Grenzgänger zwischen Theater und Kino: Schauspielerporträts aus dem Berlin der Zwanziger Jahre*, Berlin: Edition Mythos Berlin.

Higson, A. (1989) 'The concept of national cinema', *Screen* vol. 30, no. 4.

Hilchenbach, M. (1982) *Kino im Exil: Die Emigration deutscher Filmkünstler 1933–1945*, Munich: Saur.

Hinton, D. B. (1991) *The Films of Leni Riefenstahl*, 2nd ed., Metuchen: Scarecrow Press.

Hochmuth, D. (ed.) (1993) *DEFA NOVA – nach wie vor? Versuch einer Spurensicherung*, Berlin: VISTAS.

Hoff, P. and Wiedemann, D. (eds) (1992) *Der DEFA Spielfilm in den 80er Jahren – Chancen für die 90er?*, Berlin: VISTAS.

Hoffmann, H. (1996) '*The Triumph of Propaganda: Film and National Socialism, 1933–1945*, trans. J. A. Broadwin and V. R. Berghahn, Providence: Berghahn.

Höfig, W. (1973) *Der deutsche Heimatfilm 1947–1960*, Stuttgart: Ferdinand Enke.

Hollstein, D. (1983) *'Jud Süss' und die Deutschen: Antisemitische Vorurteile im nationalsozialistischen Spielfilm*, Frankfurt am Main: Ullstein.

Horak, J.-C. (1984) *Fluchtpunkt Hollywood: Eine Dokumentation zur Filmemigration nach 1933*, Münster: MAkS.

Horak, J.-C. (1993) 'Rin-Tin-Tin in Berlin or American cinema in Weimar', *Film History* vol. 5, pp. 49–62.

Horak, J.-C. (1996) 'German exile cinema, 1933–1950', *Film History* vol. 8, pp. 373–89.

Hull, D. S. (1973) *Film in the Third Reich: A Study of the German Cinema 1933–1945*, New York: Simon & Schuster.

Hurst, H. and Gassen, H. (eds) (1991) *Kameradschaft – Querelle: Kino zwischen Deutschland und Frankreich*, Munich: Institut Français.

Jacobi, R. and Janssen, H. (eds) (1987) *Filme in der DDR 1945–1986: Kritische Notizen aus 42 Kinojahren*, Cologne: Verlag Katholisches Institut für Medieninformation.

Jacobsen, W. (1989) *Erich Pommer: Ein Filmproduzent macht Filmgeschichte*, Berlin: Argon.

Jacobsen, W. (ed.) (1992) *Babelsberg: Ein Filmstudio 1912–1992*, Berlin: Argon.

Jacobsen, W. and Prinzler, H. H. (eds) (1992) *Käutner*, Berlin: Volker Spiess.

Jansen, P. W. and Schütte, W. (eds) (1977) *Film in der DDR*, Munich: Hanser.

Jary, M. (1993) *Traumfabriken made in Germany: Die Geschichte des deutschen Nachkriegsfilms 1945–1960*, Berlin: edition q.

Jochum, N. (ed.) (1979) *Das wandelnde Bild: Der Filmpionier Guido Seeber 1879–1940*, Berlin: Elefanten Press.

Jordan, G. and Schenk, R. (eds) (1996) *Schwarzweiss und Farbe: DEFA-Dokumentarfilm 1946–92*, Berlin: Henschel.

Jörg, H. (1994) *Die sagen- und märchenhafte Leinwand: Erzählstoffe, Motive und narrative Strukturen der Volksprosa im 'klassischen' deutschen Stummfilm (1910–1930)*, Sinzheim: Pro Universitate.

Jung, U. (ed.) (1993) *Der deutsche Film: Aspekte seiner Geschichte von den Anfängen bis zur Gegenwart*, Trier: WVT Wissenschaftlicher Verlag.

Jung, U. and Schatzberg, W. (eds) (1992) *Filmkultur zur Zeit der Weimarer Republik*, Munich: K. G. Saur.

Jung, U. and Schatzberg, W. (1999) *Beyond Caligari: The Films of Robert Wiene*, New York: Berghahn.

Kaes, A. (ed. and intro.) (1978) *Kino-Debatte: Texte zum Verhältnis von Literatur und Film 1909–1929*, Tübingen: Max Niemeyer.

Kaes, A. (1989) From *'Hitler' to 'Heimat': The Return of History as Film*, Cambridge, Mass.: Harvard University Press.

Kaes, A. (1995) 'German cultural history and the study of film: ten theses and a postscript', *New German Critique* no. 65.

Kaes, A. (2000) *M*, London: bfi Publishing.

Kaes, A. (2002) *Shell Shock: Film and Trauma in Weimar Germany*, Princeton: Princeton University Press (forthcoming).

Kannapin, D. (1997) *Antifaschismus im Film der DDR: DEFA-Spielfilme 1945–1955/56*, Cologne: PapyRossa.

Kanzog, K. (1994) *'Staatspolitisch besonders wertvoll'. Ein Handbuch zu 30 deutschen Spielfilmen der Jahre 1934 bis 1945*, Munich: diskurs film.

Kasten, J. (1990) *Der expressionistische Film: Abgefilmtes Theater oder avantgardistisches Erzählkino? Eine stil-, produktions- und rezeptionsgeschichtliche Untersuchung*, Münster: MAkS.

Kelson, J. F. (1996) *Catalogue of Forbidden German Feature and Short Film Productions held in Zonal Film Archives of Film Section, Information Services Division, Control Commission for Germany (BE)*, Westport: Greenwood Press.

Katz, R. (1987) *Love is Colder than Death: The Life and Times of Rainer Werner Fassbinder*, New York: Random House.

Keiner, R. (1987) *Hanns Heinz Ewers und der phantastische Film*, Hildesheim: Olms.

Keiner, R. (1991) *Thea von Harbou und der deutsche Film bis 1933*, Hildesheim: Olms.

Kessler, F. et al. (eds) (1992) *Früher Film in Deutschland*, Frankfurt am Main: Stroemfeld/Roter Stern (*Kintop* 1).

Kessler, F. et al. (eds) (1994a) *Oskar Messter – Filmpionier der Kaiserzeit*, Frankfurt am Main: Stroemfeld/Roter Stern (*Kintop* 2).

Kessler, F. et al. (eds) (1994b) *Oskar Messter – Erfinder und Geschäftsmann*, Frankfurt am Main: Stroemfeld/Roter Stern (*Kintop* 2).

Kilchenstein, G. (1997) *Frühe Filmzensur in Deutschland: Eine vergleichende Studie zur Prüfungsarbeit in Berlin und München (1906–1914)*, Munich: diskurs film.

Kinter, J. (1985) *Arbeiterbewegung und Film (1895–1933): Zur Geschichte der Arbeiter- und Alltagskultur und der gewerkschaftlichen und sozialdemokratischen Kultur- und Medienarbeit*, Hamburg: Medienpädagogik-Zentrum.

Klaus, U. J. (1988–92) *Deutsche Tonfilme: Filmlexikon der abendfüllenden und deutschsprachigen Tonfilme nach ihren deutschen Uraufführungen*, 3 vols (for 1929/30, 1931, and 1932) Berlin and Berchtesgaden: Klaus.

Kluge, A. (1983) *Bestandaufnahme Utopie Film: Zwanzig Jahre neuer deutscher Film*, Frankfurt am Main: Zweitausendeins.

Kluge, A. (1999) *In Gefahr und grösster Not bringt der Mittelweg den Tod: Texte zu Kino, Film, Politik*, ed. C. Schulte, Berlin: Vorwerk.

Knight, J. (1992) *Women and the New German Cinema*, London: Verso.

Koch, K. (1985) *Die Bedeutung des 'Oberhausener Manifestes' für die Filmentwicklung in der BRD*, Frankfurt am Main: Peter Lang.

Koebner, T. (ed.) (1997) *Idole des deutschen Film: Eine Galerie von Schlüsselfiguren*, Munich: edition text + kritik.

Koepnick, L. (2002) *The Dark Mirror: German Cinema Between Hitler and Hollywood*, Berkeley: University of California Press (forthcoming).

Kolker, R. and Beicken, P. (1993) *The Films of Wim Wenders: Cinema as Vision and Desire*, Cambridge: Cambridge University Press.

König, I. et al. (ed.) (1995) *Zwischen Bluejeans and Blauhemden: Jugendfilm in Ost und West*, Berlin: Henschel.

König, I. et al. (ed.) (1996) *Zwischen Marx und Muck: DEFA-Filme für Kinder*, Berlin: Henschel.

Korte, H. (ed.) (1980) *Film und Realität in der Weimarer Republik*, Frankfurt am Main: Fischer.

Korte, H. (1998) *Der Spielfilm und das Ende der Weimarer Republik: Ein rezeptionshistorischer Versuch*, Göttingen: Vanderhoeck und Ruprecht.

Kosta, B. (1994) *Recasting Autobiography: Women's Counterfictions in Contemporary German Literature and Film*, Ithaca: Cornell University Press.

Kracauer, S. (1995) *The Mass Ornament*, ed. and trans. T. Y. Levin, Cambridge: Harvard University Press.

Kracauer, S. (1974) *From Caligari to Hitler: A Psychological History of the German Film*, Princeton: Princeton University Press.

Kracauer, S. (1990) *Schriften* 5, 3 vols, ed. I. Mülder-Bach, Frankfurt am Main: Suhrkamp.

Krah, H. (ed.) (1999) *Geschichte(n) NS-Film – NS-Spuren heute*, Kiel: Ludwig.

Kreimeier, K. (1973) *Kino und Filmindustrie in der BRD: Ideologieproduktion und Klassenwirklichkeit nach 1945*, Kronsberg: Scriptor.

Kreimeier, K. (1996) *The Ufa Story: A History of Germany's Greatest Film Company, 1918–1945*, trans. R. and R. Kimber, New York: Hill and Wang.

Kühn, G. et al. (eds) (1975) *Film und revolutionäre Arbeiterbewegung in Deutschland 1918–1932: Dokumente und Materialien*, 2 vols, Berlin: Henschel.

Kuzniar, A. (2000) *The Queer German Cinema*, Stanford: Stanford University Press.

Ledig, E. (ed.) (1988) *Der Stummfilm: Konstruktion und Rekonstruktion*, Munich: diskurs film.

Ledig, E. (1990) *Paul Wegeners Golem-Filme im Kontext fantastischer Literatur*, Munich: diskurs film.

Leiser, E. (1974) *Nazi Cinema*, trans. G. Mander and D. Wilson, New York: Macmillan.

Leonhardt, S. (1989) 'Testing the Borders: East German film between individualism and social commitment', in Goulding, D. G. (ed.), *Post New Wave Cinema in the Soviet Union and Eastern Europe*, Bloomington: Indiana University Press.

Linville, S. (1998) *Feminism, Film, Fascism: Women's Autobiographical Film in Postwar Germany*, Austin: University of Texas Press.

Loacker, A. and Prucha, M. (eds) (2000) *Unerwünschtes Kino: Der deutschsprachige Emigrantenfilm 1934–1937*, Vienna: Filmarchiv Austria.

Loiperdinger, M. (ed.) (1991) *Märtyrerlegenden im NS-Film*, Opladen: Leske + Budrich.

Lowry, S. (1991) *Pathos und Politik: Ideologie in Spielfilmen des Nationalsozialismus*, Tübingen: Niemeyer.

Lüdeke, W. (1973) *Der Film in Agitation und Propaganda der revolutionären deutschen Arbeiterbewegung (1919–1933)*, Berlin/West: Oberbaumverlag.

Lutze, P. C. (1998) *Alexander Kluge: The Last Modernist*, Detroit: Wayne State University Press.

McCarthy, M. and Halle, R. (eds) (2002) *Popular German Cinema*, Detroit: Wayne State University Press (forthcoming).

McCormick, R. (1991) *Politics of the Self: Feminism and the Postmodern in West German Literature and Film*, Princeton: Princeton University Press.

McCormick, R. (2002) *Emancipation and Crisis: Gender, Sexuality, and 'New Objectivity' in Weimar Film and Literature*, New York: Palgrave and St Martin's Press.

Maiwald, K.-J. (1983) *Filmzensur im NS-Staat*, Dortmund: Nowotny.

Majer O'Sickey, I. and von Zadow, I. (eds) (1998) *Triangulated Visions: Women in Recent German Cinema*, Albany: State University of New York Press.

Manvell, R. and Fraenkel, H. (1971) *The German Cinema*, New York: Praeger.

Marquardt, A. and Rathsack, H. (eds) (1981) *Preussen im Film*, Reinbek: Rowohlt.

Marsiske, H.-A. (ed.) (1992) *Zeitmaschine Kino: Darstellungen von Geschichte im Film*, Marburg: Hitzeroth.

Meurer, H. J. (2000) *Cinema and National Identity in a Divided Germany, 1979–1989*, Lewiston: Edwin Mellen Press.

Minden, M and Bachmann, H. (eds) (2000) *Fritz Lang's 'Metropolis': Cinematic Visions of Technology and Fear*, Rochester: Camden House.

Möbius, H. and Vogt, G. (1990) *Drehort Stadt: Das Thema 'Grossstadt' im deutschen Film*, Marburg: Hitzeroth.

Moeller, F. (1998) *Der Filmminister: Goebbels und der Film im Dritten Reich*, Berlin: Henschel.

Möhrmann, R. (1980) *Die Frau mit der Kamera: Filmemacherinnen in der Bundesrepublik Deutschland: Situationen, Perspektiven. Zehn exemplarische Lebensläufe*, Munich: Hanser.

Moldenhauer, G. and Zimmermann, P. (2000) *Der geteilte Himmel: Arbeit, Alltag und Geschichte im ost- und westdeutschen Film*, Constance: UVK Medien.

Moltke, J. von (1996) 'Trapped in America: the Americanization of the Trapp Family, or "Papa's Kino" revisited', *German Studies Review* vol. 19, no. 5.

Monaco, P. (1976) *Cinema and Society: France and Germany during the Twenties*, New York: Elsevier.

Mückenberger, C. (ed.) (1990) *Prädikat: Besonders schädlich: 'Das Kaninchen bin ich' 'Denk bloss nicht dass ich heule'*, Berlin: Henschel.

Mückenberger, C. and Jordan, G. (1994) *'Sie sehen selbst, Sie hören selbst' . . . Die DEFA von ihren Anfängen bis 1949*, Marburg: Hitzeroth.

Mueller, R. (1989) *Bertolt Brecht and the Theory of Media*, Lincoln: University of Nebraska Press.

Mühl-Benninghaus, W. (1997) 'German film censorship during World War I', *Film History* vol. 9, pp. 71–94.

Mühl-Benninghaus, W. (1999) *Das Ringen um den Tonfilm: Strategien der Elektro- und der Filmindustrie in den 20er und 30er Jahren*, Düsseldorf: Droste.

Müller, C. (1994) *Frühe deutsche Kinematographie: Formale, wirtschaftliche, und kulturelle Entwicklungen 1907–1912*, Stuttgart: Metzler.

Murray, B. (1990) *Film and the German Left in the Weimar Republic*, Austin: University of Texas Press.

Murray, B. and Wickham, C. (eds) (1992) *Framing the Past: The Historiography of German Cinema and Television*, Carbondale: University of Southern Illinois Press.

Neale, S. (1977) 'Propaganda', *Screen* vol. 18, no. 3.

Negt, O. and Kluge, A. (1993) *The Public Sphere and Experience: Toward an Analysis of the Bourgeois and Proletarian Public Sphere*, trans. P. Labanyi et al., Minneapolis: University of Minnesota Press.

Noack, F. (2000) *Veit Harlan: 'Des Teufels Regisseur'*. Munich: belleville.

Orbanz, E. (ed.) (1977) *Wolfgang Staudte*, Berlin: Volker Spiess.

Osten, U. von der (1998) *NS-Filme im Kontext sehen! 'Staatspolitisch besonders wertvolle' Filme der Jahre 1934–1938*, Munich: diskurs film.

Ott, F. W. (1986) *The Great German Films: From Before World War I to the Present*, Secaucus: Citadel.

Paech, A. and Paech, J. (2000) *Menschen im Kino: Film und Literatur erzählen*, Stuttgart: Metzler.

Paech, J. (1988) *Literatur und Film*, Stuttgart: Metzler.

Petermann, W. and Thoms, R. (eds) (1988) *Kino Fronten: 20 Jahre '68 und das Kino*, Munich: Trickster.

Petley, J. (1979) *Capital and Culture: German Cinema 1933–45*, London: British Film Institute.

Petro, P. (1989) *Joyless Streets: Women and Melodramatic Representation in Weimar Germany*, Princeton: Princeton University Press.

Pflaum, H. G. (1990) *Germany on Film: Theme and Content in Cinema of the Federal Republic of Germany*, trans. R. Helt and R. Richter, Detroit: Wayne State University Press.

Pflaum, H. G. and Prinzler, H. H. (1983) *Cinema in the Federal Republic of Germany*, Bonn: Inter Nationes.

Phillips, K. (ed.) (1984) *New German Filmmakers: From Oberhausen Through the 1970s*, New York: Frederick Ungar.

Pinthus, K. (ed.) (1983) *Das Kinobuch*, afterword W. Schobert, Frankfurt am Main: Fischer.

Plummer, T. G. et al. (eds) (1982) *Film and Politics in the Weimar Republic*, New York: Holmes & Meier.

Pommer, E. (1999) *Kinobesuch im Lebenslauf: Eine historische und medienbiographische Studie*, Constance: UVK Medien.

Poss, I. (ed.) (1997) *DEFA 50: Gespräche aus acht Filmnächten*, Brandenburgische Zentrale für Politische Bildung.

Prawer, S. S. (1980) *Caligari's Children: The Film as Tale of Terror*, London: Oxford University Press.

Prinzler, H. H. and Patalas, E. (eds) (1984) *Lubitsch*, Munich: C. J. Bucher.

Prümm, K. and Wenz, B. (eds) (1991) *Willy Haas: Der Kritiker als Mitproduzent, Texte zum Film 1920–1933*, Berlin: Edition Hentrich.

Rayns, T. (ed.) (1979) *Fassbinder*, London: British Film Institute.

Reeves, N. (1999) *The Power of Film Propaganda: Myth or Reality?*, London and New York: Cassell.

Reichmann, H.-P. and Schobert, W. (eds) (1991) *Abschied von gestern: Bundesdeutscher Film der sechziger und siebziger Jahre*, Frankfurt am Main: Deutsches Filmmuseum.

Reimer, R. C. (ed.) (2000) *Cultural History through a National Socialist Lens: Essays on the Cinema of Nazi Germany*, Rochester: Camden House.

Reimer, R. and Reimer, C. (1992) *Nazi-Retro Films: How German Narrative Cinema Remembers the Past*, New York: Twayne.

Reiss, E. (1979) *'Wir senden Frohsinn': Fernsehen unterm Faschismus*, Berlin: Elefanten Press.

Rentschler, E. (1984) *West German Cinema in the Course of Time*, Bedford Hills: Redgrave.

Rentschler, E. (ed.) (1986) *German Film and Literature: Adaptations and Transformations*, London and New York: Methuen.

Rentschler, E. (ed.) (1988) *West German Filmmakers on Film*, New York: Holmes & Meier.

Rentschler, E. (ed.) (1990) *The Films of G. W. Pabst: An Extraterritorial Cinema*, New Brunswick: Rutgers University Press.

Rentschler, E. (1996) *The Ministry of Illusion: Nazi Cinema and its Afterlife*, Cambridge: Harvard University Press.

Rentschler, E. (2000) 'From New German Cinema to the postwall cinema of consensus', in Hjort, M. and MacKenzie, S. (eds) *Cinema and Nation*, London: Routledge.

Richter, H. (1986) *The Struggle for the Film: Towards a Socially Responsible Film*, ed. J. Römhild, trans. B. Brewster, foreword A. L. Rees, New York: St Martin's Press.

Richter, H. (1968) *Filmgegner von heute – Filmfreunde von morgen*, intro. W. Schobert, Frankfurt am Main: Fischer.

Richter, R. (ed.) (1983) *DEFA-Spielfilm-Regisseure und ihre Kritiker*, 2 vols, Berlin: Henschel.

Riecke, C. (1998) *Feministische Filmtheorie in der Bundesrepublik Deutschland*, New York: Peter Lang.

Riefenstahl, L. (1993) *Leni Riefenstahl: A Memoir*, New York: St Martin's Press.

Riess, C. (1985) *Das gab's nur einmal: Die grosse Zeit des deutschen Films*, 3 vols, Frankfurt am Main: Ullstein.

Romani, C. (1992) *Tainted Goddesses: Female Film Stars of the Third Reich*, trans. R. Connolly, New York: Sarpedon.

Rosen, P. (1984) 'History, textuality, nation: Kracauer, Burch, and some problems in the study of national cinemas', *Iris* vol. 2, no. 2.

Rossell, D. (1998) 'Beyond Messter: aspects of early cinema in Berlin', *Film History* vol. 10, pp. 52–69.

Rossell, D. (2001) *Faszination der Bewegung: Ottomar Anschütz zwischen Photographie und Kino*, Frankfurt am Main: Stroemfeld.

Rother, R. (2000) *Leni Riefenstahl: Die Verführung des Talents*, Berlin: Henschel.

Rügner, U. (1988) *Filmmusik in Deutschland zwischen 1924 und 1934*, Hildesheim: Olms.

Rutz, G.-P. (2000) *Darstellungen von Film in literarischen Fiktionen der zwanziger und dreissiger Jahre*, Münster: LIT.

Salt, B. (1979) 'From *Caligari* to who?', *Sight and Sound* vol. 48, no. 2.

Sanford, J. (1980) *The New German Cinema*, Totowa: Barnes and Noble.

Santner, E. (1990) *Stranded Objects: Mourning, Memory, and Film in Post-war Germany*, Ithaca: Cornell University Press.

Saunders, T. J. (1994) *From Berlin to Hollywood: American Cinema and Weimar Germany*, Berkeley: University of California Press.

Saunders, T. J. (1997). 'The German–Russian film (mis)alliance (DERUSSA): commerce & politics in German–Soviet cinema ties', *Film History* vol. 9, pp. 168–88.

Schacht, D. A. (1991) *Fluchtpunkt Provinz: Der neue Heimatfilm zwischen 1968 und 1972*, Münster: MAkS.

Schaudig, M. (ed.) (1996) *Positionen deutscher Filmgeschichte: 100 Jahre Kinematographie: Strukturen, Diskurse, Kontexte*, Munich: diskurs film.

Schebera, J. (1990) *Damals in Neubabelsberg: Studios, Stars und Kinopaläste im Berlin der zwanziger Jahre*, Leipzig: Edition Leipzig.

Schenk, I. (ed.) *Dschungel Grossstadt: Kino und Modernisierung*, Marburg: Schüren.

Schenk, R. (ed.) (1994) *Das zweite Leben der Filmstadt Babelsberg, DEFA 1946–92*, Berlin: Henschel.

Schenk, R. (ed.) (1995a) *Regie: Frank Beyer*, Berlin: Edition Hentrich.

Schenk, R. (ed.) (1995b) *Vor der Kamera: Fünfzig Schauspieler in Babelsberg*, Berlin: Henschel.

Schlüpmann, H. (1990) *Unheimlichkeit des Blicks: Das Drama des frühen deutschen Kinos*, Frankfurt am Main: Stroemfeld/Roter Stern.

Schmid, M. and Gehr, H. (eds) (1992) *Rainer Werner Fassbinder: Dichter, Schauspieler, Filmemacher*, Berlin: Argon.

Schmieding, W. (1961) *Kunst oder Kasse: Der Ärger mit dem deutschen Film*, Hamburg: Rütting & Loening.

Schmitt-Sasse, J. (ed.) (1993) *Widergänger: Faschismus und Antifaschismus im Film*, Münster: MAkS.

Schobert, W. and Hoffmann, H. (eds) (1989) *Zwischen gestern und morgen: Westdeutscher Nachkriegsfilm 1946–1962*, Frankfurt am Main: Deutsches Filmmuseum.

Schönemann, H. (1992) *Fritz Lang: Filmbilder Vorbilder*, Berlin: Hentrich.

Schöning, J. (ed.) (1989) *Reinhold Schünzel: Schauspieler und Regisseur*, Munich: edition text + kritik.

Schöning, J. (ed.) (1995) *Fantaisies russes: Russische Filmmacher in Berlin und Paris 1920–1930*, Munich: edition text + kritik.

Schulte-Sasse, L. (1996) *Entertaining the Third Reich: Illusions of Wholeness in Nazi Cinema*, Durham: Duke University Press.

Schulz, G. (ed.) (1989) *DEFA-Spielfilme 1946–1964: Filmografie*, Berlin: Staatliches Filmarchiv.

Schuster, A. (1999) *Zerfall oder Wandel der Kultur? Eine kultursoziologische Interpretation des deutschen Films*, Wiesbaden: DUV.

Schütz, R. (1990) 'Zur Erkundung individueller Glücksansprüche in DEFA-Spielfilmen der achtziger Jahre' in *Junge Filmemacher zwischen Innovation und Tradition*, Berlin: VISTAS.

Schweinitz, J. (ed.) (1992) *Prolog vor dem Film: Nachdenken über ein neues Medium 1909–1914*, Leipzig: Reclam.

Segeberg, H. (ed.) (1996, 1998, 2000) *Mediengeschichte des Films*, 3 vols: *Die Mobilisierung des Sehens. Die Modellierung des Kinofilms. Die Perfektionierung des Scheins*, Munich: Wilhelm Fink.

Seidl, C. (1987) *Der deutsche Film der fünfziger Jahre*, Munich: Heyne.

Shandley, R. (2001) *Rubble Films: German Cinema in the Shadows of the Third Reich*, Philadelphia: Temple University Press.

Shattuc, J. (1995) *Television, Tabloids, and Tears: Fassbinder und Popular Culture*, Minneapolis: University of Minnesota Press.

Sigl, K. et al. (1990). *Jede Menge Kohle? Kunst und Kommerz auf dem deutschen Filmmarkt der Nachkriegszeit*, Munich: Filmland Presse.

Silberman, M. (1990) 'Remembering history: the filmmaker Konrad Wolf', *New German Critique* no. 49.

Silberman, M. (1994) 'Post-wall documentaries: new images from a new Germany', *Cinema Journal* vol. 33, no. 2.

Silberman, M. (1995) *German Cinema: Texts and Contexts*, Detroit: Wayne State University Press.

Silberman, M. (1996) 'What is German in the German cinema?', *Film History* vol. 8, pp. 297–315.

Silberman, M. (ed. and trans.) (2000) *Bertolt Brecht on Film & Radio*, London: Methuen.

Soldovieri, S. (1998) 'Socialists in outer space', *Film History* vol. 10, pp. 382–98.

Spieker, M. (1999) *Hollywood unterm Hakenkreuz: Der amerikanische Spielfilm im Dritten Reich*, Trier: WVT Wissenschaftlicher Verlag.

Spielhagen, E. (ed.) (1993) *So durften wir glauben zu kämpfen . . . Erfahrungen mit DDR-Medien*, Berlin: VISTAS.

Spiker, J. (1975) *Film und Kapital: Der Weg der deutschen Filmwirtschaft zum nationalsozialistischen Einheitskonzern*, Berlin: Volker Spiess.

Stationen der Moderne im Film II: Texte Manifeste Pamphlete (1989) Berlin: Freunde der Deutschen Kinemathek.

Stettner, P. (1992) *Vom Trümmerfilm zur Traumfabrik: Die 'Junge Film-Union' 1947–1952*, Hildesheim: Olms.

Strauss, A. (1996) *Frauen im deutschen Film*, Frankfurt am Main: Peter Lang.

Sturm, S. and Wohlgemuth, A. (eds) (1996) *Hallo? Berlin? Ici Paris! Deutsch-Französische Filmbeziehungen 1918–1939*, Munich: edition text + kritik.

Syberberg, H.-J. (1982) *Hitler: A Film from Germany*, trans. J. Neugroschel, New York: Farrar, Straus and Giroux.

Thomas, H. A. (1962) *Die deutsche Tonfilmmusik: Von den Anfängen bis 1956*, Gütersloh: Bertelsmann.

Thompson, K. (1996) 'National or international films? The European debates during the 1920s', *Film History* vol. 8, pp. 281–96.

Tornow, I. (1990) *Piroschka und Wunderkinder oder: Von der Unvereinbarkeit von Idylle und Satire. Der Regisseur Kurt Hoffmann*, Munich: Filmland Presse.

Töteberg, M. (ed.) *Szenenwechsel: Momentaufnahmen des jungen deutschen Films*, Reinbek: Rowohlt.

Traudisch, D. (1993) *Mutterschaft mit Zuckerguss? Frauenfeindliche Propaganda im NS-Spielfilm*, Pfaffenweiler: Centaurus.

Trumpener, K. (2001) *Divided Screens: Postwar Cinema in East and West*, Princeton: Princeton University Press (forthcoming).

Turner, G. (1986) *National Fictions*, Sydney: Allan Unwin.

Uhlenbrok, K. (ed.) (1998) *MusikSpektakelFilm: Musiktheater und Tanzkultur im deutschen Film*, Munich: edition text + kritik.

Usai, P. C. and Codelli, L. (eds) (1990) *Before Caligari: German Cinema 1895–1920*, Pordenone: Le Giornate del Cinema Muto.

Vogelsang, K. (1990) *Filmmusik im Dritten Reich: Eine Dokumentation*, Hamburg: Facta Oblita.

Wager, J. B. (1999) *Dangerous Dames: Women and Representation in the Weimar Street Film and Film Noir*, Athens: Ohio State University Press.

Walsh, M. (1996) 'National cinema, national imaginary', *Film History* vol. 8, no. 3.

Warstat, D. H. (1982) *Frühes Kino der Kleinstadt*, Berlin: Volker Spiess.

Wedel, M. (1996) *Max Mack: Showmann im Glashaus*, Berlin: Freunde der Deutschen Kinemathek.

Weinberger, G. (1992) *Nazi Germany and Its Aftermath in Women Directors' Autobiographical Films of the late 1970s: In the Murderer's House*, San Francisco: Mellen Research University Press.

Welch, D. (1985) *Propaganda and the German Cinema 1933–1945*, Oxford: Oxford University Press.

Welch, D. (1993). *The Third Reich: Politics and Propaganda*, London: Routledge.

Wenders, W. (1989) *Emotion Pictures: Reflections on the Cinema*, trans. S. Whiteside, London: Faber and Faber.

Werner, P. (1990) *Die Skandalchronik des deutschen Films*, Frankfurt am Main: Fischer.

Westermann, B. (1990) *Nationale Identität im Spielfilm der fünfziger Jahre*, Frankfurt am Main: Peter Lang.

Wetzel, K. and Hagemann, P. A. (1982) *Zensur – verbotene deutsche Filme 1933–1945*, Berlin: Volker Spiess.

Willemen, P. (1994) 'The national', in *Looks and Frictions: Essays in Cultural Studies and Film Theory*, London: bfi Publishing.

Wilmesmeier, H. (1994) *Deutsche Avantgarde und Film: Die Filmmatinee 'Der absolute Film' 3. und 10. Mai 1925*, Münster: LIT.

Witte, K. (1995) *Lachende Erben, toller Tag: Filmkomödie im Dritten Reich*, Munich: Vorwerk.

Worschech, R. et al. (ed.) (1995) *Lebende Bilder einer Stadt: Kino und Film in Frankfurt am Main*, Frankfurt am Main: Deutsches Filmmuseum.

Wulf, J. (1989) *Theater und Film im Dritten Reich: Eine Dokumentation*, Frankfurt am Main: Ullstein.

Wuss, P. (1990) *Kunstwert des Films und Massencharakter des Mediums*, Berlin: Henschel.

Zeutschner, H. (1995) *Die braune Mattscheibe: Fernsehen im Nationalsozialismus*, Hamburg: Rotbuch.

Zglinicki, F. von (1986) *Die Wege der Traumfabrik: Von Guckkästen, Zauberscheiben und bewegten Bildern*, Berlin: Transit.

Zilinski, L. et al. (ed.) (1970) *Spielfilme der DEFA im Spiegel der Kritik*, Berlin: Henschel.

The following German-language journals and newsletters regularly publish articles and special issues on all aspects and periods of German cinema:

Augen-Blick, Marburg: Marburger Hefte zur Medienwissenschaft.

diskurs film, Munich: Münchener Beiträge zur Filmphilologie.

Kinemathek, Berlin: Freunde der Deutschen Kinemathek.

Kintop, Frankfurt am Main: Stroemfeld/Roter Stern.

Filmexil, Berlin: Stiftung Deutsche Kinemathek.

Filmblatt, Berlin: Cinegraph Babelsberg, Berlin-Brandenburgisches Centrum für Filmforschung.

Filmgeschichte, Berlin: Newsletter des Filmmuseums Berlin.

Film und Kritik, Frankfurt am Main: Stroemfeld/Roter Stern.

Frauen und Film, Frankfurt am Main: Stroemfeld/Roter Stern.

montage/av, Zeitschrift für Theorie & Geschichte audiovisueller Kommunikation, Berlin.

The following English-language journals have published special issues on German cinema:

Arachne, vol. 3, no. 2 (1996), ed. U. Lischke Mc-Nab and C. Flinn, special issue on German film and culture.
Camera Obsura, no. 44 (2000), special issue on post-Wall German cinema.
Discourse, no. 6 (1983), ed. R. Mueller, special issue on German avant-garde cinema.
German Quarterly, vol. 64, no. 1 (1991), special issue on literature and film.
Film Criticism, vol. 23 (1999), nos. 2–3, ed. G. Gemünden, special issue on Detlef Sierck/Douglas Sirk.
Monatshefte, vol. 82, no. 3 (1990), special issue on German film studies.
New German Critique, nos. 24–25 (1981–82), ed. D. Bathrick and M. Hansen, special double issue on New German Cinema.
New German Critique, no. 49 (1990), ed M. Hansen, special issue on Alexander Kluge.
New German Critique, no. 60 (1993), ed. D. Bathrick and E. Rentschler, special issue on German film history.
New German Critique, no. 63 (1994), ed. D. Bathrick and G. Gemünden, special issue on Rainer Werner Fassbinder.
New German Critique, no. 74 (1998), ed. D. Bathrick and E. Rentschler, special issue on Nazi cinema.
October, no. 21 (1982), ed. D. Crimp, special issue on Rainer Werner Fassbinder.
October, no. 46 (1988), ed. S. Liebman, special issue on Alexander Kluge.
October, no. 72 (1995), ed. S. Liebman, special issue on 'Berlin 1945: war and rape in *Liberators Take Liberties*'.
Quarterly Review of Film Studies, vol. 5, no. 2 (1980), ed. E. Rentschler, special issue on West German film in the 1970s.
Seminar: A Journal of Germanic Studies, vol. 33, no. 4 (1997), ed. U. Lischke-McNab and K. Hanson, special issue on recent German film.
Wide Angle, vol. 12, no. 1 (1990), ed. J. Shattuc, special issue on 'the other Fassbinder'.

The following websites offer information on all aspects of German film history cinema and provide links to other German film sites:

www.cinegraph.de
www.defa-stiftung.de
www.filmmuseum-berlin.de
www.filminstitut.de
www.filmmuseum-potsdam.de

SUBJECT INDEX

abstract film 38–9
action adventures 18, 76, 164
actors: character actors 44, 68, 69; in exile
    62, 96, 130–1; female stars 16–17,
    43–4, 52, 68–9, 74, 102, 106, 130,
    163; male stars 16, 44, 52, 69, 76, 102,
    107, 130, 163; as muses 155;
    popularity polls 44–5; reception of
    foreign stars 16, 68, 74; star system
    15–17, 43–4, 68–9, 105, 107, 129–31,
    185–6
America *see* Hollywood
animation 23, 38–9
audiences: attendance patterns 11, 47, 51,
    65–6, 67, 104–5, 113–14, 122, 126,
    129, 139, 163, 181; lower middle class
    11, 47, 72–3; middle class 21, 37, 47,
    72–3, 114, 163; postwar tastes 102–3,
    104–5; reception of Hollywood films
    41, 44, 45, 97, 181–2; spectatorship
    theories 14, 28, 72–3, 151; women as
    8, 28; working class 11, 72–3; *see also*
    cinemas
authorship, theories of 15, 121, 144,
    154–9
avante-garde cinema 38–9, 121–2, 139,
    149, 150

Berlin films 39, 101, 158, 191–2;
    representation of divided city 125, 158,
    172; unified city 158, 172
biographical films 66, 101–2, 166, 167,
    170; famous writers and artists 70, 136,
    137, 161; genius films 83, 95, 105,
    137; political leaders 70, 82, 94–5,
    105–6
broadcasting 74, 80, 88, 113, 129, 161–2,
    168, 181, 187

censorship 11–12, 31, 45, 49–50, 62–3,
    89, 92–3, 121, 138
chamber play films 19, 36, 40–1
children's films 64, 103–4, 142
chronicle films 94
cinemas: art houses 162, 163; communal
    cinemas 163; flickers (Kientopp) 11;
    movie palaces 11;
    multiscreens/multiplexes 163, 181; in
    postwar FRG 104, 163, 181; Third
    Reich period 67; Weimar period 33, 47;
    Wilhelmine period 8, 10, 11, 23; *see also*
    audiences; distribution system
cinematography 9–10, 15, 31–2, 33, 42,
    62, 105, 148, 155–6, 173
class representations: middle class 37; petty
    bourgeoisie 19, 40, 69, 111–12, 127,
    184; white-collar workers 53, 73;
    working class 50, 92–3, 94, 95, 101–2,
    161; yuppies 182–3, 184, 186
colonialism 13, 24, 70, 82
comedies 169; ethnic comedies 18–19; of
    everyday life in GDR 134–5; petty-
    bourgeois 69, 111–12, 127, 184;
    proletarian comedies 184–5; romantic
    comedies 33, 102, 103, 130, 173–4,
    182–4; slapstick 19, 33, 45; Third
    Reich period 71,
    73–4; white-collar comedies 53,
    73
contemporary dramas 103, 104–5, 107–8,
    127, 132–8, 140
co-productions: European 2, 32, 46–7,
    51–2, 90, 114; German–Austrian 46,
    65; German–German 98, 128, 137;
    German–Swiss 169
costume dramas 18, 33, 37, 41–2, 106,
    127–8

style: expressionism 8, 9, 28–30, 35, 40,
71; fascist aesthetics 78–9, 100, 123;
modernism 27, 28, 34, 43, 79–80,
93–4, 122–4, 149; post-modernism
159, 163–4; social realism 36, 39, 41,
71, 148, 149; socialist realism 93–4,
100–2, 132

technology: colour 114; early cameras 10,
32; film sound 36–7, 49, 51–3
television: cable television 168; in FRG
161–2, 168, 171, 181, 187; in GDR
113, 129; in Third Reich 80
theatre: film and drama 20–1, 37, 71; stage
actors on the screen 21, 44, 69
theory: Critical Theory 151; notion of
authorship 15, 121, 144, 154–5; silent
film theory 20–1
thrillers 18, 35, 40, 150, 186, 192
travel films 110–11

United States *see* Hollywood

visual arts: architecture 31, 83, 141, 143,
179; painting 35, 70, 137; photography
39

war films: World War I 23–4, 36, 49, 80,
81; World War II 67, 79, 97, 101,
123–4, 137–8, 142–3, 169–71, 187
westerns 17, 128, 153
women: as audience 8, 28; *Frauenfilm*
165–8; representations of motherhood
16–17, 75; representations of women
41, 68–9, 75–6, 106, 108–9, 124,
135–6, 140, 147–8, 182–3; *see also*
feminist film; gender

Young German Cinema 86, 144, 145,
146–53
youth: children's films 64, 103–4, 142;
fairytale films 103–4; family conflicts
108, 109–10, 146, 148; youth culture
101, 107–8, 113–14, 125, 127, 129,
135, 141, 152, 164

NAME INDEX

INDEX OF FILMS

NOTE: Film titles consisting of numerals are filed as spelled out in German, e.g. *08/15* is filed as Nullachtfünfzehn. Film titles beginning with a German definite article have the article transposed to the end of the heading, e.g. *Bergkatze, Die*, but film titles beginning with an indefinite article do not, e.g. *Ein Walzertraum*.